THE CHRISTIAN WORKER

A *Life* Essentials BOOK

THE CHRISTIAN WORKER

R. A. TORREY

MOODY PRESS
CHICAGO

Moody Press, a ministry of Moody Bible Institute,
is designed for education, evangelization, and edification.
If we may assist you in knowing more about Christ
and the Christian life, please write us without obligation:
Moody Press, c/o MLM, Chicago, Illinois 60610.

Originally published in 1901
as the Practical Christian Work Course
offered by the Moody Bible Institute of Chicago
Correspondence School

Also published earlier as
How to Work for Christ
by Fleming Revell,
now a division of Baker Books

Updated edition 2001 by
THE MOODY BIBLE INSTITUTE
OF CHICAGO

Library of Congress Cataloging-in-Publicaton Data

Torrey, R. A. (Reuben Archer), 1856–1928
    The Christian worker / R. A. Torrey.—Updated ed.
      p. cm. — (a life essentials book)
    Rev. ed. of: Practical Christian work course. 1901.
    ISBN 0-8024-5218-3
      1. Evangelistic work. I. Torrey, R. A. (Reuben Archer), 1856–1928. Practical Christian work course. II. Title. III. Series.

BV3790 .T575 2001
253—dc21

2001032678

1 3 5 7 9 10 8 6 4 2

Printed in the United States of America

CONTENTS

FOREWORD

WHEN I WAS A TEENAGER IN ARGENTINA, a missionary graciously gave me a beaten up copy of "Practical Christian Work," a study course published by Moody Bible Institute. The author was Dr. R. A. Torrey, the former superintendent (president) of Moody Bible Institute. I was so thrilled to get it. In those days we had very little Christian literature in Argentina. This volume sent me on my way with confident service to Jesus Christ from my teenage years to this day. How thrilled I am that at last Moody Press and Moody External Studies are reprinting it.

I studied every inch of the lessons, from beginning to end, underlining profusely, and I memorized just about every Bible verse that's included in this amazing course. Dr. Torrey's lessons taught me the basics of the Gospel, how to prepare Bible teaching messages, and how to prepare evangelistic sermons. I learned how to "work for Christ" in a park, on a train, in a big city, or out in the countryside. I learned how to deal with children and adults, with Christians and non-Christians.

Through the anointed teachings of this book, two major lessons struck home to me as a teenager:

One condition of success was that I needed to have a definite experience of being filled with the Holy Spirit of God. I could not launch out into winning souls one-on-one, in small groups or in large campaigns, without a special and definite experience of being filled with the Holy Spirit. This is not related to the gifts of the Spirit, but to the definite infilling and clear anointing of His power.

In the very first pages of this book was the concept of how to get a passion for those who are lost without Jesus Christ. D. L. Moody's most repeated verse was Luke 19:10, "For the Son of Man came to seek and to save those who were lost." Acts 20:31, where the apostle Paul says, "I never stopped warning each of you night and day with tears," was another verse that became real to me.

In the first chapter, Dr. Torrey makes three basic points. How do we get real power and compassion for men and women who are eternally lost without Christ?

- By studying what the Bible has to say about the present standing and condition and the future destiny of those who are outside of Christ.
- By believing what the Bible says on these points without trying to tone it down or make it fit the popular notions of the day.
- By dwelling upon these truths about the lost condition of men and women who are apart from Christ until they take hold of our hearts and we understand their meaning.

These truths vitally propelled me into out-and-out evangelism. The fire of those days has never died out. It has increased. But these were some of the basic truths that gave me joy and confidence in practicing evangelism of all sorts.

The section on agnostics and atheists has served me well. During our crusades around the world, I host a live television program called *Night Talk with Luis Palau*. Many a time I have turned to Dr. Torrey's suggestions to respond to a skeptic's question or accusation and have seen a startling change in the caller's attitude toward God. Maria, a leftist guerrilla in Ecuador, was converted and radically changed. In counseling her, I used the practical and clear guidance from Holy Scripture as Dr. Torrey taught me in the book that you now have in your hands.

In the section on "Some Hints and Suggestions for Personal Work," Dr. Torrey said, "It is oftentimes well to use but a single passage of Scripture." In my first face-to-face encounter with Maria, I used Hebrews 10:17, "Their sins and their lawless deeds I will remember no more." Maria kept arguing. "But I blasphemed the name of God when I was a teenager," she said.

I replied, "God says, 'Their sins and their lawless deeds I will remember no more.'"

"But I stabbed a man who tried to rape me, and he committed suicide," Maria said.

I replied, "God says, 'Your sins and evil deeds I will remember no more.'"

She tried over and over. Seventeen times I quoted Hebrews 10:17 based on Dr. Torrey's wise counsel. Finally Maria, with tears flowing down her face, said, "If God can change me, He can change anyone!"

"Maria, God can change anyone and He will change you right now," I said, and I led her to the feet of Christ.

I reread this compendium from time to time to be reminded of its effectiveness. Every time I do, I am thrilled at its wisdom and endless suggestions.

Most of all, I learned from Dr. Torrey's course to "correctly handle the word of truth" (2 Timothy 2:15), the Bible, so as to lead people to Jesus Christ and fix the assurance of their salvation exclusively on the holy Word of God. Planted in the mind and heart of people we're seeking to lead to the Savior, the Word of God has enormous, eternal power.

These lessons have been with me now for more than forty years. I have applied the doctrine. I have preached the outlines. In all sorts of cultures in seventy countries around the world, I have practiced the methodology, and God has graciously granted a harvest of souls. Because the methods Dr. Torrey taught are biblical, they fit just about any culture in any society at any point in history. The teaching and the practical counsel in this course fit every nation—in Africa, Asia, Australia, the Americas, and Europe. This book has never failed me.

I am so glad that Moody has chosen to reprint it. This course is going to motivate evangelists, Sunday school teachers, youth workers, and all outreach-minded Christians in the workplace and their neighborhood to study the Word of God more. They will want to know the basics of the good news of Jesus Christ that turns people to faith and repentance and the fundamentals of the faith that nurture and bring to maturity the men, women, and children who find forgiveness and eternal life in Christ.

I believe that if we could put this course into the hands of Christians all around the world—in every major language—the effectiveness of evangelism would increase, the depth of discipleship would grow, and the spiritual and numerical growth in the churches would be astonishing. I hope and pray that the lessons Dr. Torrey wrote a century ago will now penetrate the world in this new millennium.

LUIS PALAU

INTRODUCTION

ON THE OCCASION OF THE 100TH ANNIVERSARY of External Studies at Moody Bible Institute, we are delighted to reissue one of the finest ministry tools ever produced. The material in this book was originally distributed in two forms. One was a book called *How to Work for Christ* and the other was a correspondence course called "Practical Christian Work," one of the first offered by Moody Bible Institute. This new book combines both forms into one. The original text has been modified only slightly, but we have added chapter introductions and footnotes in order to help you appreciate the contributions of each lesson. We have also added learning activities for each lesson in order to help you put the material into practice, study as a group, or participate in the revised correspondence course.

The impact of this material is seen vividly in the life and ministry of Luis Palau. Early in his ministry career, he was given a copy of the original correspondence course. Although he never enrolled in the course with Moody, he studied diligently on his own and found the teaching of the course to be of enormous benefit to his ministry. He still gives testimony to the power of this material in his current ministry. (See the foreword written by him.)

It is appropriate that the reissue of this material is a joint effort of Moody Press and Moody External Studies, both ministries of Moody Bible Institute, because of the influence of D. L. Moody on the life of R. A. Torrey, especially regarding personal work. Torrey accepted Christ while a student at Yale. In the next year, D. L. Moody preached at Yale, and Torrey asked him how to bring people to Christ. "He said a few words, gave a few texts of Scripture, and said 'You go at it.'" That night, Torrey led his first soul to Christ!

After serving as pastor in Garrettsville, Ohio, for four years, Torrey went overseas to study at the University of Leipzig and the University of Erlangen. Upon his return to the United States, he served as pastor of the People's Church in Minneapolis. It was his excellent work as secretary of the International Christian Workers' Association that brought him again to the attention of D. L. Moody. Moody called him to Chicago, laid his plans for the Bible institute in front of Torrey, and said simply, "I want you to take this." In 1889, Torrey, at age thirty-four, became superintendent of what is now known as Moody Bible Institute. Later, he was also used by God to found the Bible Institute of Los Angeles, now known as Biola University. Both while in Chicago and Los Angeles, Torrey served as pastor of a local church.

Torrey is probably best known as an evangelist. He followed the example of Moody and conducted numerous evangelistic campaigns, including some that went around the world. One man said, "Dr. Torrey did more to emphasize and promote personal evangelism than any one other man since the days of the apostle Paul."[1] This book is the continued manifestation of the abundant work of Torrey as an author. He wrote more than seventy books and countless articles.

Torrey was ahead of his time in terms of education. As early as December 1900, he identified the enormous potential of distance education. He wrote, "Education by correspondence is no longer an experiment" in explanation for the founding of a Correspondence School Department of Moody Bible Institute. Torrey saw that "All over the land are those who would with a little well-directed study and training, become efficient lay workers in the cause of Christ." Since that time, Moody's External Studies Division has had more than 1.5 million enrollments. In Torrey's mind, the use of distance education methods was a matter of ministry economics.

There is a crying need for competent Bible teachers and also for those who understand the Word of God and know how to use it in bringing others to Christ. On the other hand, all over the land are those who would with a little well-directed study and training, become efficient lay workers in the cause of Christ. The Moody Bible Institute was founded to solve this problem of supply and demand.[2]

He was also ahead of his time in terms of lifestyle evangelism and seeker sensitivity. As you will see in this book, Torrey viewed evangelism and personal work as a way of life. He was also very aware of the fallen world in which we minister, and he provides very practical instruction on how to meet needy people in service where they are. Torrey never viewed ministry as something to be done only by the formally credentialed pastoral staff. This book was written to equip the masses of Christian workers in the work that many of them were already doing.

The practical nature of this book may take some readers by surprise. Many contemporary books focus so much on the principles of ministry that they don't make clear applications. Torrey tries to help you see the principles, but he does so from within the context of real situations. Although he provides very specific instructions on what you may do in certain circumstances, he doesn't intend for you to be restricted by his instructions. Rather, they are intended to train you in how to go about personal work so that you can be well-equipped for common situations and ready to adapt as necessary. Many of his illustrations may sound quaint, and a number of his instructions wouldn't work in the very different world of the twenty-first century. For one thing, Torrey lived in a world that was still heavily influenced by the church; even those who were not Christians knew something of the biblical story, respected Judeo-Christian ethics, and understood Christian terminology. Nevertheless, the principles are sound, and many of the examples can easily be made workable with a little creativity. In a few places, we've added a note explaining a term or suggesting a modern application of an example.

One constant throughout this book is the extreme priority of the Word of God in ministry. The book is filled with instruction on how to use particular Scripture passages that are relevant to the aspect of ministry at hand. Torrey stresses the power of having people read the Bible for themselves as you minister to them. It is not the "right answers" of the Christian worker that bring the results, but the power of God through His Word.

Another distinctive of Torrey's approach is his tremendous dependence on the Holy Spirit. Prayer is a vital component of one's ministry. Torrey's writings have been avoided in some contexts because of his statements regarding the Holy Spirit. Particularly, he writes often about the importance of the "baptism of the Holy Spirit." This phrase has taken on various meanings in the decades since Torrey's writing. It is now used commonly by those in a Holiness tradition to mean a "special sanctification that relieves one from even the temptation to sin" and by those in a Pentecostal tradition to mean a "confirmation of the presence of the Holy Spirit through the expression of sign gifts like speaking in tongues." The teaching of Moody Bible Institute is that the baptism of the Holy Spirit is something that happens in one's soul at the time of putting faith in Christ for salvation. Torrey used this term to refer to something special that happened after conversion. His understanding of the baptism of the Holy Spirit doesn't fit neatly within any of the common theological systems. However, it is important to note exactly what he meant when he used the term. Torrey was referring to a special empowerment of God for effectiveness in ministry. In this book, it is clear that he does not espouse the teachings of what became the Pentecostal or charismatic movement. He also didn't see Spirit baptism as a relief from even the temptation to sin. Rather, every reference he makes to the baptism of the Holy Spirit is connected to his teaching about how God may provide special empowerment for effectiveness in ministry. Thus, we have substituted the word "power" or "empowerment" for "baptism" in many of these references so that you will be able to focus on the significance of what he says, not the words he uses to say it.

This book is a great tool to keep alongside other tools. It provides the wisdom of an age gone by and captures the contributions of one of the most effective ministers ever. However, it certainly doesn't replace many of the other tools that are available today. It is best used alongside other tools.

The original text of this book has been modified only slightly. Introductions have been added to each chapter to provide special insights to make the contributions of Torrey most helpful. Footnotes are provided with the first occurrences of terms that are important but not widely known in contemporary society. Footnotes are also used to provide contemporary counterparts to resources that are no longer available. The lessons have been regrouped in order to provide chapters with better balance and flow. We have also been more consistent in the use of gender-inclusive language. Some Scripture passages in the original text have been removed due to space consideration, though the references remain. The original Scripture passages were from the King James Version, but we have used the *New King James Version*. Torrey himself made several references to the use of other versions, and we think that the NKJV fits the effort we are making to be historical and contemporary at the same time.

As you will soon see, Torrey wants the reader to use Scripture extensively and encourages the memorization of numerous passages for use in dozens of possible scenarios. If you are just learning your way around the Bible, you may find yourself intimidated at times by the sheer quantity of verses he suggests. You may find it helpful to highlight or underline particular discussions you are most likely to find useful, memorize the most useful of these, and make notes for some scenarios on a page in your Bible.

The learning activities at the end of each lesson are provided to help you put this material to use in your own personal work, in group studies, and/or as part of a correspondence course with Moody (if you choose to enroll). It is our desire to help you master the content but also move forward in its use. We think that the best learning comes from content mastery, critical thinking, collaborative interaction, and practical application. Hopefully, the material in the chapters and the learning activities will be used by God to make you a more effective Christian worker.

Of course, thanks goes first to R. A. Torrey who had not only such insight into practical Christian ministry, but also vision for how to teach others regarding it. Other thanks goes to several colleagues at Moody Bible Institute who have supported this project. Jay Fernlund has provided tremendous tangible and intangible support for Moody's historic distance education ministry. Randy Dattoli provided special encouragement that some of the original Moody correspondence courses had value for contemporary society. Debbie Ellis did most of the work getting Torrey's material in clean digital form. Greg Thornton shared the vision that a joint Moody Press/Moody External Studies project was a worthwhile idea. Cheryl Dunlop provided the insightful and penetrating editorial analysis that helped deliver Torrey's contribution to the readers of a new century. We hope and pray that the timeless truth and power of God's Word will be found effective as you prepare for and engage in your Practical Christian Work.

STEPHEN KEMP

NOTES
1. Faris David Whitesell, *Great Personal Workers* (Chicago: Moody, 1956), 56.
2. "Correspondence Course," *The Institute Tie*, December 1900, 105.

CHAPTER ONE

PREPARING FOR PRACTICAL CHRISTIAN WORK

ONE OF THE JOYS OF THE CHRISTIAN LIFE is the opportunity to be an ambassador for Christ. Practical Christian Work is for every believer. Some have professional training for specialized aspects of ministry, but everyone is called, gifted, and mandated to serve. This chapter presents the basics for personal work. However, it is not just a theoretical introduction. By the end of this chapter, you will already be equipped and launched into significant, practical Christian ministry. The rest of the book provides training to fill in the gaps in order to make you even more effective, but you are unlikely to benefit from the rest of the book if you don't immediately start putting this chapter into action.

The potential power of global transformation is not unleashed through the massive capacity of technology or even widely popular evangelists. God's plan is to use every one of us, as well as technology and prominent ministers. Jesus Himself used this approach. Although He ministered to the masses, it was His influence on twelve men that led to the global impact. One-on-one ministry may not seem as glamorous as preaching on TV that is being beamed around the world by satellite, but it is God's plan. Even the most prominent preachers who have ever lived were also called to be active in personal work for Christ.

Sometimes training for ministry takes a one-size-fits-all approach. R. A. Torrey has not done this in this book. Although he deals very specifically with situations and suggestions, a great deal of sensitivity underlies this training. As you read it, you will discover that the training is not just trying to give you the exact right answer for certain situations (though it does this well). Rather, it is trying to help you to grow into the kind of person who is able to draw on a wide range of resources (starting with the Holy Spirit and the Bible) as needed in situations that are foreseen and unforeseen. The impact comes from your being the minister that God wants you to be, not from having all the right answers.

Many of the examples in this chapter involve modes of transportation that were prevalent in the 1890s. The advent of the automobile has made transportation much more private, but there are still many ways that these instructions can be adapted for modern transportation, such as airplanes, and other social contexts. The point is clear that Torrey thinks that personal work is for everyone, everywhere, all the time.

The practical orientation of this book is wasted if you don't use it in a practical manner. At the end of each section are questions and learning activities that will help you to learn the content and also grow in your ability to use it. These opportunities for mastery of the content through active learning are key to your development as a Practical Christian Worker. It is our hope that God will use this experience to move you into more effective ministry. It follows the model established in the original curriculum of Moody Bible Institute. Students met in classes during the morning, ministered in the afternoon, and met together for testimonies and prayer in the evening.

THE IMPORTANCE AND ADVANTAGES OF PERSONAL WORK

IN OUR STUDY OF THE VARIOUS FORMS of Christian activity, we begin with "personal work"; that is, hand to hand dealing with men, women, and children. We begin with it because it is the simplest form of Christian work and one that everyone can do. It is also the most effective method of winning lost souls.

⟶ *Personal work is another term for Practical Christian Work, with both referring to dealing with a person's spiritual needs, particularly salvation, in a one-on-one counseling opportunity. Torrey uses them both throughout the book.*

The apostle Peter was brought to Jesus by the hand-to-hand work of his brother Andrew. Andrew first found Christ himself; then he went to Peter quietly and told him of his great find, and thus he led Peter to the Savior he himself had found. I do not know that Andrew ever preached a sermon—if he did, it is not recorded— but he did a great day's work when he led his brother Peter to Jesus. Peter preached a sermon that led to the conversion of three thousand people, but where would Peter's great sermon have been if Andrew had not first led him to Christ by quiet personal work? Mr. Edward Kimball, a Boston businessman, led D. L. Moody, a young Boston shoe clerk, to the Savior. Where would all Mr. Moody's wonderful work for Christ have been if he himself had not been led to the Savior by the faithful personal work of his Sunday school teacher?

I believe in preaching. It is a great privilege to preach the Gospel, but this world can be reached and evangelized far more quickly and thoroughly by personal work than by public preaching. Indeed, it can only be reached and evangelized by personal work. When the whole church of Jesus Christ shall rouse to its responsibility and privilege in this matter, and every individual Christian becomes a personal worker, the evangelization of the world will be close at hand. When the membership of any local church shall rouse to its responsibility and privilege in this matter, and each member becomes a personal worker in the power of the Holy Spirit, a great revival will be close at hand for the community in which that church is located. Personal work is a work that wins but little applause from men, but it accomplishes great things for God.

There are many who think personal work beneath their dignity and their gifts. A blind woman once came to me and said, "Do you think that my blindness will hinder me from working for the Master?" "Not at all; it may be a great help to you, for others seeing your blindness will come and speak to you, and then you will have an opportunity of giving your testimony for Christ, and of leading them to the Savior." "Oh, that is not what I want," she replied. "It seems to me a waste of time when one might be speaking to five or six hundred at once, just to be speaking to an individual." I answered that our Lord and Savior Jesus Christ was able to speak to more than five thousand at once, and yet He never thought personal work beneath His dignity or His gifts. Indeed, it was the work the Savior loved to do. We have more instances of our Savior's personal work recorded in the Gospels than of His preaching. The one who is above personal work is above his Master.

I. THE ADVANTAGES OF PERSONAL WORK

A. All can do it.

In an average congregation there are not more than four or five who can preach to edification. It would be a great pity, too, should all attempt to become preachers; it would be a great blessing if all would become personal workers. Any child of God can do personal work, and all can learn to do effective personal work. The mother who is confined at home by a multiplicity of home duties can still do personal work, first of all with her own children, and then with the servants in the home, with the butcher, the grocer, the tramp who calls at the door—in fact, with everybody who comes within reach. I once knew a mother very gifted in the matter of bringing her own children up in the nurture and admonition of the Lord who lamented that she could not do some work for Christ. I watched this woman carefully and found that almost everyone who came to the house in any capacity was spoken to about the Savior, and she was, in point of fact, doing more for Christ in the way of direct evangelistic work than most pastors.

Even the one shut up at home by sickness can do personal work. As friends come to the sickbed, a word of testimony can be given for Christ, or even an extended conversation can be held. A little girl of twelve, the child of very poor parents, lay dying in the city of Minneapolis. She let her light shine for the Master and spoke, among others, to a godless physician to whom, perhaps, no one else had ever spoken about Christ. A poor girl in New York City, who was rescued from the slums and died a year or two afterward, was used of God to lead about one hundred men and women to Christ while lying upon her dying bed.

Even the servant girl can do effective personal work. Lord Shaftsbury, the great English philanthropist, was won to Christ in a godless home by the effective work of a nurse girl.

Those who travel have unusually good opportunities for doing personal work as they travel on the trains from town to town, as they stop in one hotel after another and go from store to store. A professional nurse once came into my Bible class in Chicago and at the close of the meeting approached me and said: "I was led to Christ by a traveling man connected with a large wholesale house. I was in a hotel parlor, and this gentleman saw me and walked across the parlor and asked me if I was a Christian, and when I told him I was not, he proceeded at once to show me the way of life. I was so startled and impressed to find a traveling man leading others to Christ that I accepted Him as my Savior then and there. The man told me if I ever came to Chicago to come to your Bible class." I have watched this woman for years since, and she herself is a most devoted Christian and effective worker.

How enormous and wonderful and glorious would be the results if all Christians should begin to be active personal workers to the extent of their abilities! Nothing else would do so much to promote a revival in any community and in the land at large. Every pastor should urge this duty upon his people, train them for it, and see that they do it.

B. It can be done anywhere.

There are but few places where one can preach. There is no place where one cannot do personal work. How often, as we pass factories, engine houses, lodging houses, and other places where crowds are gathered, do we wish that we might get into them and preach the Gospel, but generally this is impossible; but it is altogether possible to go in and do personal work. Furthermore, we can do personal work on the street, whether street meetings are allowed or not. We can do personal work in the homes of the poor and in the homes of the rich, in hospitals, workhouses, jails, station houses, and all sorts of institutions—in a word, everywhere.

C. It can be done at any time.

The times when we can have preaching services and Sunday schools are quite limited. As a rule, in most communities, we cannot have services more than two or three days in the week and only three or four hours in the day, but personal work can be done seven days in the week and any time of day or night. Some of the best personal work done in this country in the last twenty years has been done on the streets at midnight and after midnight. Those who love souls have walked the streets looking for wanderers and have gone into dens of vice seeking the lost sheep, and hundreds upon hundreds of them have thus been found.

D. It reaches all classes.

There are large classes that no other method will reach. There are the shut-ins who cannot get out to church, the streetcar workers, the police, railroad conductors, sleeping-car workers, the very poor, and the very rich. Some cannot and others will not attend church or a cottage meeting or mission meeting, but personal work can reach them all.

> *Streetcars were a combination of trains and buses. In Chicago, they ran on rails down the middle of main streets and made frequent stops for passengers. Sleeping cars were train cars specially made to allow passengers to sleep comfortably during long trips. Some of the most popular and best ones were manufactured in Chicago at this time by the Pullman Company.*

E. It hits the mark.

Preaching is necessarily general; personal work is direct and personal. There is no mistaking who is meant; there is no dodging the arrow; there is no possibility of applying what is said to someone else. Many whom even so expert a Gospel preacher as Mr. Moody has missed have been afterward reached by personal work.

F. It meets the definite need, and every need, of the person dealt with.

Even when someone is aroused and convicted—and perhaps converted—by a sermon, personal work is necessary to bring out into clear light and into a satisfactory experience one whom the sermon has thus aroused, convicted, and converted.

G. It avails where other methods fail.

One of my best workers told me a few weeks ago that she had attended church for years and had wanted to become a Christian. She had listened to some of the best-known preachers and still was unsaved, but the very first inquiry meeting she went into she was saved because someone came and dealt with her personally.

H. It produces very large results.

There is no comparison whatever between what will be effected by good preaching and what will be effected by constant personal work. Take a church of one hundred members; such a church under an excellent pastor would be considered as doing an exceptionally good work if, on an average, fifty were added annually to this membership. But suppose that that church was trained to do personal work and that fifty of the one hundred members actually went at it. Certainly one a month won to Christ by each one would not be a large average. That would be six hundred a year instead of the fifty mentioned above. A church of many members—with the most powerful preaching possible—that depends upon the minister alone to win folks to Christ by his preaching, would not accomplish anything like what would be accomplished by a church with a comparatively poor preacher where the membership generally were personal workers.

LEARNING ACTIVITIES

1. Review the stories of successful personal work given in this section. Identify two or three additional stories from your church or elsewhere, perhaps even your own life. Ponder the importance of the ministry of normal people in their lives. Spend a few minutes in prayer, thanking God for His powerful work in these lives.

2. List the eight advantages of personal work. What other advantages might you add to the list? Which ones do you think are the most important for you and your personal work?

3. What excuses might you (or those in your church) give for not taking personal work seriously? How might R. A. Torrey respond to these excuses? What would be the impact on your church, home, job, and community if you (and believers around you) took personal work seriously?

4. Are you a believer? Have you personally accepted Christ as your Savior? If not, your first point of application of this material needs to be for yourself. You should jump to chapter 2 and follow Torrey's instructions for how to become a Christian.

THE CONDITIONS OF SUCCESS

I. A PERSONAL KNOWLEDGE OF CHRIST

The first condition of success in personal work, and in all soul-saving work, is a personal, experiential knowledge of Jesus Christ as Savior. It was because the apostle Paul could say: "This is a faithful saying and worthy of all acceptance, that Christ Jesus came into the world to save sinners, of whom I am chief" (1 Timothy 1:15) that he had power in bringing other men to that Savior. It is the one who knows Jesus as his own Savior who will have a longing to bring others to this wonderful Savior whom he has himself found, and it is the one who knows Jesus as his Savior who will understand how to bring others to the Savior whom he has found. Many today who are trying to save others are not saved themselves. Others, while they are probably saved, have such a vague knowledge of Christ as their own Savior that they cannot hope to make the way of salvation clear to others. A personal, experiential knowledge of Jesus Christ as Savior includes three things: a knowledge that our own sins have been forgiven because Jesus bore them in His own body on the cross; a knowledge that the risen Christ is delivering us daily from the power of sin; and an absolute surrender of our wills to Jesus Christ as our Lord and Master.

II. A CLEAN LIFE

The second condition of success in personal work is really involved in the first, and is a life clean within and without. In 2 Timothy 2:21 we read, "Therefore if anyone cleanses himself . . . he will be a vessel for honor, sanctified and useful for the Master, prepared for every good work." If a person is to be used of God, his life must be clean—not only his outward life as the world sees it, but his inward secret life as it is known only to God and to himself. One who holds on to any sin of act or thought or affection cannot expect to have power with a holy God, and consequently cannot expect to have power for God. Many a man and woman of great natural gifts and unusual knowledge of the Bible are trying to do work for God and meet with little or no success. People wonder why it is that their work is so devoid of results, but if we knew their secret life as God knows it, we would understand their failure; there is sin before God. It has been often said, and well said, that "God does not demand a beautiful vessel for His work, but He does demand a clean one." Many are working on in disappointment and failure, working hard but accomplishing nothing, because God sees sin in their inner life that they will not give up.

III. A SURRENDERED LIFE

The third condition of success in personal work is a surrendered life, a life wholly given up to God. Paul was mighty as a worker for Christ because he could say, "For to me, to live is Christ." The miracle of the five loaves and two fishes (Matthew 14:17–20) is deeply significant. The disciples said unto Jesus, "We have here only five loaves and two fish." He said, "Bring them here to me." We are told He took all that they had. It was not much, but they brought it all. Then He blessed it and broke it, and there was an abundance for all. But if one of those insignificant barley loaves had been kept back, or one of those little fishes, there would not have been enough to go around. We too may not have much—it may be only five barley crackers and two little fishes—but if we will bring them all—absolutely all—to Christ, He will take them, bless them, and multiply them; but if we hold back one cracker or one fish, He will not bless and multiply. Here lies the secret of failure in many a one who would work for Christ; there is one cracker kept back or one little fish. We talk very lightly of absolute surrender to God, but it means more than most people who profess it seem to realize. I would ask each reader of these pages, Have you brought all to Christ—absolutely all—absolutely ALL?

IV. A RECOGNITION OF MAN'S LOSTNESS

The one who would have success in personal work must have a deep realization that those out of Christ are lost. Jesus had this. He said, "For the Son of Man has come to seek and to save that which was *lost*" (Luke 19:10). When He looked upon men living in sin, He knew and realized the utter ruin of their condition. The same thing was true of Paul. We read in Acts 20:31 that he "did not cease to warn everyone night and day with tears." He knew that if one had not a saving knowledge of Jesus Christ, he was eternally lost. This overwhelming conviction that men and women out of Christ are eternally lost seems to be very rare in our day, and this is one great reason why so few have real power in soul-winning. How can we get this realization?

⌁ *Soul-winning was a common term at this time for assertive, confrontational evangelism.*

A. First of all, by studying what the Bible has to say about the present standing and condition and future destiny of those who are out of Christ.

B. By believing what the Bible says upon these points without trying to tone it down and make it fit in with the popular notions of the day.

C. By dwelling upon these truths about the lost condition of those out of Christ until they take hold upon our hearts and we realize their meaning.

These things are not pleasant to think about, but they are true, and we ought to think about them until our souls are on fire to save people from the awful condition of utter ruin in which they now are, and from the destiny of eternal shame and despair to which they are hurrying.

V. LOVE OF PEOPLE

The fifth condition of success in personal work is love. Nothing wins like love. In the first place, it leads to untiring effort for the salvation of others. If I really love others, I cannot bear the thought that they should be lost forever, and I will be willing to work day and night to save them from such an awful destiny. In the second place, love attracts others to us. There is nothing so irresistible as love. It is Jesus Christ lifted up on the cross, a revelation of God's love and of His own love to man, that draws all unto Him (John 12:32). Folks will not put you off if they really believe that you love them, but they will never believe that you love them unless you really do. We need not only love for others, but love for Christ. It was the love of Christ that constrained Paul to his untiring efforts to bring men to a knowledge of Christ. The great men and women of Christian history have been the men and women who have had a great love for Christ, men and women whose hearts were all aglow with love for the glorious Son of God.

But how can we get love? First of all, by dwelling upon Christ's love to us. "We love Him because He first loved us" (1 John 4:19). We shall never appreciate Christ's love to us until we see it against the black background of our own sin. It is the one who is forgiven much who loves much (Luke 7:47). The one who has never been brought to a deep realization of his own sinfulness before God will have no warmth of love for that Savior who, by His own atoning death on the cross, redeemed him from the awful depth to which he had sunk. The apostle Paul realized that he was the chief of sinners, and that Jesus loved him and gave Himself for him, so he was full of love to Jesus Christ. This is a faithful saying, and worthy of being accepted, "that Christ Jesus came into the world to save sinners, of whom I am chief" (1 Timothy 1:15). "I have been crucified with Christ; it is no longer I who live, but Christ lives in me; and the life which I now live in the flesh I live by faith in the Son of God, who loved me and gave Himself for me" (Galatians 2:20).

If we are to have love to Christ and love to men, the Holy Ghost must impart it. The first fruit of the Spirit is love: "But the fruit of the Spirit is love, joy, peace, longsuffering, kindness, goodness, faithfulness" (Galatians 5:22). If we will look to the Holy Spirit to do His whole work in our hearts, He will soon fill them with love of Christ and love of others.

VI. PERSEVERANCE AND PATIENCE

The sixth condition of success in personal work is perseverance. No work requires so much patience and perseverance as soul-winning. People are not usually won to Christ in a day. You must hold on to them day after day, week after week, month after month, and if need be, year after year. You must not give them up even though you seem to make absolutely no headway at first, and even though you seem to do more harm than good.

When you start out to lead someone to Christ, keep after him until he is saved, no matter how long it takes. Study how to get at those who are unreachable. Someone who cannot be reached in one way can in another. There are very few in the world to whose hearts there is not an open door somewhere, if we will only search diligently until we find it. If we cannot get in at the door, perhaps we can break up the roof and get in that way. Anyone who wishes to win souls at the rate of one every fifteen minutes had better go into some other business. Take time; never give up; and do thorough work.

I waited and watched fifteen long years to get my chance with one man. Never a day passed for all those fifteen years that I did not speak to God about that man. At last my chance came, and it was my privilege to lead him to Christ. He afterward became a preacher of the Gospel, and is now in heaven. I was with him the day before he died and shall never forget that day as long as I live. When you undertake to bring a man to Christ, never give up.

VII. A PRACTICAL BIBLE KNOWLEDGE

The seventh condition of success in personal work is a practical knowledge of the Bible. "All Scripture is given by inspiration of God, and is profitable for doctrine, for reproof, for correction, for instruction in righteousness, that the man of God may be complete, thoroughly equipped for every good work" (2 Timothy 3:16–17). In the Bible is all the truth we need. The Word of God is the only instrument that God has appointed for salvation, and the only instrument He honors is the Word. It is the Word that produces conviction of sin. It is the Word that regenerates. It is the Word that produces faith (Acts 2:37; Romans 10:17; 1 Peter 1:23). If, then, we are to be used in soul-winning, we must know the Bible. Five texts ought to sink deep into the heart of every personal worker. They are:

A. "So then faith comes by hearing, and hearing by the word of God" (Romans 10:17).

B. "The seed is the word of God" (Luke 8:11b).

C. "Having been born again, not of corruptible seed but incorruptible, through the word of God which lives and abides forever" (1 Peter 1:23).

D. "And take the helmet of salvation, and the sword of the Spirit, which is the word of God" (Ephesians 6:17).

E. "'Is not My word like a fire?' says the Lord, 'and like a hammer that breaks the rock in pieces?'" (Jeremiah 23:29).

The personal worker who depends upon any other instrument than the Word of God is doomed to failure. But we must have a practical knowledge of the Bible; that is, we must know how to use it for definite results. A great many have a large theoretical knowledge of the Bible, but no practical knowledge. They do not know how to use the Bible so as to accomplish anything definite by its use. In an inquiry meeting one evening, I asked one of the best Bible scholars in America to speak to an inquirer and show her the way of life, and he whispered in my ear, "I don't know how to do that." A small practical knowledge of the Bible is better in personal work than a large theoretical knowledge.

⟶ The inquiry room was a designated place where those under conviction or wanting to inquire further about Christ could come and meet personally with someone about their questions or needs following a church service or Gospel meeting. It was often located a short distance from the platform so that it could be easily accessed after an invitation by inquirers who came forward during a service.

A practical knowledge of the Bible involves four things:

A. A knowledge of how to so use the Bible as to show people, and make them realize, their need of a Savior.

B. A knowledge of how to use the Bible so as to show people Jesus as the Savior who meets their need.

C. A knowledge of how to use the Bible so as to show people how to make Jesus their own Savior.

D. A knowledge of how to use the Bible so as to meet the difficulties that stand in the way of people accepting Christ.

A large part of the following pages will be devoted to imparting this particular kind of Bible knowledge.

VIII. AN ACTIVE LIFE OF PRAYER

The eighth condition of success in personal work is prayer. God honors prayer. In nothing does He honor it more than in the matter of soul-winning. The one who is to be much used of God in soul-winning must spend much time in prayer. There are four things for which we must especially pray:

A. We must ask God to bring to us, or us to, the right persons.

We cannot speak with everyone. If we attempt it, we will spend much time in speaking where we can do no good that we might have used in speaking where we could have accomplished something for Christ. God alone knows the one to whom He intends us to speak, and we must ask Him to point him out to us and expect Him to do it (Acts 8:29).

B. We should ask God to give us the right message in each case where we do speak with anyone.

We can learn much by studying what is the right message for any given class, but after all our study, we must look directly to God for the right message in each individual case. Many cases will baffle us, but no case will baffle God. We need and must have the direct guidance of the Holy Spirit in each individual case. Every experienced worker could testify to many instances in which God has led him to use some text of Scripture that he would not otherwise have used, but which proved to be just the one needed.

C. We must pray to God to give power to that which He has given us to say.

We need not only a message from God, but power from God to send the message home. Most workers have to learn this lesson by humiliating experiences. They sit down beside an unsaved person and reason and plead and bring forth texts from the Word of God, but the person does not accept Christ. At last it dawns upon the workers that they are trying to convert in their own strength, and they lift a short but humble prayer to God for His strength, and in a very little while this "very difficult case" has settled the matter and is rejoicing in Christ.

D. We must pray to God to carry on the work.

After having done that which seems to have been our whole duty in any given instance, whatever may have been the apparent result of our work, whether successful or unsuccessful, we should definitely commit the case to God in prayer. If there is anything the average worker in this hurrying age needs to have impressed upon him, it is the necessity of much prayer. By praying more, we will not work any less, and we will accomplish vastly more.

IX. POWER OF THE HOLY GHOST

The ninth condition of success in personal work is the power of the Holy Ghost. In Acts 1:8 we read, "But you shall receive power when the Holy Spirit has come upon you." The supreme condition of power in the early church was the definite empowerment by the Holy Ghost. The supreme condition of success in soul-winning is the same today. Many in these days are trying to prove that there is no such thing as a special empowerment by the Holy Spirit, but a candid and careful study of the Acts of the Apostles will show that there is. Very many in our day also know by blessed experience that the power of the Holy Spirit is a present-day reality. One ounce of believing experience along this line is worth whole tons of unbelieving exegesis, no matter how subtle and learned it may be. There are thousands of men and women—in this and other lands—who have been brought out of a place of powerlessness into a place of power in the Lord's service through meeting the conditions plainly laid down in the Bible for receiving the empowerment of the Holy Ghost. This empowerment by the Holy Spirit is for every child of God, and the one who would be largely used of God in personal work must get it at any cost.

R. A. Torrey often refers to a special baptism of the Holy Spirit. Since he was clearly not referring to the second blessing or baptism of the Holy Spirit with the meaning that was made common by the Pentecostals who would soon follow, we have usually changed the wording to refer to the power of the Holy Spirit. Clearly, Torrey's emphasis was on the concept of a special provision of God's power for service, but not a "baptism" that resulted in what is commonly known as the sign gifts, such as speaking in tongues.

LEARNING ACTIVITIES

1. Review the nine conditions of success in personal work. Evaluate yourself using these conditions. Which conditions do you consider to be your strengths? Which conditions do you consider to be your weaknesses? Perhaps you could use a rating system to evaluate yourself on each one (1 to 10, weak/moderate/strong).

2. Make a list of areas in which you know you need to grow in order to be more effective in personal work. Share this list with a trusted fellow believer, and allow that believer to help you refine the list. Give this person a copy of the list, and invite him or her to check up on you every few weeks for the next three months.

3. What does a personal, experiential knowledge of Jesus Christ as Savior include? Do you have this knowledge for yourself? If not, please pause right now to receive it. God wants you to have it for your benefit as well as for the benefit of those you serve.

4. How can we get a realization that men and women outside of Christ are lost? If your passion for lost souls is not sufficient, pause right now and follow the instructions of this lesson. Study what the Bible says, identify those in your life who are lost, meditate upon the sad reality of their condition, and ask God to give you a passion for souls.

5. How can we get love for Christ? How can we get love for people? Identify one or two practical steps for each that you can take to improve your love for Christ and your love for people.

6. What four things does a practical knowledge of the Bible involve? Keep these in mind as you proceed through the rest of the book, since they are keys to being effective in personal work.

7. Review the four things for which we should pray, then take a good bit of time to pray for them. Consider how you might add these things to your prayer life.

8. Does your current personal work reflect the power of the Holy Spirit? Identify ways that you can become more dependent on God through prayer, everyday behavior, and special behavior that draws you closer to God.

WHERE TO DO
PERSONAL WORK

I. AFTER A GOSPEL MEETING

Perhaps the easiest and most natural place to do personal work is after a Gospel meeting. Whenever you attend a meeting, watch for someone to deal with after the meeting is over. Do not trust to chance in the matter, but as the minister preaches the sermon keep your eyes on the audience, and watch who it is who is hit and what hits them; then you can follow up the work that the minister has already done by his sermon. You will soon acquire good judgment in deciding with whom it is wisest to speak. Of course, one must be on his guard against being obtrusive in watching others. Before you go to the meeting, pray definitely to God to give you someone at the meeting, and then watch for an answer to your prayer. When you have found your man, go for him, and do not let him slip away under any consideration. It is often well to go as quickly as possible to one of the doors of the meeting house, and without making oneself too prominent, watch people as they come out, and then gently and courteously approach someone, and deal with him about his soul.

Gospel meetings were common evangelistic services held for the purpose of attracting those who needed to hear the Gospel.

There is a great difference in Christian workers. Some seem to never get anyone at the close of a meeting unless someone else takes them to them. They wait around with their Bibles under their arms for someone to come to them and take them to an inquirer; others keep their eyes open for themselves and almost always manage to get hold of someone. In many of the more active churches, the church is divided into sections with an overseer over each division of the church and individual workers under the overseer. This is an excellent plan. When it is well carried out, it prevents any hopeful cases from getting out without being dealt with personally.

II. IN HOMES

The apostle Paul tells us that he preached the Gospel not only publicly, but "from house to house" (Acts 20:20). There is far too little Christian work done in the home. The best home to begin with is your own. Jesus bade the demoniac of Gadara when he was healed to return to his own house and show what great things God had done unto him (Luke 8:39). Everyone who is converted should begin to tell the saving power of Christ first at home, to relatives and friends. Many regret not having a wider field of labor for Christ, but anyone can find one of the grandest of all fields at home.

But we should not limit our personal work to our own homes; we should do it in the homes where we visit. In this way, those who make us partakers of their hospitality will entertain angels unawares (Hebrews 13:2). A godly man who once visited in the home of Spurgeon's parents, by a few words to the little boy, made an impression upon that boy that went far toward making him the mighty minister of the Gospel that he became in later years.

Then we should do personal work in the houses that we enter in our house-to-house visitation. That man or woman is a poor church visitor who simply makes a pleasant call or talks upon religious generalities. The true visitor will find frequent opportunities for doing effective personal work with some of the inhabitants of the home or with strangers they may find calling upon them.

III. ON THE STREETS

Here again, we have the apostle Paul for an example. Not only did he reason "in the synagogue with the Jews and with the *Gentile* worshipers," but also "in the marketplace daily with those who happened to be there" (Acts 17:17). As you walk the streets, be listening for the voice of God to say, "Go and speak to that man." Very often, as one walks the streets of a crowded city or the lonely roads of the country, if he is walking with God, the leading will come to speak to someone that he meets by the way; and countless are the souls that have been led out of darkness into light in this way. As you look upon the surging crowd, ask God if there is someone in this crowd with whom He desires you to speak. Sometimes it is well to stand to one side and watch the people as they pass. Soon there will come a face that interests you, a face it may be that tells a story of sin, or sorrow, and need. You can quietly follow this person and watch for an opportunity to engage him in conversation, and then point him to the One who says, "Come to Me, all you who labor and are heavy laden, and I will give you rest."

IV. IN THE PARKS AND OTHER RESORTS

The parks are often full of people who have plenty of leisure and are willing to talk upon almost any subject. Go through the park and find someone; engage in a conversation and, as quickly as you can, lead up to the great subject that is burning in your own heart. Oftentimes, it is well to begin to talk about matters of passing interest, the burning questions of the day, then lead by the shortest possible route to the great question. Sometimes show the one with whom you are talking a tract, and ask for an opinion of it, and this will lead easily to the matter uppermost in your mind. Not infrequently, if you sit down in a park, someone will come and sit down beside you and begin to talk to you; then, of course, it is very easy to lead the person into a conversation about his own soul's need.

V. ON A WALK OR RIDE.

In this we have our Savior's own example. He made the hearts of the two disciples burn within them while He spoke to them in the way and opened to them the Scriptures (Luke 24:32). We also have the example of Philip the evangelist. The Spirit bade him go and join himself to the chariot of Queen Candace's treasurer. The treasurer invited him up into the chariot to ride with him, and the memorable conversation and personal dealing that followed led to the conversion and baptism of the treasurer and the carrying of the Gospel into Ethiopia (Acts 8:27–38). There are few more favorable places to do personal work than on a walk or ride with a friend, or even with a stranger.

VI. AT THE PLACE OF BUSINESS

Here again we have the Savior's example. "As He passed by, He saw Levi the son of Alphaeus sitting at the tax office, and said to him, 'Follow Me.' And he arose and followed Him" (Mark 2:14). Of course, we ought not to interrupt people and hinder their proper performance of their business duties. Many a worker has special opportunities to speak with fellow workers, sometimes during work hours, sometimes during the noon rest. One of the most earnest Christian ministers I ever knew had been a godless employee in a factory, but the man who worked next to him was a Christian, took an interest in his fellow employee's soul, and was instrumental under God in leading him to Christ. I have met a good many from one of the largest business institutions in our city who have been led to Christ by one consecrated young man in the establishment. This young man has since gone as a foreign missionary, but he was used of God to lead many of his fellow employees to Christ before he went. It is well, wherever possible, to go into stores and factories and other places of business for the deliberate purpose of leading those who work there to Christ. Of course, as already said, it will not do to interrupt a man at his business; neither will it do generally to deal with him when others are around and listening; nor should he be taken at an hour when he is in a bad temper; but one who has that discretion that God is so ready to give (James 1:5) will find many opportunities for doing the Master's work. It is quite possible oftentimes to drop a word, or even to have a little talk—when there is not a great pressure of business—with the clerk who sells us goods, or with the barber who shaves us, or with the one who shines our shoes. There are five marks of a good opportunity: when one is alone, unoccupied, in good humor, communicative, and in a serious mood.

VII. ON CARS AND BOATS

Traveling on the steam cars affords a very rare opportunity for personal work. Travelers usually have much time that hangs heavily upon their hands and are glad to get into conversation with anyone, but if one is a real Christian, there is one subject always uppermost in his mind, one subject that one would rather talk about than any other, and that is Jesus Christ. When you get into a train, get as good a seat for yourself as you can, put your coat out of the way, move away over to the farther side of the seat, and make the vacant space beside you look as inviting as possible. If the car is at all crowded, you will soon have a fellow passenger and the desired opportunity for personal work. Sometimes it is well to keep your coat in the seat beside you until you see the man or woman that you want coming, and then remove it and move along in a way of silent invitation.

Steam cars were trains that operated on steam power.

It is well to talk with the workers on the train. They are usually willing to talk, and many of them have been led to Christ by Spirit-filled workers who were traveling with them. Many Christian workers go through trains and give tracts to everyone on the train. I am not sure that this is the wisest thing to do, but I know that great blessing has come from it in many cases. Certainly it is well to carry a good supply of religious literature with you when you travel. Some of the books of the Bible Institute Colportage Association are excellent for this purpose. People are willing to read almost anything on a train, and these books without any comment oftentimes will lead the reader to Christ, and when they do not do this they pave the way for a conversation.

The Bible Institute Colportage Association was the historic precursor to Moody Press. It was a publishing house that focused on materials that could be used in personal work. An excellent current resource for this purpose is the small book by Ray Pritchard called An Anchor for the Soul.

Streetcars are not as favorable a place for personal work as steam cars. One does not have the time or opportunity that he does on a train, and yet good work can be done on a streetcar, both with the passengers and with the motorman and conductor. A minister once said to me, "I was greatly ashamed last night going down on the streetcar. I was sitting inside the car talking on unimportant matters with friends, and as I looked to the front end of the car, I saw one member of my church talking with the driver about his soul, and when I looked to the other end of the car, I saw another member of my church talking to the conductor; and there I, the pastor of the church, was doing nothing but wasting my time."

VIII. IN PRISONS, HOSPITALS, AND OTHER PUBLIC INSTITUTIONS

A fine place to do personal work is in public institutions, such as prisons and hospitals, where many people are gathered together and are at leisure from morning till night. Every Sunday, all over this land, devoted men and women are going into prisons, jails, and hospitals carrying the glad tidings of salvation, and thousands are being converted to God through their faithful personal work. Many of the best Christians that I know today were brought to Christ in prison, not so much through the public preaching as through the personal work of some devoted child of God who went from cell to cell and talked to the men about Christ. But while so much is being done already in this direction, there are many prisons and jails and hospitals where little or nothing is done.

Nurses in hospitals have a rare opportunity of doing personal work in the institutions where they are employed. Fortunately, a very large proportion of trained nurses are devoted Christian women, and yet many of them do not realize the opportunities that God has put within their reach. A very unusual opportunity is also open to the Christian physician. Indeed, a true Christian physician will oftentimes find opportunities for doing personal work that even the minister of the Gospel cannot find. Sometimes it will be with the patient, sometimes with the relatives and friends of the patient who are in deep anxiety as to the outcome of the sickness.

What has been said does not, of course, cover all the places where personal work can be done, but it will suggest rich fields of opportunity. To put it in a word, personal work should be done everywhere. We read of the early disciples that "those who were scattered went everywhere preaching the word" (Acts 8:4); that is, talking to individuals about Jesus, showing them the Word of Truth as it is found in the Bible, and leading them to accept it. Every child of God should be at all times on the lookout for opportunities to speak personally to some other man or woman about Christ.

LEARNING ACTIVITIES

1. List eight places in which personal work can be profitably done, including one or two in addition to those listed by Torrey. Which of these places are available for you to use for personal work?

2. Have you ever dealt with anyone for salvation after an evangelistic meeting? How did you (or how would you) go about doing so? How might you use this book as a reference to help you?

3. Give scriptural proof of the importance of personal work in the home. How active are you in your home? As you proceed through this book, keep a list of how you might minister more effectively in your own home.

4. Have you ever dealt with anyone on the street, in a park, or during some other spontaneous public encounter? Describe the encounter and compare it to the biblical illustrations and comments in this lesson.

5. Review the places in which personal work can be done (including Torrey's and yours). Identify the places where you think that you will be most effective. Jot down a few of Torrey's instructions (or instructions that you think of for yourself) and put them where you are likely to find them and be reminded of what to do when you are in those places.

HOW
TO BEGIN

ONE OF THE MOST DIFFICULT POINTS in personal work is beginning. It is comparatively easy to go on after one has got an opening.

I. THE FIRST THING IS TO FIND THE ONE TO DEAL WITH.

As has already been said, we should pray God to lead us to someone, or someone to us. When we go to church or when we walk the street, when we are in the park or on the train or calling, in a word, whenever we have time that is not demanded by other duties, we should look up to God and definitely ask Him to lead us to the one with whom we are to speak, if it is His will that we employ that time in work for Him. Further than this, we should be on the lookout for opportunities. A fisherman cultivates a keen eye for opportunities to catch fish, and a soul-winner should cultivate a keen eye for opportunities for soul-winning. Whenever we are thrown into the company of a man or woman, the great probability is that it is a providential opening, and we should be ready to meet it as such.

It is said of one of the most distinguished Sunday school workers in this country that he makes it a point whenever he is alone with any individual to speak to him about his soul. The story is told of a man, that being left alone in a hotel parlor with a strange lady he at once approached her and began to speak to her about her soul. After he had gone, the woman's husband returned, and she told him what had happened. The husband was in a great rage and said, "If I had been here, I would have sent him about his business." His wife replied, "If you had been here, you would have thought he was about his business." We ought to make soul-winning our business and improve every possible opportunity.

II. HAVING FOUND SOMEONE, BEGIN A CONVERSATION.

How shall that be done? In the inquiry room, by asking at once a few leading questions to find out just where the person stands; for example: "Are you a Christian?" "Are you saved?" "Have you been born again?" "Upon what do you base your hope of eternal life?" "Are you confessing Christ openly before the world?" "Have you surrendered all you have and are to Christ?"

Sometimes it is well to begin in this direct way even when you meet someone casually. The question "Are you saved?" is as a general rule a better one to ask than "Are you a Christian?" It is more likely to set one to thinking. It is more definite and pointed. Many will take the asking of such a question as an impertinence, but that will not prove that the question has not done good. Not a few people who have become angry at a stranger putting a question like this to them have afterward been converted in consequence of it. There are many other questions that one may ask that will set one to thinking and open the way for further conversation. For example, you can ask, "Do you think that life is worth living?" and after you have engaged in conversation on this point, you can lead on and tell of the life that really is worth living. Or you can ask an utter stranger, "How do you think someone can get the most real satisfaction out of life?" The answer is, of course, by accepting Jesus Christ as Savior. Or you can say, "I have learned the great secret of happiness," and when asked to tell what it is, you can do so. Of course, these are only offered as suggestions of ways in which to begin a conversation.

A good way to begin is by handing the person with whom you wish to deal a well-chosen tract to read. When he is finished with the tract, you can ask what he thinks about it, and thus the way is opened to a conversation on the great subject. It is often well to begin by engaging the person in a general conversation, perhaps on subjects quite remote from religion, and gradually working around to the point. It was thus that Christ engaged the woman of Samaria, making a very simple request of her, that she would give Him a drink (John 4:7), but before long He was telling her of the Living Water. If the person with whom you wish to deal is older than yourself, you might begin by saying, "There is a subject in which I am deeply interested, and I am trying to get all the light upon it that I can. You are older than I, and perhaps you can help me. The subject is 'How to Be Saved.'"

Showing people little kindnesses very often opens the way for a conversation on the great subject. For example, in a crowded car one can move along and invite someone who is standing to a seat by your side. It is the most natural thing in the world then to get into conversation. The favor of the person who has been standing is gained, and it will be very easy to lead on to the great subject. When one is riding and sees someone else walking, an invitation to the walker to ride will afford a splendid opportunity for approaching him on the subject of his soul's salvation. Mr. Moody made a constant practice of inviting those with whom he wished to deal out riding with him. As he drew near to some quiet spot, he would speak to them of what was upon his heart and then stop the horse and have a season of prayer. No one can tell how many were thus led to Christ.

Sometimes it is well to show the people that you would lead to Christ kindnesses for days and weeks, and even years, waiting for your opportunity to say a word. A devoted Chinese missionary, who had made great sacrifices to go to that land, was received by the people with bitterest hatred, but he simply gave himself up to live among them and live for them. One by one, opportunities came of showing them kindnesses, and after years of self-sacrificing living he had so won their confidence that it was an easy matter for him to lead them to Christ; but he had to begin by showing them the most ordinary, everyday kindnesses, far away, apparently, from the subject that was closest to his heart.

Sometimes a person's face will tell the story of discontent, unhappiness, or unrest. In such a case, it is easy to ask if the person is happy, and if not, tell about the One who can make him happy. Tact in beginning will come with experience, but it is better to begin awkwardly than not to begin at all. I do not think that anyone could begin more awkwardly in this work than I did with the first person whom I led to Christ. I felt that God wanted me to speak to this young man, and I called on him for that purpose, but when I met him I had not the slightest idea what to say. I talked on and on waiting for an opportunity, and at last blundered out awkwardly what I had come for. God blessed the awkward but honest effort, and the young man was saved and has become a very active and efficient worker for Christ. The best way to learn how to do personal work is by doing it, gaining wisdom from your mistakes.

III. FIND OUT AS SOON AS POSSIBLE WHERE THE PERSON STANDS.

In order to treat a case intelligently, you need just as much as a physician to know exactly where the person is at present. But how can we find out to what class any person belongs?

A. By asking questions

First of all, by asking questions, such as "Are you saved?" "Have you eternal life?" "Have you been born again?" "Do you know that you are a great sinner before God?" "Do you know that your sins are forgiven?" Or you can ask a person directly, "Where do you stand; what do you believe?" These questions may be answered untruthfully, either from ignorance or a desire to mislead you; nevertheless, the answers and manner of giving them will show you a great deal about a person's real state.

B. By watching the inquirer's face

A face will often reveal that which words try to conceal. Anyone who cultivates a study of the faces of those with whom he is dealing will soon be able to tell—in many instances—their exact state, irrespective of anything they may say.

C. By observing the inquirer's tone and manner

A tone or manner often tells more than words. People who are not saved will very likely tell you that they are, but their tone and manner will reveal plainly that they are not. If one gets angry at you for asking these questions, that of itself may reveal an uneasy conscience.

D. By the Holy Spirit

The Holy Spirit, if we look to Him to do it, will often flash into our minds a view of the person's position and just the Scripture that he needs.

IV. LEAD THE PERSON TO CHRIST.

When we have learned where the person with whom we are dealing stands, the next thing to do is to lead the person as directly as we can to accept Jesus Christ as his personal Savior, and to surrender to Him as his Lord and Master. We must always bear in mind that the primary purpose of our work is not to get people to join the church, or to give up their bad habits, or to do anything else than this: to accept Jesus Christ as their Savior, the One who bore their sins in His own body on the tree, and the One through whom they can have immediate and entire forgiveness, and as their Master, to whom they surrender absolutely the guidance of their thoughts, purposes, feelings, and actions.

V. NEXT, SHOW FROM GOD'S WORD THAT THERE IS NOW FORGIVENESS OF SINS AND ETERNAL LIFE.

Acts 10:43; 13:39; John 3:36; 5:24 will answer for this purpose. The next step will be to show how to make a success of the Christian life that has been entered.

LEARNING ACTIVITIES

1. Identify a specific situation and/or a specific person with whom you want to begin personal work. Apply the instructions of Torrey to this situation using the questions below. What leading questions might you use?

2. What is the first thing that Torrey suggests you find out when you have begun to deal with this person? How might you use Torrey's advice or other ideas to learn where this person stands spiritually? What needs to be your first priority in dealing with this person? When this person accepts Christ, what further steps need to be taken?

3. Develop a plan for beginning personal work in your specific situation and/or with a specific person. Include steps that you can take in the next few hours or days, including prayer to the Lord to strengthen you for the task.

4. Ask someone in your church or another fellow believer to hold you accountable for putting the plan into action. A regular system of training, activity, and reporting will prove to be of great value. Establish specific places, times, and questions to be asked so that you can make sure that you are putting into practice what you are learning.

CHAPTER TWO

LEADING PEOPLE TO CHRIST, PART 1

THIS CHAPTER MOVES RIGHT INTO the most important thing that we can do in personal work, namely, leading others to salvation in Christ. It deals with the easiest and largest groups, those who are ready to respond and those who have no concern. If one only studies this chapter, it will provide an excellent basic framework for presenting the Gospel. In dealing with both of these groups, the presentation of the Gospel is straightforward. In the next chapter, one must deal with the complicating factors that cause difficulties. However, even in dealing with those who have difficulties, one will constantly need to come back to the basics of the Gospel as presented in this chapter.

It is important to note that although salvation is a simple matter of belief, Torrey does not teach an "easy believism." This chapter shows that salvation is the beginning of God's work in a person's life. Torrey provides instruction on how to launch the new believer in the victorious Christian life of holiness and service through the continuous ministry of the Holy Spirit and the Bible in one's life.

Torrey's teaching provides very precise guidance in having the right conversations regarding the Gospel. In many instances, he leads you through common conversations. These models are of great assistance in being able to anticipate the flow of the discussion and be prepared to make the next step toward acceptance of Christ as Savior. However, the instructions are not tight protocol that must be followed precisely in every situation. Rather, they are very practical instructions that allow you to mix, match, adjust, and adapt as necessary.

Lastly, it is significant to see how heavily these instructions depend on Scripture. The concept of personal work is firmly founded in the Bible, but so is the process. In every situation, Torrey doesn't just provide you with the right answer, he gives you a word from Scripture that can be used. A vast portion of your personal work is simply being able to present the right portions of the Bible at the right time. In this way, your personal work is truly God's personal work.

HOW TO DEAL WITH THOSE WHO REALIZE THEIR NEED OF A SAVIOR AND REALLY DESIRE TO BE SAVED

WE COME NOW TO THE QUESTION of how to deal with individual cases. We begin with those who realize their need of a Savior, and really desire to be saved. We begin with these because they are the easiest class to deal with.

I. SHOW THEM JESUS AS A SIN-BEARER.

The first thing to show one who realizes a need of a Savior is that Jesus has borne our sins in His own body on the cross. A good verse for this purpose is Isaiah 53:6: "All we like sheep have gone astray; we have turned, every one, to his own way; and the Lord has laid on Him the iniquity of us all." Get the inquirer to read the verse, then say, "The first half of this verse shows you your need of salvation; the second half shows you the provision that God has made for your salvation. Read again the first half of the verse. Is this true of you? Have you gone astray like a sheep? Have you turned to your own way?" "Yes." "Then what are you?" Get the inquirer to say, "I am lost." "We will now look at the provision God has made for your salvation. Read the last half of the verse. Who is the One in this verse upon whom our iniquity has been laid?" "Christ." "What then has God done with your sin?" "Laid it on Christ." "Is it then on you any longer?" Go over it again and again until it is seen that his sin is on Christ and has been settled forever.

I often use a simple illustration in making the meaning of the verse plain. I let my right hand represent the inquirer, my left hand represent Christ, and my Bible represent the inquirer's sin. I first lay the Bible on my right hand and say, "Now where is your sin?" The inquires replies, of course, "On me." I then repeat the last half of the verse, "the Lord has *laid on him* the iniquity of us all," and transfer the Bible from my right hand to my left, and ask, "Where is your sin now?" The inquirer replies, "On Him, of course." I then ask, "Is it on you any longer?" "No, on Christ." Very many people have been led out into light and joy by this simple illustration.

I sometimes put it in this way, in using this verse: "There are two things that a person needs to know, and one thing a person needs to do in order to be saved. A person needs to know, first, that he or she is a lost sinner, and this verse says that; and second, that Christ is an all-sufficient Savior, and this verse also says that. What he or she needs to do is to accept this all-sufficient Savior whom God has provided. Now will you accept Him right here and now?"

Another excellent verse to show Jesus as a Sin-Bearer is Galatians 3:13: "Christ has redeemed us from the curse of the law, *having become a curse for us* (for it is written, 'Cursed is everyone who hangs on a tree')." Inquirers should be given the verse to read for themselves. When it has been read, you may ask something like this: "What does this verse tell us that Christ has redeemed us from?" "Whom has He redeemed?" "How has He redeemed us from the curse of the law?" "Do you believe that Christ has redeemed you from the curse of the law by being made a curse in your place?" "Will you read it then in the singular instead of in the plural?" Make it clear what you mean, until the inquirer reads the verse in this way: "Christ has redeemed me from the curse of the law, being made a curse for me; for it is written, cursed is everyone who hangs on a tree."

Another good verse for this purpose is 2 Corinthians 5:21: "For He made Him who knew no sin to be sin for us, that we might become the righteousness of God in Him." Have the person read the verse, and then ask questions somewhat as follows: "Who is it who has been made sin for us?" "For whom has Christ been made sin?" "For what purpose is it that Christ has been made sin for us?" "Can you put this verse in the singular and read it this way: 'For He made Him who knew no sin to be sin for me, that I might be made the righteousness of God in Him'?"

Sometimes it will be well to use all three of these passages, but as a rule the first is sufficient. As far as my own experience goes, it is more effective than either of the other passages—in fact, I deal with very few with whom I do not use Isaiah 53:6 sooner or later.

II. SHOW THEM JESUS AS A RISEN SAVIOR, ABLE TO SAVE TO THE UTTERMOST.

It is not enough to show them Jesus as a Sin-Bearer, for through believing in Jesus as a Sin-Bearer one merely gets pardon from sin, but there is something else that the sinner needs, that is deliverance from sin's power. In order to get this, he needs to see Jesus as a risen Savior, able to save to the uttermost. By believing in Christ crucified, we get pardon, but by believing in Christ risen, we get deliverance from sin's power. One of the best verses to use for this purpose is Hebrews 7:25: "Therefore He is also able to save to the uttermost those who come to God through Him, since He always lives to make intercession for them." When the inquirer has read the passage, ask him who it is that is able to save, and to what extent He is able to save. Explain to the inquirer what "to the uttermost" means. Many read this passage as though it taught that Jesus was able to save from the uttermost. This is true, but it is not the truth of this text, it is *save to* the uttermost. Then ask the inquirer why it is that Jesus is able to save to the uttermost. Dwell upon this thought, that *Jesus ever lives*, that He is not only a Savior who once died and made atonement for sin, but that He is a Savior who lives today and is able to keep from sin's power. Then ask the inquirer if he or she is willing to trust Jesus as a living Savior, One to whom he or she can look day by day for victory over sin.

Another good verse to use for this purpose is Jude 24: "Now to Him who *is able to keep you from stumbling*, and to present you faultless before the presence of His glory with exceeding joy." When the inquirer has read the verse, ask what this verse says Jesus is able to do; emphasize "to keep you from stumbling." Explain why it is that Jesus is able to keep him from falling or stumbling, because He is a risen, living Savior today; and get the inquirer to see plainly that he is to look to the risen Christ to keep him from falling.

Matthew 28:18 is a good verse to use to bring out the extent of Christ's power. A young convert needs to realize that one is to stand, not in one's own strength, but in the strength of Christ, and it is a great help to see that the One in whom we trust has all power in heaven and on earth. One can also use to advantage 1 Peter 1:5 and 1 Corinthians 15:1–4. The latter passage brings out clearly the thought that the doctrine that Christ died for our sins, as blessed as it is, is not the whole Gospel, but only half of it; that the rest of the Gospel is that He was buried and that He rose again. Always get an inquirer to believe not only in Christ crucified, but in Christ risen as well.

A man once came to me in deep distress of soul. He was a perfect stranger to me, but told me that he had come quite a distance to tell me his story. He said, "When I was a boy seven years of age, I started to read the Bible through. I had not gotten through Deuteronomy before I found that if one kept the whole law of God for one hundred years, and then broke it at one point, he was under the curse of a broken law. Was that right?" "Yes," I replied, "that is substantially the teaching of the law." He then continued that he was in deep distress of soul for about a year, but as a boy of eight, he read John 3:16 and saw how Jesus Christ had died in his place, and borne the curse of the broken law for him, and he added, "My burden rolled away, and I had great joy. Was I converted?" I replied that that sounded very much like an evangelical conversion.

"Well," he said, "let me tell you the rest of my story. Years passed by; I came to Chicago to live; I worked in the stockyards and lived in the stockyards region among many godless men. I fell into drink and I cannot break away; every little while this sin gets the mastery of me, and what I have come to ask you is, is there any way in which I can get the victory over sin?"

I replied, "There is. I am glad you have come to me; let me show you the way." I opened my Bible to 1 Corinthians 15:1–4, and had him read. Then I said to him, "What is the Gospel that Paul preached?" He answered, "That Christ died for our sins according to the Scriptures, was buried, and rose again." "That is right," I said. Then I said, "Now you have believed the first part of this Gospel, that Christ died for your sins." "Yes." "Through believing that, you have found peace." "Yes." "Well," I continued, "this is only half the Gospel. If you will really believe the other half from your heart, you will get victory over your sin. Do you believe that Jesus rose again?" "Yes, I believe everything in the Bible." "Do you believe that Jesus is today in the place of power at the right hand of God?" "I do." "Do you believe that He has all power in heaven and on earth?" "I do." "Do you believe that this risen Christ, with all power in heaven and on earth, has power to set you free from the power of your sin?" "Yes," he said slowly, "I do." "Will you ask Him to do it, and trust Him to do it right now?" "I will." We knelt in prayer. I prayed and then he followed. He asked the risen Christ to set him free from the power of sin. I asked him if he really believed He had power to do it. "Yes." "Do you believe He will do it?" "Yes, I do." We rose and parted. Some time after, I received a very joyous letter from him, telling me how glad he was that he had come to see me, and how the message he had heard was just the one that he needed.

There are thousands of professing Christians today who know Jesus as a crucified Savior, and have found pardon and peace through believing in Him, but they have never been brought to a definite, clear faith in Jesus as a risen Savior who can save from the power of sin.

III. SHOW THEM JESUS AS LORD.

It is not enough to know Jesus as Savior; we must know Him as Lord also. A good verse for this purpose is Acts 2:36: "Therefore let all the house of Israel know assuredly that *God has made this Jesus*, whom you crucified, *both Lord and Christ*." When the inquirer has read the verse, ask what God made Jesus, and hold to it until you get the reply, "Both Lord and Christ." Then say, "Are you willing to accept Him as your Divine Lord, the One to whom you will surrender your heart, your every thought and word and act?"

Another good verse for this purpose is Romans 10:9: "That if you confess with your mouth *the Lord* Jesus and believe in your heart that God has raised Him from the dead, you will be saved." When the inquirer has read the verse, ask what we are to confess Jesus as. If the reply is not "Lord," ask other questions until the answer is given. Then ask, "Do you really believe that Jesus is Lord, that He is Lord of all, that He is rightfully the absolute Lord and Master of your life and person?" Perhaps it will be well to use Acts 10:36.

IV. SHOW THEM HOW TO MAKE JESUS THEIR OWN.

It is not enough to see that Jesus is a Sin-Bearer, and that Jesus is a risen Savior, and that Jesus is Lord; one must also see how to make this Jesus his own Sin-Bearer, his own risen Savior, and his own Lord. There is perhaps no better verse to use for this purpose than John 1:12: "But *as many as received Him*, to them He gave the right to become children of God, to those who believe in His name." When one has read the verse, you can ask to whom it is Jesus gave power to become the sons of God. "As many as received Him." "Received Him as what?" Then make it clear from what you have already said under the preceding points, that it is to receive Him as Sin-Bearer, to receive Him as risen Savior, to receive Him as our Lord and Master. "Will you just take Him as your Sin-Bearer now, as your risen Savior, as your Lord and Master? Will you take Him to be whatever He offers Himself to you to be?" "I will." "Then what does this verse show you that you have a right to call yourself?" "A child of God." "Are you a child of God?" Oftentimes the inquirer will hesitate, but go over it again and again until it is as clear as day to him.

Another excellent passage to use for this purpose is John 3:16: "For God so loved the world that He gave His only begotten Son, that *whoever believes in Him* should not perish but have everlasting life." Ask the inquirer who it is that receives eternal life. "Whoever believes in Him." "Do you believe in Him as your Sin-Bearer? Do you believe in Him as your risen Savior? Do you believe in Him as your Lord? Well, then, what do you have?"

Other good passages to use are Acts 10:43 and Acts 13:39.

V. SHOW THE NEED OF CONFESSING CHRIST WITH THE MOUTH.

No conversion is clear and satisfactory until one has been led to confess Christ with the mouth before men. Perhaps the best passage to show the need of such open confession with the mouth is Romans 10:9–10: "That if you confess with your mouth the Lord Jesus and believe in your heart that God has raised Him from the dead, you will be saved. For with the heart one believes unto righteousness, and with the mouth confession is made unto salvation." When the inquirer has read it, ask what is the first thing this verse tells us we must do if we are to be saved. "Confess with your mouth the Lord Jesus." "Well, will you confess Jesus as your Lord with the mouth now?" Wherever possible, it is good to get the person dealt with to make a public confession of Jesus just as soon as possible. If you are dealing with people in an after meeting, have them make this confession right then and there; if somewhere else, bring them to a prayer meeting, or some other service where they can make the confession as soon as possible.

VI. LEAD INTO ASSURANCE.

It is not enough that one should be saved. One ought to have the assurance of salvation. One ought to be brought to a place where it can be said confidently and joyously, "*I know* I am saved; *I know* I have everlasting life." After an inquirer has been led to the acceptance and confession of Christ, an excellent passage to use for this purpose is John 3:36: "He who believes in the Son *has everlasting life*; and he who does not believe the Son shall not see life, but the wrath of God abides on him." When the inquirer has read the passage, you can say, "Now this passage tells us that there is someone who has everlasting life; who is it?" "He who believes on the Son." "What does God say in this passage that everyone who believes on the Son has?" "Everlasting life." "Is it absolutely sure that everyone who believes on the Son has everlasting life?" "It is; God says so." "Well, do you believe on the Son?" "Yes." "What have you then?" "Everlasting life." "Are you absolutely sure that you have everlasting life?" "Yes." "Why are you sure?" "Because God says so here." In many cases, probably in the majority of cases, it will be necessary to go over this again and again, before the inquirer says that he or she is absolutely sure of having everlasting life because of belief on the Son, but do not let him or her go until thus absolutely sure.

VII. GIVE DIRECTIONS AS TO HOW TO LIVE THE CHRISTIAN LIFE.

It is not enough that a person be led to accept Christ; that is only the beginning of the Christian life, and if one is not shown how to lead the Christian life that has begun, life is likely to be largely one of failure. The reason so many Christian lives are comparative failures is because of a lack of definite and full instruction to the young convert as to how to lead the life that he has begun. The following instructions should be given to everyone who has been dealt with as described above; and not only to them, but to every other class of inquirers that may be led to the acceptance of Christ by the methods described in the following pages or in any other way. You will speak to the inquirer somewhat as follows: "You have just begun the Christian life; now you wish to make a success of it. There are six very simple things to do, and it is absolutely sure that anyone who does these six things will make a success of the Christian life."

Although Torrey doesn't explicitly mention it, he clearly assumes that the new believer will be active in church. Torrey served as a pastor of a local church throughout his ministry. In our day with television preachers and busy lives, new believers may need additional encouragement to help them make a local church a primary context in which to follow these six steps.

A. "Confess Christ before others."

"You will find the first of these in Matthew 10:32. Please read it very carefully": "Therefore whoever confesses Me before men, him I will also confess before My Father who is in heaven." "This verse tells us that Christ confesses before the Father those who confess Him before men. You will make a success of the Christian life only if Christ confesses you before the Father, so if you wish to succeed in this life that you have begun, *you must make a constant practice of confessing Christ before men.* Improve every opportunity that you get of showing your colors, and stating that you are upon Christ's side, and of telling what the Lord has done for your soul."

B. "Study the Word of God regularly, and hide it in your heart."

To make this point clear, use the following passages: *"Your word I have hidden in my heart*, that I might not sin against You" (Psalm 119:11). "As newborn babes, desire the pure milk of the word, that you may grow thereby" (1 Peter 2:2). One of the most frequent causes of failure in the Christian life is neglect of the Word of God. One can no more thrive spiritually without regular spiritual food than he can thrive physically without regular and proper physical nourishment.

C. "Pray without ceasing."

To make this point clear, use "Pray without ceasing" (1 Thessalonians 5:17). "But those who wait on the Lord shall renew their strength; they shall mount up with wings like eagles, they shall run and not be weary, they shall walk and not faint" (Isaiah 40:31). Have the young converts read these verses again and again and mark them in their own Bibles.

D. "Surrender your will absolutely to God, and obey Him in all things."

To make this plain use Acts 5:32: "And we are His witnesses to these things, and so also is the Holy Spirit whom God has given to *those who obey Him.*" Show that obedience is a matter of the will more than of the outward life, and that God gives His Holy Spirit to them who obey Him, or surrender their will absolutely to Him. Insist upon the need of this absolute surrender of the will to God.

E. "Be a constant and generous giver."

To make the necessity of this plain to the convert, use 2 Corinthians 9:6–8: "But this I say: He who sows sparingly will also reap sparingly, and he who sows bountifully will also reap bountifully. So let each one give as he purposes in his heart, not grudgingly or of necessity; for God loves a cheerful giver. And God is able to make all grace abound toward you, that you, always having all sufficiency in all things, may have an abundance for every good work." Go over it again until it is fixed in the young convert's mind that in order to enjoy the fullness of God's blessing, if God is to make all grace abound, he or she must give to the Lord's work as the Lord prospers, that he or she must be a constant and generous giver. Many young Christians make little headway in the Christian life because they are not plainly instructed on the necessity of regular, systematic, and generous giving to the Lord.

F. "Go to work for Christ, and keep working for Christ."

To show the necessity of this, use Matthew 25:14–30, explaining the teaching of the parable, that it is the one who uses what one has who gets more, but the one who neglects to use what one has, loses even that.

Go over these six points again and again; write them down with the texts, and give them to the young convert to take. The directions given above may seem to be very full, and it may occur to the reader that it will take a long time to follow them out. This is true, and oftentimes it will not be necessary to use all the texts, but at the same time it is best to be sure that you do thorough work. There is a great deal of superficial and shoddy work done in soul-winning today, and this kind of work does not stand. It is better to spend an hour, or two hours, on one person, in order for him or her to be really rooted and grounded in the truth, than it is to get a dozen or more to say that they accept Christ, when they do not really understand what they are doing. One of the most common and greatest of faults in Christian work today is superficial dealing with souls.

LEARNING ACTIVITIES

1. Review the seven steps in dealing with one who realizes a need of a Savior and really desires to be saved. Memorize one or two verses of Scripture for each step, and state how you would use one of them for each step. If you are studying with someone else, quiz each other on these steps and Scripture passages over the next few weeks.

2. Go through all seven steps one at a time and describe what would be lost in the process if any step was missed. What difficulties might develop in the evangelistic discussion or in the Christian life of the new believer?

3. State the six things that one must do in order to make a success of the Christian life. Give a Scripture passage for each. How will the new believer's Christian life be weak if any of the six are missing? Discuss the temptations that are likely to face new believers in each of these areas.

4. Who in your life seems ready to receive Christ? How might you prepare to make sure that you are ready to lead them to Christ?

5. Pray for the Lord to bring into your life others who are ready to accept Christ as Savior. Then make sure that you are ready when He answers your prayer.

HOW TO DEAL WITH THOSE WHO HAVE LITTLE OR NO CONCERN ABOUT THEIR SOULS

THE LARGEST CLASS OF MEN AND WOMEN are those who have little or no concern about their salvation. Some contend that there is no use dealing with such, but there is. It is our business when a person has no concern about his salvation to go to work to produce that concern. How shall we do it?

I. SHOW HIM THAT HE IS A GREAT SINNER BEFORE GOD.

There is no better verse for this purpose than Matthew 22:37–38: "Jesus said to him, '"You shall love the Lord your God with all your heart, with all your soul, and with all your mind." *This is the first and great commandment.*'" Before the one with whom you are dealing reads these verses, you can say, "Do you know that you are a great sinner before God?" Very likely the reply will be, "I suppose I am a sinner, but I do not know that I am such a great sinner." "Do you know that you have committed the greatest sin that can possibly be committed?" "No, I certainly have not." "What do you think is the greatest sin that can possibly be committed?" Probably one will answer, "Murder." "You are greatly mistaken; let us see what God says about it." Then have him or her read the passage. When read, ask, "What is the first and great commandment?" "You shall love the Lord your God with all your heart, with all your soul, and with all your mind." "Which commandment is this?" "The first and great commandment." "If this is the first and great commandment, what is the first and great sin?" "Not to keep this commandment." "Have you kept it? Have you put

God first in everything: first in your affections, first in your thoughts, first in your pleasures, first in your business, first in everything?" "No, I have not." "What commandment, then, have you broken?" "The first and great commandment."

Some time ago, a young man came into our inquiry meeting. I asked him if he was a Christian, and he replied that he was not. I asked him if he would like to be, and he said that he would. I said, "Why, then, do you not become a Christian tonight?" He replied, "I have no special interest in the matter." I said, "Do you mean that you have no conviction of sin?" "Yes," he said, "I have no conviction of sin, and am not much concerned about the whole matter." I said, "I hold in my hand a Book which God has given us for the purpose of producing conviction of sin; would you like to have me use it upon you?" Half laughing, he replied, "Yes." When he had taken a seat, I had him read Matthew 22:37–38. When he had read the passage, I said to him, "What is the first and great commandment?" He read it from the Bible. I said, "If this is the first and great commandment, what is the first and great sin?" He replied, "Not to keep this commandment." I asked, "Have you kept it?" "I have not." "What have you done then?" Said he, "I have broken the first and greatest of God's commandments," and broken down with a sense of sin, then and there he went down before God and asked Him for mercy and accepted Christ as his Savior.

Another excellent passage to use to produce conviction of sin is Romans 14:12: "So then each of us shall give account of himself to God." The great object in using this passage is to bring careless persons face-to-face with God, and make them realize that they must give account to God. When they have read it, ask, "Who has to give account?" "Every one of us." "Who does that take in?" "Me." "Who, then, is to give account?" "I am." "To whom are you to give account?" "To God." "Of what are you to give account?" "Of myself." "Read it that way." "I shall give account of myself to God." "Now just let that thought sink into your heart. Say it over to yourself again and again, 'I am to give account of myself to God. I am to give account of myself to God.' Are you ready to do it?"

Other passages, such as Amos 4:12b and Romans 2:16, can be used in much the same way.

II. SHOW THE AWFUL CONSEQUENCES OF SIN.

A very effective passage for this purpose is Romans 6:23, "For the wages of sin is death, but the gift of God is eternal life in Christ Jesus our Lord." When the passage has been read, ask, "What is the wages of sin?" "Death." Explain the meaning of death—literal death, spiritual death, eternal death. Now say, "This is the wages of sin. Have you earned these wages?" "Yes." "Are you willing to take them?" "No." "Well, there is one alternative; read the remainder of the verse." "The gift of God is eternal life in Christ Jesus our Lord." "Now you have your choice between the two, the wages that you have earned by sin, and the gift of God; which will you choose?"

Other very useful passages along this line are Isaiah 57:21, John 8:34, and Romans 6:16.

III. SHOW HIM THE AWFULNESS OF UNBELIEF IN JESUS CHRIST.

Very few out of Christ realize that unbelief in Jesus Christ is anything very bad. Of course, they know it is not just right, but that it is something awful and appalling, they do not dream for a moment. They should be shown that there is nothing more appalling than unbelief in Jesus Christ. A good passage for this purpose is John 3:18–19: "He who believes in Him is not condemned; but he who does not believe is condemned already, because he has not believed in the name of the only begotten Son of God. And this is the condemnation, that the light has come into the world, and men loved darkness rather than light, because their deeds were evil." When the passage has been read, say, "Now this verse tells us of someone who is condemned already. Who is it?" "He who does not believe." "Does not believe in whom?" "Jesus." "How many who do not believe in Jesus are condemned already?" "Everyone." "Why is everyone who does not believe in Jesus condemned already?" "Because they have not believed on the name of the only begotten Son of God." "Why is this such an awful thing in the sight of God?" "Because light has come into the world, and people loved darkness rather than light because their deeds are evil." "In whom did the light come into the world?" "In Jesus." "Jesus, then, is the incarnation of light, God's fullest revelation. To reject Jesus, then, is the deliberate rejection of what?" "Light." "The choice of what?" "Darkness." "In rejecting Jesus, what are you rejecting?" "Light." "And what are you choosing?" "Darkness rather than light." Ask all the questions that are necessary to impress this truth upon the mind of the unbeliever, that he or she is deliberately rejecting the light of God, and choosing darkness rather than light.

Other very useful passages for the same purpose are Acts 2:36–37, John 16:8–9, and Hebrews 10:28–29.

IV. SHOW THE AWFUL CONSEQUENCES OF UNBELIEF.

For this purpose begin by using Hebrews 11:6, the first part of the verse: "But without faith it is impossible to please Him." "Now this verse tells you that there is one thing that God absolutely requires if we are to please Him: What is it?" "Faith." "And no matter what else we do, if we have not faith, what is impossible for us?" "To please Him."

Follow this up by John 8:24: "Therefore I said to you that you will die in your sins; for if you do not believe that I am He, you will die in your sins." "What does this verse tell us will happen to you if you do not believe in Jesus?" "I will die in my sins." Then have the inquirer read verse 21, "Then Jesus said to them again, 'I am going away, and you will seek Me, and will die in your sin. Where I go you cannot come.'" That will show the result of one dying in his sins.

Further, follow this up by 2 Thessalonians 1:7–9: "And to give you who are troubled rest with us when the Lord Jesus is revealed from heaven with His mighty angels, in flaming fire taking vengeance on those who do not know not God, and on those who do not obey the gospel of our Lord Jesus Christ. These shall be punished with everlasting destruction from the presence of the Lord and from the glory of His power." Say to the inquirer, "This verse tells us of a coming day in which Jesus is to take vengeance upon a certain class of people, and they are to be punished with everlasting destruction from the presence of the Lord and the glory of His power. Who is it that are to be thus punished?" "Those who do not know not God and do not obey the Gospel of our Lord Jesus Christ." "Are you obeying the Gospel of the Lord Jesus Christ?" "No." "If, then, Christ should come now, what would be your destiny?" "I should be punished with everlasting destruction from the presence of the Lord and the glory of His power."

Then turn to Revelation 21:8. This verse needs no comment; it tells its own story: "But the cowardly, unbelieving, abominable, murderers, sexually immoral, sorcerers, idolaters, and all liars shall have their part in the lake which burns with fire and brimstone, which is the second death." Revelation 20:15 may also be used.

V. SHOW THAT ALL ONE HAS TO DO TO BE LOST IS SIMPLY TO NEGLECT THE SALVATION THAT IS OFFERED IN CHRIST.

A verse that will serve for this purpose is Hebrews 2:3: "How shall we escape if we neglect so great a salvation, which at the first began to be spoken by the Lord, and was confirmed to us by those who heard Him." When the verse has been read, ask, "What does this verse tell us is all that is necessary to be done in order to be lost?" "Simply neglect the great salvation." "That is the very thing that you are doing today; you are already lost. God has provided salvation for you at great cost: All you need to do to be saved is to accept the salvation, but you cannot be saved any other way; and all you need to do to be lost is simply to neglect it. You do not need to plunge into desperate vices; you do not need to be an open and avowed atheist; you do not need even to refuse to accept salvation. If you simply neglect it, you will be lost forever. Will you not let the question of the text sink deep into your heart? 'How shall we escape if we neglect so great a salvation?' "

Other passages to use for this purpose are Acts 3:22–23, Acts 13:38–41, and John 3:36.

VI. SHOW THE WONDERFUL LOVE OF GOD.

Oftentimes, when every other method of dealing with the careless fails, a realization of the love of God breaks the heart and leads to an acceptance of Christ. There is no better passage to show the love of God than John 3:16: "For God so loved the world that He gave His only begotten Son, that whoever believes in Him should not perish but have everlasting life." Generally it will need no comment. I was once dealing with one of the most careless and vile women I ever met. She moved in good society, but in her secret life was as vile as a woman of the street. She told me the story of her life in a most shameless and unblushing way, half laughing as she did it. I made no further reply than to ask her to read John 3:16 to which I had opened my Bible. Before she had read the passage through, she burst into tears, her heart broken by the love of God for her.

Another excellent passage to use in the same way is Isaiah 53:5: "But He was wounded for our transgressions, He was bruised for our iniquities; the chastisement for our peace was upon Him, and by His stripes we are healed." God used this passage one night to bring to tears and penitence one of the most stubborn and wayward young women with whom I ever dealt. I made almost no comment, simply read the passage to her. The Spirit of God seemed to hold up before her her Savior, wounded for her transgressions, and bruised for her iniquities. Her stubborn will gave way, and before many days she was rejoicing in Christ. Two other passages that can be used in the same way are Galatians 3:13 and 1 Peter 2:24.

After showing the love of God through the use of such passages as these mentioned, it is oftentimes well to clinch this truth by using Romans 2:4–5. Before having the passage read, say, "Now we have been looking at the love of

God to you; let us see what God tells us is the purpose of that love, and what will be the result of our despising it." Then have one with whom you are dealing read the passage, Romans 2:4–5. When read, ask what is the purpose of God's goodness. "To lead to repentance." "If it does not lead us to repentance, what does it show us about our hearts?" "That they are very hard and impenitent." "And if we refuse to let the goodness of God lead us to repentance, what will be the result?" "We treasure up wrath unto ourselves against the day of wrath and revelation of the righteous judgment of God."

Of course, it will not always be possible to get a person who has little or no concern about salvation to talk with you long enough to go over all these passages, but not infrequently they will become so interested after the use of the first or second passage that they will be glad to go through the rest. Oftentimes, it is not at all necessary to use all these passages. Not infrequently I find that the first passage, Matthew 22:37–38, does the desired work, but it is well to be thorough and to use all the passages necessary.

Sometimes, one will not talk with you for any length of time at all. In such a case, the best thing to do is to select a very pointed and searching passage and give it to the person, repeating it again and again, and then as he goes, say to him something like this, "I am going to ask God to burn that passage into your heart"; and then do not forget to do what you said you were going to do. Good passages for this purpose are Romans 6:23, Mark 16:16, John 3:36, and Isaiah 57:21.

When the inquirer has been led by the use of any or all of these passages to realize the need of a Savior, and really desires to be saved, of course he or she comes under the class treated in the preceding chapter, and should be dealt with accordingly. It is not intended that the worker shall follow the precise method laid down here; it is given rather by way of suggestion, but the general plan here outlined has been honored of God to the salvation of very many. But let us be sure, whether we use this method or some other, to do thoroughgoing and lasting work.

Of course, it is not supposed that the inquirer will always answer you exactly as stated above. If he or she does not, make use of the answers given, or if necessary ask the same question another way until answered correctly. The answers given to the questions are found in the text, but people have a great habit of not seeing what is plainly stated in a Scripture text. Oftentimes when they do not answer right, it is well to ask them to look at the verse again, and repeat the question, and keep asking questions until they do give the right answer. Perhaps the inquirer will try to switch you off on to some side track. Do not permit him or her to do this, but hold right to the matter in hand.

LEARNING ACTIVITIES

1. Review Torrey's six steps in dealing with one who has little or no concern about his soul. Memorize one passage of Scripture for each step, and explain how you would use it. If you are studying with someone else, quiz each other on these steps and Scripture passages over the next few weeks.

2. What would you do with one who refused to talk with you for any length of time? Is there someone in your life who fits this description? Consider how the truths of this lesson might apply specifically to this person. Pray for this person, prepare for how to deal with him or her, and look for the opportunities that God may give you to do so.

3. Find a Christian friend to role-play with you. Practice responding to ones who have little or no concern about their souls, but also practice leading them to Christ after you have been able to show them their need.

CHAPTER THREE

LEADING PEOPLE TO CHRIST,
PART 2

PEOPLE ARE AT ALL SORTS OF DIFFERENT STAGES in the process of considering Christ as their Savior. In this chapter, Torrey addresses a wide range of difficulties that honestly keep people from dealing with the truth of Scripture. However, it is important to note that this chapter deals with sincere concerns. Torrey deals later with those who raise difficulties just for the sake of being resistant. In this chapter, those who have difficulties are still close to coming to Christ. Torrey helps you to be sensitive to their needs, but keep bringing them back to the Cross and the opportunity of personal salvation.

The range of issues that people may raise is quite wide. This chapter covers a variety of topics, but certainly doesn't cover all of them. Although it provides specific instructions for specific difficulties, it is not simply a step-by-step guide. Rather, it continues to reinforce a key dimension of personal Christian work, namely, dependence on the Scripture. One could easily add several more pages to this chapter by stating other difficulties, identifying relevant Scripture, and walking the seeker through the passages. The importance of Bible knowledge, skill in using

Scripture, and dependence on God's Word more than one's own wisdom is on every page of this chapter.

Another key dimension is mentioned occasionally, but is assumed throughout. One should always handle these discussions with courtesy. There is a temptation to come across as cold, mechanical, or uncaring in the asking of questions and the pressing for responses. Torrey's emphasis on respect for the one with whom you are dealing must not be overlooked.

As you read this chapter, you will find that Torrey is giving instructions for dealing with folks whom you might not expect to meet. For instance, he is very forthright in how to deal with murderers. Torrey didn't live in utopian "good ol' days." He wrote from the perspective of a minister who was right in the middle of all that was happening in Chicago in the 1890s. The testimonies of his own personal work show that he was not a respecter of persons. He dealt with the most esteemed people and the most despised. One should read this chapter not focused just on the situations that are familiar or already identified, but in recognition that whole new situations may be just around the corner.

HOW TO DEAL
WITH THOSE WHO
HAVE DIFFICULTIES

WE WILL FIND THAT A VERY LARGE NUMBER of the persons whom we try to lead to Christ are really anxious to be saved, and know how, but are confronted with difficulties which they deem important or even insurmountable. Whenever it is possible, it is well to show such persons their need of Christ before taking up a specific difficulty. In this way, many of the supposed difficulties are dissipated. Oftentimes, even when people really are anxious to be saved, there is not that deep, clear, and intelligent knowledge of their need of Christ that is desirable. It is usually a waste of time to take up specific difficulties until there is this clear and definite sense of need.

I. "I AM TOO GREAT A SINNER."

This is a difficulty that is very real, and very often met, but fortunately it is also one with which it is very easy to deal. The method of treatment is as follows:

A. General treatment

There is no better passage to use to meet this difficulty than 1 Timothy 1:15: "This is a faithful saying and worthy of all acceptance, that Christ Jesus came into the world to save sinners, of whom I am chief." This verse so exactly fits the case that there is little need for comment. At the close of a Sunday morning service, I spoke to a man of intelligence and ability, but who had gone down into the deepest depth of sin. When asked why he was not a Christian, he replied, "I am too great a sinner to be saved." I turned him at once to 1 Timothy 1:15. No sooner had I read the verse than he replied, "Well, I am the chief of sinners." "That verse means you, then." He replied, "It is a precious promise." I said, "Will you accept it now?" "I will." Then I said, "Let us kneel down and tell God so." We knelt down, and he confessed to God his sins and asked God for Christ's sake to forgive him. When he had finished his prayer, I asked him if he really had accepted Christ, and he said that he had. I asked him if he really believed that he was accepted, and he said he did. He took the first opportunity afforded him of confessing Christ, and became an active Christian. His broken home was restored, and every day he was found witnessing for his Master. Other useful passages in dealing with this class are Matthew 9:12–13 and Romans 5:6–8.

At the close of an evening service in Minneapolis, a man who had raised his hand for prayer hurried away as soon as the benediction was pronounced. I hastened after him, laid my hand upon his shoulder, and said, "Did you not hold your hand up tonight for prayer?" "Yes." "Why, then, are you hurrying away?" He replied, "There is no use talking to me." I said, "God loves you." He replied, "You do not know whom you are talking to." "I do not care whom I am talking to, but I know God loves you." He said, "I am the meanest thief in Minneapolis." I said, "Then I know God loves you," and I opened my Bible to Romans 5:6–8 and read the passage through. "Now," I said, "if you are the meanest thief in Minneapolis, you are a sinner, and this verse tells us that God loves sinners."

The Spirit of God carried the message of love home to his heart; he broke down, and going with me into another room, he told me the story of his life. He had been released from confinement that day, and had started out that night to commit what he said would have been one of the most daring burglaries ever committed in Minneapolis. With his two companions in crime, he was passing a corner where we were holding an open-air meeting. He stopped a few moments to hear what was going on, and in spite of the protests of his companions, stayed through the meeting, and went with us into the mission. It so happened that a few days earlier he had dreamed in confinement of his mother, and the hearing of the Gospel added to this, and the few words that had been spoken to him personally had completed the work. After he had told me his story, we knelt in prayer. Utterly overcome with emotion, through falling tears he looked to God for pardon, and left the room rejoicing in the assurance that his sins had all been forgiven.

It is often well to say, "Your sins are great, greater far than you think, but they are all settled." In order to show how they are settled, and to make it clear that they are settled, turn to Isaiah 53:6.

B. Special cases

Among those who regard themselves as too great sinners to be saved, there are special cases:

1. *The one who says, "I am lost."*

If the difficulty is stated in this way, it is well to use Luke 19:10, as that fits so exactly the inquirer's statement of the case; for the verse says: "For the Son of Man has come to seek and to save that which was lost." I was once speaking to a young man who was the complete slave of drink and other sins, and urging him to accept the Savior. He turned to me in a despairing way and said, "Mr. Torrey, go talk to those other men; there is no use talking to me; I am lost." I replied, "If you are lost, I have a message from God's Word addressed directly to you." I turned to Luke 19:10 and read, "For the Son of Man has come to seek and to save that which was lost." The text fitted the case so exactly that there was no need of comment or explanation on my part.

2. *Murderers*

Among those who think that they are too great sinners to be saved, murderers form a special class. I find that not a few who have stained their hands with the blood of another have a deep-seated impression that there is no hope for one who has committed this sin. Isaiah 1:18 is very useful in such a case. One night I was dealing with a man who was sure that he was beyond all hope. I asked him why he thought so, and he replied that it was because he had taken the life of another. I said, "Let me read you something from God's Word," and I read: "'Come now, and let us reason together,' says the Lord, 'Though your sins are like scarlet, they shall be as white as snow; though they are red like crimson, they shall be as wool.'" I said, "If you have taken the life of a fellowman, your sins are as scarlet." "Oh," he cried, "the bullet was scarlet; I can see it now." Then I asked him to listen again to the promise, "Though your sins are like scarlet, they shall be as white as snow; though they are red like crimson, they shall be as wool." He saw how the promise exactly covered his case, and it brought hope into a heart that had been filled with despair. Another useful passage is Psalm 51:14.

C. General remarks

1. *Never give false comfort by telling the inquirer, "You are not a very great sinner."*

This mistake is often made. Tenderhearted people are greatly disturbed over the deep conviction of sin that the Spirit of God produces in hearts, and try to give comfort by telling the inquirer that he or she is not so great a sinner, after all. This is false comfort. There is no one but who is a greater sinner than ever thought or realized.

2. *After meeting the specific difficulty, show the inquirer how to be saved.*

This remark applies not only to this difficulty, but to all the difficulties that follow. It is not enough to remove difficulties; we must bring inquirers to a saving knowledge of Christ.

II. "MY HEART IS TOO HARD."

One of the passages given under the former difficulty will also be useful here: Luke 19:10. Before using it, it may be well to say, "Well then, if your heart is so hard and wicked, you must be lost." "Yes, I am lost." "Very well, I have a promise for you." Turn to Luke 19:10 and let the person read. "You said that your heart was so hard and wicked that you were lost." "Yes." "And this verse tells us that Jesus Christ is come to seek and to save whom?" "The lost." "And that means you. Will you let Him save you now?"

Another useful passage is John 6:37, the last half of the verse, "The one who comes to Me I will by no means cast out." You can say, "You think your heart is so hard and wicked that you cannot be saved, but would you be willing to come to Christ if He would accept you?" "Yes." "Well, let us listen to what He says." Then read the passage, "The one who comes to Me I will by no means cast out." "Whom does Jesus say here that He will receive?" "Anyone who comes." "Does He say He will receive anyone who comes provided their heart is not too hard and wicked?" "No." "What does He say?" "That He will receive anyone who comes." "Then He will receive anyone who comes, no matter how hard and wicked their heart?" "Yes." "Will you come now?"

Other passages are Ezekiel 36:26 and 2 Corinthians 5:17.

III. "I MUST BECOME BETTER BEFORE I BECOME A CHRISTIAN."

This is a very real difficulty with many people. They sincerely believe that

74

they cannot come to Christ just as they are in their sins, that they must do something to make themselves better before they can come to Him. You can show them that they are utterly mistaken in this by having them read Matthew 9:12–13: "When Jesus heard that, He said to them, 'Those who are well have no need of a physician, but those who are sick. But go and learn what this means: "I desire mercy and not sacrifice." For I did not come to call the righteous, but sinners, to repentance.'" When inquirers have read it, if they do not see the point for themselves, you can ask, "To what does Jesus compare Himself in this verse?" "To a physician." "Who is it who needs a physician, well people or sick people?" "Sick people." "Ought a person who is sick to wait until he gets well before he gets to the doctor?" "No, of course not." "Ought a person who is spiritually sick to wait until he is better before he comes to Jesus?" "No." "Who is it Jesus invites to come to Himself, good people or bad people?" "Bad people." "Is then the fact that you are not good a reason for waiting or a reason for coming to Jesus at once?"

Luke 15:18–24 and Luke 18:10–14 also fit the case.

IV. "I CANNOT HOLD OUT" (OR "I AM AFRAID I SHALL FAIL IF I TRY").

A. General treatment

First, see if the inquirer is in dead earnest, and if there is not some other difficulty lying back of this. Many give this as a difficulty, when perhaps it is not the real one. There is perhaps no better verse in the Bible for this difficulty than Jude 24: "Now to Him who is able to keep you from stumbling, and to present you faultless before the presence of His glory with exceeding joy."

Another useful passage is 1 Peter 1:5: "Who are kept by the power of God through faith for salvation ready to be revealed in the last time." When the inquirer has read it, ask him by whose power it is that we are kept. Then you can say, "It is not then a question of our strength at all, but of God's strength. Do you think that God is able to keep you?"

Other passages that are helpful along the same line are 2 Timothy 1:12; Isaiah 41:10, 13; John 10:28–29; and Hebrews 7:25.

B. Special cases

1. *Those afraid of some temptation that will prove too strong*

The best passage to use in such a case is 1 Corinthians 10:13: "No temptation has overtaken you except such as is common to man; but God is faithful, who will not allow you to be tempted beyond what you are able, but with the temptation will also make the way of escape, that you may be able to bear it."

2. *Those who dwell upon their own weakness*

"And He said to me, 'My grace is sufficient for you, for My strength is made perfect in weakness.' Therefore most gladly I will rather boast in my infirmities, that the power of Christ may rest upon me. Therefore I take pleasure in infirmities, in reproaches, in needs, in persecutions, in distresses, for Christ's sake. For when I am weak, then I am strong" (2 Corinthians 12:9–10). "He gives power to the weak, and to those who have no might He increases strength. Even the youths shall faint and be weary, and the young men shall utterly fall, but those who wait on the Lord shall renew their strength; they shall mount up with wings like eagles, they shall run and not be weary, they shall walk and not faint" (Isaiah 40:29–31).

One evening, a lady called me to a man whom she was trying to lead to Christ and asked me if I could help him. I said to him, "What is your difficulty?" He replied, "I have no strength." "Ah," I said, "I have a message that exactly fits your case," and read Isaiah 40:29. "You say you have no strength, that is no might; now this verse tells us that to those who have no might, that is, to people just like you, God increases strength." The Holy Spirit took the word of comfort home to his heart at once, and he put his trust in Jesus Christ then and there.

V. "I CANNOT GIVE UP MY EVIL WAYS."

A. "You must or perish."

In order to prove this statement, use: "For the wages of sin is death, but the gift of God is eternal life in Christ Jesus our Lord" (Romans 6:23). Also use Galatians 6:7–8 and Revelation 21:8. Drive this thought home. Show the inquirer rest, but keep calling for a change of thought: "You must give up your evil ways or perish." Emphasize it by Scripture. When the inquirer sees and realizes this, then you can pass on to the next thought.

B. "You can in the strength of Jesus Christ."

To prove this, have the inquirer read Philippians 4:13 and John 8:36: "I can do all things through Christ who strengthens me" and "Therefore if the Son makes you free, you shall be free indeed."

C. Show the risen Christ with all power in heaven and on earth.

It is in the power of the risen Christ, and through union with Him, that we are enabled to give up our evil ways, so the one who has this difficulty should have the fact that Christ is risen made clear to him. The following passage will serve well for this purpose. "And Jesus came and spoke to them, saying, 'All authority has been given to Me in heaven and on earth" (Matthew 28:18). Other passages are 1 Corinthians 15:1–4 and Hebrews 7:25.

D. Show how to get victory over sin.

There is perhaps nothing in the Bible that makes the way of victory over sin more plain and simple than Romans 6:12–14: "Therefore do not let sin reign in your mortal body, that you should obey it in its lusts. And do not present your members as instruments of unrighteousness to sin, but present yourselves to God as being alive from the dead, and your members as instruments of righteousness to God. For sin shall not have dominion over you, for you are not under law but under grace." You can say to the inquirer, "In this verse we are told how to get victory over sin: We are told what not to do and what to do. What is it we are told not to do?" "Not to let sin reign in our mortal body; not to yield our members as instruments of unrighteousness to sin." "What are we told to do?" "To yield ourselves to God as those that are alive from the dead; and to yield our members as instruments of righteousness to God." "Now do you believe that through union with the risen Christ your Savior, you are alive from the dead? Will you yield or present yourself to God as one alive from the dead? Will you now and here present the parts of your body as instruments of righteousness to God?" After the inquirer has been led to do this, show him that whatever we yield to God, God accepts, and that he can now trust God for victory over sin and have deliverance from his evil ways.

VI. "I HAVE TRIED BEFORE AND FAILED."

Those who have tried to be Christians and have failed in the attempt, very naturally hesitate about trying again, and such a case needs to be handled with great care, wisdom, and thoroughness.

A. The first thing to do is to say to such a one, "I can show you how to try and not fail."

Then point him to 2 Corinthians 9:8: "And God is able to make all grace abound toward you, that you, always having all sufficiency in all things, may have an abundance for every good work." When the person has read the verse, to be sure that he gets its meaning, you can say, "This verse tells us that God is able to make all grace abound toward us, that we, 'always having all sufficiency in all things, may have an abundance for every good work.' It is clear, then, that there is a way to try and not fail."

B. Find out the cause of failure.

In finding out the cause of failure, there are seven points to be looked into:

1. *"Did you put all your trust for pardon in the finished work of Christ?"*

This is a very frequent cause of failure in the attempt to be a Christian: The person has never been led to see clearly the ground of his salvation, and to trust wholly in the finished work of Christ for pardon. Isaiah 53:6 is a useful passage at this point.

2. *"Did you surrender absolutely to God?"*

Many are led to make a profession of faith in Christ without having been led to absolute surrender; the Christian life thus begun is very likely to prove a failure. The passage to use at this point is Acts 5:32.

3. *"Did you confess Christ openly before men?"*

This is one of the most frequent causes of failure. I have talked with very many who have said that they have tried to be Christians and failed, and a very large proportion of them I have found failed at this very point, the lack of a constant, open confession of Christ. Good passages to use at this point are Matthew 10:32–33 and Romans 10:10.

4. *"Did you study the Word of God daily?"*

Here is another frequent cause of failure, neglect of the Bible. Very few of those who have really begun the Christian life, and who have made a practice of daily study of the Word, fail in their attempt to be Christians. Good passages to use at this point are 1 Peter 2:2 and Psalm 119:11.

5. *"Did you look each day to God alone, and not to self at all, for strength and victory?"*

To emphasize this question, use Isaiah 40:29, 2 Corinthians 12:9, and 1 Peter 5:5b.

6. *"Did you pray constantly?"*

Use at this point 1 Thessalonians 5:17, Isaiah 40:29–31, and Hebrews 4:16.

7. *"Did you go to work for Christ?"*

Here use Matthew 25:14–29.

VII. "THE CHRISTIAN LIFE IS TOO HARD."

A. If a person states this as his difficulty, first show him that the Christian life is not hard.

In Matthew 11:30, Christ tells us His yoke is easy. Proverbs 3:17 shows us that wisdom's ways are ways of pleasantness. First John 5:3 says that God's commandments are not burdensome. First Peter 1:8 pictures the Christian life as a life of joy unspeakable and full of glory. In using the latter passage you might say, "We have a picture of the Christian life in 1 Peter 1:8; let us see if it is a hard life." Have the inquirer read the verse, and then ask, "What kind of a life, according to this passage, is the Christian life?" "A life of joy inexpressible and full of glory." "Do you think that is hard?"

B. Show him that the way of sin is hard.

It is not the Christian life, but the life without Christ that is the hard life. For this purpose, use the last half of Proverbs 13:15 and Isaiah 57:21: "But the way of the unfaithful is hard" and "'There is no peace,' says my God, 'for the wicked.'"

VIII. "THERE IS TOO MUCH TO GIVE UP."

This is often the difficulty even when not stated.

A. First show that no matter how much there may be to give up, it is better to give up anything than to lose one's soul.

For this purpose, use Mark 8:36: "For what will it profit a man if he gains the whole world, and loses his own soul?"

B. Show the inquirer that the only things we have to give up are the things that will harm us.

This is made clear by Psalm 84:11: "For the Lord God is a sun and shield;

the Lord will give grace and glory; no good thing will He withhold from those who walk uprightly." When the inquirer has read the verse, ask, "What does this verse tell us that God will not withhold from us?" "Any good thing." "The things then that God asks you to give up are what kind of things?" "Evil things." "Then all God asks you to give up are the things that are harmful to you. Do you wish to keep them?" I have also found Romans 8:32 very effective, for it emphasizes the thought that if God loved us enough to give His Son to die for us on the cross, He will freely give us all things.

I once had a long conversation with a young woman who was having a great struggle about accepting Christ. She was very fond of the world and certain forms of amusement, which she felt she would have to give up if she became a Christian. Finally I said to her, "Do you think God loves you?" "Yes, I know He does." "How much does God love you?" "Enough to give His Son to die for me," she replied. "Do you think if God loved you enough to give His Son to die for you, He will ask you to give up anything that is for your good?" "No, certainly He will not." "Do you wish to keep anything not for your good?" "No." "Then do you not think you had better accept Jesus Christ right here and now?" "Yes," and she did.

Another verse that is useful as showing the inquirer that the things to give up are the things that are passing away is 1 John 2:15–17.

C. Show the inquirer that what we give up is nothing to what we get.

For this purpose, use Philippians 3:7–8: "But what things were gain to me, these I have counted loss for Christ. Yet indeed I also count all things loss for the excellence of the knowledge of Christ Jesus my Lord, for whom I have suffered the loss of all things, and count them as rubbish, that I may gain Christ." You can call the inquirer's attention to the fact that it was Paul who spoke these words, that perhaps no one ever gave up more for Christ than he did, and yet he here tells us that what he gave up was to what he got only as the garbage of the street.

D. Show the inquirer that if one rejects Christ for fear of what will have to be given up, he will make a terrible mistake.

Then you can say, "The Bible pictures to us a man who made this very mistake. Will you read the story of his folly and its consequences?" Then turn to Luke 12:16–21 and let the inquirer read it. When it has been read, ask if he or she is willing to follow in the footsteps of the man in the passage.

IX. "I CANNOT BE A CHRISTIAN IN MY BUSINESS" (OR "IT WILL HURT MY BUSINESS," OR "I WILL LOSE MY POSITION").

This is a very real difficulty with many, and must be met honestly and squarely.

A. Even when someone really thinks this is true, it is not always so.

Many people have an idea that it is impossible to be a Christian in any line of business except Christian work. They must be shown that this is a mistake. When one makes this excuse, it is often well to ask about the nature of his or her employment, and why one cannot be a Christian in it. Sometimes you will find that it is a business in which there are many Christians, and you can tell him that there are many Christians in the same business.

B. But oftentimes it is true that it is a business in which it is impossible to be a Christian.

In that case, say, "You had better lose your business (or position) than to lose your soul." To drive this statement home, use Mark 8:36: "For what will it profit a man if he gains the whole world, and loses his own soul?" Do not pass on to the next point until this is seen and realized. Make the person feel that he would be better losing every dollar he has in the world than to lose his soul. When he sees this, you can use Matthew 6:33: "But seek first the kingdom of God and His righteousness, and all these things shall be added to you." This verse will show that if one puts God and His kingdom first, all needful things will be supplied. It is better to starve than to reject Christ, but no one who accepts Christ will be left to starve. Another very useful passage is Mark 10:29–30.

X. "I WILL LOSE MY FRIENDS."

Many a person who contemplates beginning the Christian life has none but ungodly companions, and sees very clearly that if he or she becomes a Christian, these friends will be lost. Since they are the only ones the person has, this difficulty is a very real one.

A. First show the inquirer that one is better off without these friends.

These friends are enemies of God. Use for this purpose James 4:4: "Adulterers and adulteresses! Do you not know that friendship with the world is enmity with God? Whoever therefore wants to be a friend of the world makes himself an enemy of God." Before giving it to the inquirer to read, say, "Yes, it may be that you will lose your friends, but if your friends are godless, you are better off without them. See what God's Word says about it." Then show the passage. If this verse does not prove sufficiently effective, follow it up with Proverbs 13:20: "He who walks with wise men will be wise, but the companion of fools will be destroyed." Follow this up with Psalm 1:1–2: "Blessed is the man who walks not in the counsel of the ungodly, nor stands in the path of sinners, nor sits in the seat of the scornful; but his delight is in the law of the Lord, and in His law he meditates day and night." Call the inquirer's attention to the fact that God has promised a special blessing to those who turn their backs upon godless friendships in order to obey Him.

B. Then you can say, "You may lose your godless friends, but you will get better friends."

Turn to 1 John 1:3: "That which we have seen and heard we declare to you, that you also may have fellowship with us; and truly our fellowship is with the Father and with his Son Jesus Christ." When the person has read it, you can say, "If you do lose your godless friends by coming to Christ, what two new friends do you get?" "The Father and His Son Jesus Christ." "Which would you rather have for friends, your godless worldly companions, or God the Father and His Son Jesus Christ?" All this may be followed up again by Mark 10:29–30.

XI. "I AM AFRAID OF RIDICULE."

A. Show the awful peril in being governed by the fear of man.

Use Proverbs 29:25: "The fear of man brings a snare, but whoever trusts in the Lord shall be safe."

You might explain that this snare into which the one who is afraid of ridicule and rejects Christ falls often results in the eternal ruin of the soul. Next use Mark 8:38: "Whoever is ashamed of Me and My words in this adulterous and sinful generation, of him the Son of Man also will be ashamed when He comes in the glory of His Father with the holy angels."

B. Show that it is a glorious privilege to be ridiculed for Christ.

Use for this purpose Matthew 5:11–12: "Blessed are you when they revile and persecute you, and say all kinds of evil against you falsely for My sake.

Rejoice and be exceedingly glad, for great is your reward in heaven, for so they persecuted the prophets who were before you."

XII. "I WILL BE PERSECUTED IF I BECOME A CHRISTIAN."

Never tell anyone that he or she will not be persecuted. On the contrary say, "Yes, I presume you will be persecuted, for God tells us in His Word that all who live godly in Christ Jesus will suffer persecution." To prove it show 2 Timothy 3:12: "Yes, and all who desire to live godly in Christ Jesus will suffer persecution." But then tell the person that it is a great privilege to be persecuted for Christ's sake, and brings an abundant reward. Read Matthew 5:10–12, and emphasize the thought that we ought to rejoice at the privilege of being persecuted rather than to shrink from being a Christian on that account. Then show the result of suffering with Christ. Turn to 2 Timothy 2:12: "If we endure, we shall also reign with Him. If we deny Him, He also will deny us." Use Romans 8:18 and 2 Corinthians 4:17 to show how small are the sufferings of this present time in comparison with the glory that we shall obtain through them. Acts 5:40–41 is useful as showing how the early church regarded persecution, rejoicing in it rather than shrinking from it. Another passage that is also useful in such a case is 1 Peter 2:20–21.

XIII. "I HAVE NO FEELING."

This is a very common difficulty. There are many who wish to come to Christ, but do not think they can come because they have not the proper feeling. The first thing to do in such a case is to find out what feeling the inquirer thinks it is necessary to have in order to become a Christian.

A. "The joy and peace that Christians tell about"

The feeling that many inquirers are waiting for is the joy and peace that Christians speak of. Of course, the thing to do in such a case is to show the inquirer that this joy and peace is the result of coming to Christ, and that we cannot expect the result before we come. The first passage to use to show this is Galatians 5:22: "But the fruit of the Spirit is love, joy, peace, longsuffering, kindness, goodness, faithfulness." This shows that joy and peace are the fruit of the Spirit. We cannot expect to have the fruit of the Spirit until we have received the Spirit, and we cannot receive the Spirit until we have accepted Christ. This is brought out very clearly in Ephesians 1:13. Emphasize the point that it is after we believe that we are sealed with the Holy Spirit of promise. Use also Acts 5:32

to show that the Holy Spirit is given to those who obey Christ, and we cannot expect to receive the Holy Spirit until we have obeyed God by putting our trust in Jesus Christ and confessing Him openly before the world. A verse that will be useful in this connection as showing that it is after we confess Christ that He confesses us before the Father is Matthew 10:32. And so we have no right to expect the sealing of the Holy Spirit until we have confessed Christ before others. It is after we have believed that we rejoice with joy inexpressible and full of glory, according to 1 Peter 1:8. Our duty is believing with the heart and confessing with the mouth, leaving the matter of feeling to God, according to Romans 10:10.

B. "Sorrow for sin"

The feeling that many are waiting for is a feeling of sorrow for sin. If you find this to be the case with any individual with whom you are dealing, proceed as follows:

1. *Use the passages already given to produce conviction of sin.*

2. *Show that it is not sorrow for sin, but turning away from sin and accepting Christ that God demands.*

For this purpose, use the following passages: Isaiah 55:7, John 1:12, Acts 16:31, and Acts 2:38.

XIV. "I HAVE BEEN SEEKING CHRIST BUT CANNOT FIND HIM."

A. "You will find Him if you seek earnestly."

It is well to say often to one who raises this difficulty, "I can tell you just when you will find Christ." This will probably awaken surprise, but insist, "Yes, I can tell you just when you will find Christ. If you will turn to Jeremiah 29:13, you will find the exact time when you will find Christ." "And you will seek Me and find Me, when you search for Me with all your heart." "Now this verse tells the time when you will find Christ. When is it?" "When you search for Me with all your heart." "The fact is, up to this time, you have not been seeking for Him with all your heart. Are you ready to let go of everything else and seek Him today with all your heart?" This passage has been used in a great many cases to lead out one who has been seeking Christ for years into a real acceptance of Him.

B. "Christ is also seeking you."

It is well sometimes to say to one who raises this difficulty, "Then you are seeking Christ? Well, did you know that Christ also is seeking you?" Then turn to Luke 19:10 (or Luke 15:3–10) and read. "Now you say you are seeking Christ, and Christ says He is seeking you—how long ought it to take for you to find one another? Will you just come to Christ and trust Him here and now?"

C. "I can show you how to find Him."

Sometimes the best thing to do is to say, "Well, if you are earnestly seeking Christ, let me show you how to find Him." Then deal with the inquirer in the way described earlier.

XV. "CHRISTIANS ARE SO INCONSISTENT."

This is one of the most common difficulties that we meet. Probably the best passage to use is Romans 14:12: "So then each of us shall give account of himself to God." When a person raises this difficulty, you can say, "So you are troubled about the sins of Christians; let me show you from God's own Word what He says about that." Then read the passage above and ask, "Who does God say you will have to give an account of?" "Myself." "Not of inconsistent Christians then?" "No." "Are you ready to give an account of yourself to God?" The mere reading of this verse without comment has led many who have been dwelling upon the inconsistency of others to see themselves lost and undone before God and to turn and accept Christ right there.

Another useful passage is Romans 2:1–5. Hand it to the inquirer to be read carefully. Ask if this passage does not describe him or her. Is he or she not judging others for doing the very things done by him or her? Then ask what God says about those who judge others for what they are doing themselves. Ask further what God says in the third verse that such a person will not escape. Ask what the fourth verse tells that he or she is really doing; and then ask what the fifth verse says he or she is treasuring up.

In many cases, Matthew 7:1–5 will be found useful.

XVI. "THERE IS SOMEONE I CANNOT FORGIVE."

This is often the difficulty even when it is not stated. I have frequently found that when people told me they could not accept Christ and did not know why, the real difficulty was here: There was someone who had wronged him, or who he thought had wronged him, and he would not forgive the person.

A. The first thing to do with such a one is to say, "You must forgive or perish."

To prove this, use Matthew 6:15: "But if you do not forgive men their trespasses, neither will your Father forgive your trespasses." Follow this up with Matthew 18:21–35.

B. Say to the person, "The wrong they have done you is nothing to the wrong you have done Jesus Christ."

Here use Ephesians 4:32: "And be kind to one another, tenderhearted, forgiving one another, even as God in Christ forgave you." You might also use Matthew 18:23–35.

C. Next show the inquirer that he can forgive the other in Christ's strength.

Use for this purpose Philippians 4:13 and Galatians 5:22–23: "I can do all things through Christ who strengthens me" and "The fruit of the Spirit is love, joy, peace, longsuffering, kindness, goodness, faithfulness, gentleness, self-control. Against such there is no law."

XVII. "A PROFESSED CHRISTIAN HAS DONE ME A GREAT WRONG."

A. "Christ has not wronged you."

First you can reply by saying, "That is no reason why you should wrong Christ; has *He* wronged you?" Use Jeremiah 2:5: "Thus says the Lord, 'What injustice have your fathers found in Me, that they have gone far from Me, have followed idols, and have become idolaters?" Ask the inquirer if he or she has found any evil in Christ. One night I turned to an aged man and asked him if he was a Christian. He replied no, that he was a backslider. I asked him why he had backslidden, and he said Christian people had treated him badly. I opened my Bible and read Jeremiah 2:5 to him, and asked him, "Did you find any iniquity in God; did God not treat you well?" With a good deal of feeling, the man admitted that God had not treated him badly. I held him right to this point of God's treatment of him and not man's, and his treatment of God. It is well to follow this passage up with Isaiah 53:5 as bringing out very vividly just what Christ's treatment of us has been.

B. "Refusing Christ is wronging yourself."

In the next place, you can say to the one who raises this difficulty, "The fact that a professed Christian has done you a great injury is no reason why you should do yourself a greater injury by refusing Christ and losing eternal life and being lost forever." Then you can say, "Let me show you what injury you are doing yourself by rejecting Christ." Use for this purpose John 3:36 and 2 Thessalonians 1:7–9.

XVIII. "I HAVE DONE A GREAT WRONG AND WILL HAVE TO MAKE IT RIGHT AND CANNOT."

Tell the inquirer to take Christ first, and leave the matter of settling the wrong with Him. Tell him that the matter cannot be settled as it ought to be settled until first taking Christ. Make it very plain that the only thing God requires of a sinner is to accept Christ, and all other questions must be left until that point has been settled. Use John 3:36 for this purpose, and Acts 10:43.

Show further that if there is any wrong to be made right, Christ will give strength to make it right, and use for this purpose Philippians 4:13.

XIX. "I HAVE SINNED AWAY THE DAY OF GRACE."

This is a very serious difficulty since this person thinks that he or she no longer even has an opportunity to accept Christ. It often arises from a poor state of health and a morbid condition of mind, but I have never found a case that would not yield to prayerful and judicious treatment. The best passage to use, and one that generally proves sufficient, is John 6:37, the last clause: "The one who comes to Me I will by no means cast out." It is oftentimes necessary to read it over and over and over again, sometimes for days and days. Hold the inquirer to the one thought that God says He is ready to receive anyone who will come, and urge him or her to come now.

Another useful passage is Romans 10:13: "For whoever calls on the name of the Lord shall be saved." Dwell upon the "whoever." The case of Manasseh as recorded in 2 Chronicles 33:1–13 is useful as showing the extent to which a person can go and yet how God will receive the person to Himself, if he only humbles himself before Him. Luke 23:39–43 is often useful as showing how one was saved even in the hour of death.

XX. "IT IS TOO LATE."

This difficulty is very much like the preceding one, and the same passage, John 6:37, is also useful in this case. Oftentimes, however, Deuteronomy 4:30–31 will prove more helpful: "When you are in distress, and all these things come upon you in the latter days, when you turn to the Lord your God and obey His voice (for the Lord your God is a merciful God), He will not forsake you nor destroy you, nor forget the covenant of your fathers which He swore to them." In using the passage, emphasize the thought, "in the latter days."

Still another passage is 2 Peter 3:9: "The Lord is not slack concerning His promise, as some count slackness, but is longsuffering toward us, not willing that any should perish but that all should come to repentance." It shows that God is not willing that any should perish, and that the reason why He delays His judgment is that people may be brought to repentance. Luke 23:39–43 is useful as showing that one was saved even as late as his dying hour, and Revelation 22:17 tells us that whosoever will may take of the Water of Life freely.

XXI. "I HAVE COMMITTED THE UNPARDONABLE SIN."

A. Show what the unpardonable sin is.

The first thing to do in this case is to show just what the unpardonable sin is. For this purpose, use Matthew 12:31–32, noting the context. This passage taken in its context makes it plain that the unpardonable sin is blasphemy against the Holy Ghost, and that blasphemy against the Holy Ghost consists in deliberately attributing to the devil the work that is known to have been wrought by the Holy Spirit. Having shown just what the unpardonable sin is, ask the inquirer, "Have you done this? Have you deliberately attributed the work that you knew to be done by the Holy Spirit to the devil?" In almost every case, if not in every case, it will be found that the inquirer has not done this.

B. Use John 6:37.

Having shown what the unpardonable sin is, and that the inquirer has not committed it, use John 6:37 as in the preceding case. Even if the inquirer thinks that he or she has committed the blasphemy against the Holy Ghost, use John 6:37. Ask the inquirer what Jesus Christ says about those who come to Him, and then ask him if he or she will come to Christ right now. If he or she says, "I have committed the unpardonable sin," reply that it does not say, "The one who has not committed the unpardonable sin that comes to Me I will by no means cast out," but, "The one who comes to Me I will by no means cast out," and put the question again, "Will you come?" To every new excuse that arises, simply repeat the promise, "The one who comes to Me I will by no means cast out," and repeat the question, "Will you come?" If he or she raises some new difficulty, as probably will happen, simply say, "Jesus says, 'The one who comes to Me I will by no means cast out.' Will you come?" Repeat and repeat and repeat, over and over again, until this promise is fairly burned into the heart, praying all the time for the Holy Spirit to carry it home.

A man was once sent to me who was in the depths of despair. He had attempted suicide some five times. He felt that he had sinned away the day of grace, and committed the unpardonable sin, and that the devil had entered into him as he did into Judas Iscariot. Day after day I dealt with him, always using John 6:37. To every excuse and difficulty he would bring up, I would simply say, "Jesus says, 'The one who comes to Me I will by no means cast out.' " I met him at last one day for a final conflict. I said to him, "Do you believe what Jesus says?" He replied, "Yes. I believe everything in the Bible." "Well," I said, "did not Jesus say, 'The one who comes to Me I will by no means cast out'?" "Yes," he replied. I said, "Will you come?" He replied, "I have committed the unpardonable sin." I said, "Jesus did not say, 'The one who has not committed the unpardonable sin and comes to Me I will by no means cast out'; He said, 'The one who comes to Me I will by no means cast out.' Will you come?"

He said, "I am possessed of the devil." I replied, "Jesus did not say, 'If a man is not possessed of the devil and comes to Me I will by no means cast him out'; He said, 'The one who comes to Me I will by no means cast out.' Will you come?" He said, "The devil has actually entered into me." I replied, "Jesus did not say, 'If the devil has not entered into a man and he comes to Me I will by no means cast him out'; He said, 'The one who comes to Me I will by no means cast out.' Will you come?" He said, "My heart is too hard to come." I replied, "Jesus did not say, 'If a man's heart is not too hard and he comes to Me, I will by no means cast him out'; He said, 'The one who comes to Me I will by no means cast out.' Will you come?"

He said, "I don't feel like coming." I replied, "Jesus did not say, 'If any man feels like coming and comes to Me, I will by no means cast him out'; He said, 'The one who comes to Me I will by no means cast out.' Will you come?" He said, "I don't know as I can come in the right way." I replied, "Jesus did not say, 'If any man comes to me in the right way, I will by no means cast him out'; He said, 'The one who comes to Me I will by no means cast out.' Will you come?" He said, "I do not know as I want to come." I replied, "Jesus did not say, 'He that wants to come, and comes to Me I will by no means cast out'; He said, 'The one who comes to Me I will by no means cast out.' Will you come?"

He said, "I don't know as I know how to come." I replied, "Jesus did not say, 'He that knows how to come, and comes to Me I will by no means cast out'; He said, 'The one who comes to Me I will by no means cast out.' Will you come? Will you get down here now and come just the best you know how?" Hesitatingly the man knelt down. I asked him to follow me in prayer. I prayed about as follows: "Lord Jesus, You have said 'The one who comes to Me I will by no means cast out'; now the best I know how, I just come." The man repeated the words after me. I said, "Did you really come?" "Yes," he said, "I did." Then I said, "What has Jesus done? Never mind what you feel, but what does Jesus say He has done? 'The one who comes to Me I will by no means cast out.' What has Jesus done; what does He say He has done?" He replied, "He has received me." I said, "Are you willing to stand there on the naked Word of God?" He replied, "I will."

"Now," I said, "you are going to your room. I have no doubt that the devil will give you an awful fight, but will you stand right there on the word of Jesus, 'The one who comes to Me I will by no means cast out'?" He replied, "I will." He went to his room. The devil did come and assail him, and try to get him to look at his own heart, his own feelings, and his doubts, but he kept looking to the promise of Jesus, "The one who comes to Me I will by no means cast out." He believed that naked promise; he came out of his struggle a victor. This was eight or nine years ago. Today he is one of the most useful men in America.

XXII. "I HAVE NO HOPE OF SALVATION."

Very many men and women are in deep distress of soul over Hebrews 6:4–6: "For it is impossible for those who were once enlightened, and have tasted the heavenly gift, and have become partakers of the Holy Spirit, and have tasted the good word of God and the powers of the age to come, if they fall away, to renew them again to repentance, since they crucify again for themselves the Son of God, and put Him to an open shame." They fear that it describes them, and that there is no hope of their salvation. The way to deal with such a person is to explain the exact meaning of the passage.

A. Show, first of all, that it is addressed to Hebrew Christians who were in danger of apostatizing, renouncing Christ and going back to Judaism. Then ask if this describes their case. Of course it does not. Furthermore, show that it does not describe a person who has merely fallen in sin, but one who has fallen away, that is apostatized, and deliberately renounced Christ. Ask if this describes their case. In most cases, of course, it will be found that it does not.

B. In the next place, show that the difficulty is not that God is not willing to receive such a one back, but that it is impossible "to renew them again to repentance." That is, that their hearts are utterly hardened, and they have no desire to come to Christ. Then show that this does not describe their case, the very fact of their being in anxiety and burden of heart proving that it does not.

C. Sometimes all of this fails; if so, simply go over the fourth verse, and ask if that has really been their experience, if they have actually been made partakers of the Holy Ghost.

D. Show by the case of Peter that one who has been a follower of Christ may fall into deep sin, and yet be restored and become more useful than ever. Use for this purpose Luke 22:31, 34; Mark 14:66–72; and John 21:15–19.

E. Finally, use John 6:37, as described above.

XXIII. "I HAVE SINNED WILLFULLY."

Many are troubled by Hebrews 10:26–27. "For if we sin willfully after we have received the knowledge of the truth, there no longer remains a sacrifice for sins, but a certain fearful expectation of judgment, and fiery indignation which will devour the adversaries." I have met many in deepest anguish because they thought that this described their experience. The way to deal with such a one is to show exactly the meaning of the verse. Explain that the word "willfully" means deliberately, and of stubborn choice. It is the same word that is translated "willingly" in 1 Peter 5:2. It does not describe one who in weakness falls into sin, but one who, with whole heart, rejects obedience to God and the service of Christ, and throws all one's soul into sin. Ask if this describes his or her case. Finally, use John 6:37.

XXIV. "GOD SEEMS TO ME UNJUST AND CRUEL."

A. "Can you speak against God?"

The shortest way of dealing with many who say this is to take them at once to Romans 9:20: "But indeed, O man, who are you to reply against God? Will the thing formed say to him who formed it, 'Why have you made me like this?'" Apply the verse directly to the inquirer's case. Ask if he or she realizes who God is, and who he or she is, and say, "You are replying against God. You are accusing God of sin. Now this is God's message to you, 'But indeed, O man, who are you to reply against God?'" This verse has been used of the Holy Spirit to break down in repentance and tears many who have complained against God.

This may be followed up by Romans 11:33. Show the inquirer that the reason God seems to him to be unjust and cruel is because such is the depth of the riches both of the wisdom and knowledge of God, and so unsearchable are His judgments, that he cannot find them out.

This can be followed up still further by Isaiah 55:8–9 and Job 40:2. When the complainer has read the verse in Job, ask if he or she wishes to contend with the Almighty. Show further that he or she is reproving God, and God says he or she must answer for it. Ask if he or she is ready to answer for it.

B. "Can today's sorrows be compared with eternity?"

If the inquirer is complaining of God's cruelty because of some sorrow or anguish in his or her own life, it is well to use Hebrews 12:5–7, 10–12:

> And you have forgotten the exhortation which speaks to you as to sons: *"My son, do not despise the chastening of the Lord, nor be discouraged when you are rebuked by Him; for whom the Lord loves He chastens, and scourges every son whom He receives."* If you endure chastening, God deals with you as with sons; for what son is there whom a father does not chasten? . . . For they indeed for a few days chastened us as seemed best to them, but He for our profit, that we may be partakers of His holiness. Now no chastening seems to be joyful for the present, but painful; nevertheless, afterward it yields the peaceable fruit of righteousness to those who have been trained by it. Therefore strengthen the hands which hang down, and the feeble knees.

One should deal very tenderly with a case like this, yet at the same time faithfully. Show the inquirer that the sorrows and disappointments and afflictions that have been suffered are God's loving dealings, to bring him or her into a life of holiness and higher joy, that God does not willingly afflict. One can follow the above passage with Isaiah 63:9. In order to lead the sorrow-stricken soul to see that the sufferings of this present time are not worthy to be compared with the glory that shall be revealed in us, use Romans 8:18 and 2 Corinthians 4:17–18.

C. "Do you know the depths of your own sin?"

Sometimes it is well to say in such a case, "You would not think that God was unjust and cruel if you only realized the depth of your own sin against Him," and use Matthew 22:37–38 to show him the greatness of his sin, in the way described on pages 60–61.

D. "Do you understand how much God loves you?"

It is a wise plan to follow up all the preceding methods by showing the complainer the wonderful love of God. John 3:16 and Isaiah 53:5 will serve well for this purpose.

XXV. "I CANNOT SEE WHY IT WAS NECESSARY THAT CHRIST SHOULD DIE IN ORDER THAT PEOPLE BE SAVED."

There are very many who will tell you this. Of course, those who say this are frequently mere triflers, and trying to find a hiding place from God's truth and their own duty, but some say this with a good deal of sincerity of purpose. I have found one of the most effective passages to use in such a case to be Romans 9:20. It is well to follow this up by showing the doubter the greatness and depth of his or her own sin in the way described earlier. No one, after being led by the Word of God and His Spirit to see oneself as God sees, will any longer have any difficulty with God's way of salvation, but will be only too glad to find that a Sin-Bearer has been provided.

XXVI. "THERE ARE SO MANY THINGS IN THE BIBLE THAT I CANNOT UNDERSTAND."

A. The first step in such a case is to show the objector why he cannot understand.

A good passage to use for this purpose is 1 Corinthians 2:14: "But the natural man does not receive the things of the Spirit of God, for they are foolishness to him; nor can he know them, because they are spiritually discerned." It can be used in this way: When one says, "There are so many things in the Bible that I cannot understand," reply, "Yes, that is just what the Bible says." Then show the passage, and say, "This verse tells you just why you cannot understand what is in the Bible, because 'the natural man does not receive the things of the Spirit of God, for they are foolishness to him,' and I suppose that many of them appear like foolishness to you." "Yes." "This verse tells you why it is: 'because they are spiritually discerned.' The truth is, you are spiritually blind. If you will turn from sin and accept Christ, you will get spiritual sight, and then many things that you cannot understand now will become as plain as day." Isaiah 55:8–9 can also be used. You can say to the one with whom you are dealing, "This tells why you cannot understand God's truth. Why is it?" "Because His thoughts are higher than my thoughts."

Daniel 12:10 is also useful. Before the person reads it, you can say, "I can show you a passage in the Bible that tells you just exactly why you cannot understand, and also how you can understand." When he or she has read it, ask who it is that does not understand. "The wicked." "And who shall understand?" "The wise." Other passages that can also be used to good effect are 2 Peter 3:16–18, 1 Corinthians 13:11–12, and Romans 11:33.

B. The second step is to show how to understand.

John 7:17 makes this plain: "If anyone wills to do His will, he shall know concerning the doctrine, whether it is from God or whether I speak on My own authority." Follow this up with Psalm 119:18 and James 1:5: "Open my eyes, that I may see wondrous things from Your law" and "If any of you lacks wisdom, let him ask of God, who gives to all liberally and without reproach, and it will be given to him."

XXVII. "I CANNOT BELIEVE."

We will take up skeptics more at length later. At this point, we take up the matter merely as an honest difficulty that some find in the way of accepting Christ.

A. Ask *what* he cannot believe.

When one states this as a difficulty, it is often well to ask what he or she cannot believe. A man once said to Mr. Moody, "I cannot believe." Mr. Moody said, "Who can't you believe?" He replied, "I cannot believe." "Who can't you believe;

can't you believe God?" "Yes," the man replied, "I can believe God, but I cannot believe myself." Mr. Moody said, "I don't want you to believe yourself; I want you to believe God." Oftentimes, the difficulty is with some doctrine that has nothing directly to do with salvation; for example, one will say, "I cannot believe the account of creation given in the first chapter of Genesis, and I cannot believe the story about Jonah and the whale." Now of course one ought to believe the Bible account of creation given in the first chapter of Genesis, and ought to believe the story about Jonah, but these are not questions to discuss with an unsaved person. When one states some such difficulty as this, the best thing to do is to say, "Can you believe in Jesus Christ?" "Yes, I can believe in Jesus Christ." "But will you believe in Him; will you accept Him as your Savior, your Sin-Bearer, and your Lord and Master?" Show that it does not say, believe this doctrine or that doctrine and you will be saved, or this incident or that incident in the Bible, but "believe on the Lord Jesus Christ, and you will be saved." For this purpose, use Acts 16:31 and John 3:16. After the man or woman has really believed on Christ and been saved, and grown somewhat in Christian knowledge, he or she will be in a position to take up secondary questions. Many a well-meaning worker makes a great mistake in discussing secondary questions with an unsaved person, when he or she is in no position to understand them at all, but should be held to the vital point of the acceptance of Jesus Christ as Savior and Lord and Master.

B. See if his sin is the real problem.

In many cases, perhaps in most cases, when one says, "I cannot believe," the real difficulty that lies back of the inability to believe is unwillingness to forsake sin. It is well to say to such a person, "Is your unbelief the real difficulty, or is there not some sin in your life that you are unwilling to give up?" I was once called to deal with a man and was told that he was a skeptic and needed help along that line. I said to him, "Are you a skeptic?" He replied, "Yes." I asked him what made him a skeptic, and he said because he could not see where Cain got his wife. I said to him, "Is that your real difficulty?" "Yes." I replied, "Then if I remove that difficulty, and show you where Cain got his wife, will you become a Christian?" He said, "Oh, no, I cannot promise that." "But," I said, "you said that was your difficulty, the thing that kept you from accepting Christ. Now, if I remove that difficulty, and you are honest, of course you will accept Christ." The man laughed and saw that he was cornered. "Now," I said, "let me ask you a question: Is not the real difficulty some sin in your life?" The man broke down and confessed that it was, and he told me what the sin was, and professed to give it up, and accepted Christ then and there. When you are convinced that the real difficulty in the case is sin, a good passage to use is John 5:44: "How can you believe, who receive honor from one another, and do not seek the honor that comes from the only God?" Before reading it, say, "Yes, I suppose you cannot believe, but Jesus Christ tells us just why it is you cannot believe," and then read the passage. Then you can say, "The reason why you cannot believe, according to this verse, is because you are seeking the honor that comes from man and not the honor that comes from God alone. Is this not so?" Be courteous, but do not let the inquirer dodge that point. Isaiah 55:7 will show that one not only needs to forsake one's own way, but one's thoughts as well. If one will return to the Lord, He will have mercy and abundantly pardon.

C. Show how to believe.

Finally, in dealing with this difficulty, it is well to show one how to believe. After dealing along the lines already mentioned, you can now say, "I can show you how to believe." Then give John 7:17: "If anyone wills to do His will, he shall know concerning the doctrine, whether it be from God or whether I speak on My own authority." Ask if he will do the will of God, if he will surrender his will to God. Then show James 1:5–7: "If any of you lacks wisdom, let him ask of God, who gives to all liberally and without reproach, and it will be given to him. But let him ask in faith, with no doubting, for he who doubts is like a wave of the sea driven and tossed by the wind. For let not that man suppose that he will receive anything from the Lord." Follow this up with John 20:31: "But these are written that you may believe that Jesus is the Christ, the Son of God, and that believing you may have life in His name." Then give the person the gospel of John to study prayerfully.

LEARNING ACTIVITIES

1. Identify three or four of the difficulties in this chapter that you have already encountered or think you are likely to encounter. If there are particular people associated with the difficulties, stop right now and pray for God to be preparing their hearts for the Gospel.

2. Find a Christian friend to role-play with you. Have this person present you with the three or four difficulties and let you practice showing the friend the scriptural answers. Make sure that you are not only responding to the difficulty, but also taking the person to the next step of considering faith in Christ as Savior.

3. After reviewing the entire chapter, ask the Christian friend to pick any of the difficulties and test how well you do in responding to it.

4. Pray for the Lord to provide you with opportunities to put this training into action. Look for the opportunities God gives you to respond to the concerns of those who are having difficulty accepting the Gospel.

5. At the end of each day for several days (or the end of each week, depending on how quickly you are moving through this material), make a brief report in a journal or to your Christian friend about how God has given you opportunities and how you have been able to respond. Which difficulties were raised? Were you able to draw on Scripture well? How did the person respond? How did your conversation compare to the material by Torrey? How might you amend the lesson to be better prepared next time?

6. Add two or three additional difficulties to this chapter that you have encountered or think that you are likely to encounter. Identify Scripture that you can use in these situations, and sketch how you think the conversation is likely to go. This will give you a customized chapter for situations in which you are likely to find yourself.

CHAPTER FOUR

DEALING WITH ISSUES OF HOPE

COMING TO CHRIST IS NOT JUST ABOUT a once-in-a-lifetime decision. It transforms one's life. This chapter deals with the extremes of hope in one's life. Many hold to false hopes that offer no real prospect of eternity. Others struggle with knowing whether or not they are really saved and can have hope. In Torrey's words, it is more dangerous to have false hopes than to struggle with assurance of salvation. However, both are important, and both rob one of the full joy of salvation.

Torrey challenges us to have "solemnness and earnestness" in using God's Word and engaging in these discussions. When we deal with someone's hope (or lack of hope) for eternal salvation, we are dealing very close to the person's innermost being. However, when we are operating in the power of the Holy Spirit and depending upon God's Word, we can be certain that God will work in us.

It was not unusual for Torrey to include stories from his own personal work or the experiences of others. As you are reading this chapter, perhaps you would benefit by pausing and thinking of stories in your own ministry experience. Or perhaps you could ask others how they were delivered from false hopes or lack of assurance.

Don't rely solely on Torrey for the good stories. It is likely that God has put some other excellent testimonies right near you.

In a postmodern world that does not find its hope in the absolute and eternal truth of God, the material in this chapter has tremendous relevance. People may express the concerns in very different ways than in Torrey's day, but issues of hope are planted deep within the heart of everyone. God's Word still speaks effectively, even to people in a postmodern culture.

HOW TO DEAL WITH THOSE WHO ENTERTAIN FALSE HOPES

I. THE HOPE OF BEING SAVED BY A RIGHTEOUS LIFE

This is the most common of false hopes. Even among those who profess to be Christians, there are many who are really depending upon their lives as Christians for their acceptance before God. Those who are depending upon their righteous lives for salvation are readily known by their saying such things as this: "I am doing the best I can." "I do more good than evil." " I am not a great sinner." "I have never done anything very bad." This mistake can be directly met by Galatians 2:16: "Knowing that a man is not justified by the works of the law but by faith in Jesus Christ, even we have believed in Christ Jesus, that we might be justified by faith in Christ and not by the works of the law; for by the works of the law no flesh shall be justified." After the passage has been read, you can say to the one with whom you are dealing, "Now you are expecting to be justified and accepted before God by what you are doing, by your own life and character; but God tells you in this passage, that 'by the works of the law no flesh shall be justified.'" Follow this up by Romans 3:19–20, Galatians 3:10, and James 2:10. Before reading the verses you can say, "Well, if you are going to be saved by your righteous life, let us see what God requires in order that one may be saved on that ground." After reading the verse in James, show that to be saved by the law, one must keep the whole law, for if one offends in a single point one is guilty of all.

A. Matthew 5:20

A verse that is useful in showing the kind of righteousness that God demands is Matthew 5:20: "For I say to you, that unless your righteousness exceeds the righteousness of the scribes and Pharisees, you will by no means enter the kingdom of heaven." This verse shows that no one's righteousness comes up to God's standard, and if someone wishes to be saved, he or she must find some other way of salvation than by his or her own deeds. It is sometimes well in using this passage to say to the inquirer, "You do not understand the kind of righteousness God demands, or you would not talk as you do. Now let us turn to God's own Word and see what kind of righteousness it is that God demands."

B. Luke 16:15 and Romans 2:16

There is another way of dealing with this class of people, by using such passages as, "And He said to them, 'You are those who justify yourselves before men, but God knows your hearts. For what is highly esteemed among men is an abomination in the sight of God'" (Luke 16:15); "In the day when God will judge the secrets of men by Jesus Christ, according to my gospel" (Romans 2:16); and "But the Lord said to Samuel, 'Do not look at his appearance or at his physical stature, because I have refused him. For the Lord does not see as man sees; for man looks at the outward appearance, but the Lord looks at the heart'" (1 Samuel 16:7). These passages show that God looks at the heart. Hold the inquirer right to that point. Everyone, when brought face-to-face with that, must tremble, for he or she knows that whatever an outward life may be, a heart will not stand the scrutiny of God's all-seeing and holy eye. No matter how self-righteous someone may appear, we need not be discouraged, for somewhere in the depths of everyone's heart is the consciousness of sin, and all we have to do is to work away until we touch that point. Everyone's conscience is on our side.

C. Matthew 22:37–39

Matthew 22:37–39 can also be used with those who expect to be saved by their righteous lives. You can say, "If you expect to be saved by your righteous life, you are greatly deceived and certainly entertain a false hope. For so far from living a righteous life, you have broken the very first and greatest of God's commandments." Of course, it may not be believed at first, but you can turn to the passage mentioned and show what the first and greatest of God's commandments is, and ask if it has been kept. This passage is especially useful if someone says, "I am doing the best I can," or "I am doing more good than evil." You can say, "You are greatly mistaken about that. So far from doing more good than evil, you have broken the first and greatest of God's laws," and then show the passage.

D. Hebrews 11:6 and John 6:29

A fourth method of dealing with this class is to use Hebrews 11:6 and John 6:29. These passages show that the one thing that God demands is faith, that the work of God is to believe on Him whom He hath sent, and that without faith it is impossible to please God whatever else one may possess. John 16:9 can also be used to show that unbelief in Christ is the greatest sin.

E. John 3:36

Still another way of dealing with this class is by the use of John 3:36: "He who believes in the Son has everlasting life; and he who does not believe the Son shall not see life, but the wrath of God abides on him." This shows that the gift of eternal life depends solely upon one's acceptance of Jesus Christ. That the sin that brings the heaviest punishment is that of treading underfoot the Son of God can be shown by Hebrews 10:28–29. Before using this passage, it is well to say, "You think you are very good, but do you know that you are committing the most awful sin in God's sight that someone can commit?" If he or she replies, "I do not think so," then say, "Let me show you from God's Word that you are." Then turn to this passage and read it with great solemnity and earnestness.

A very useful passage with many a self-righteous person is Luke 18:10–14. You can say, "There is a picture in the Bible of someone just like you, who expected to be accepted before God on the grounds of his righteousness, and who had much righteousness to present to God, but let us see what God says." Then have him or her read the passage.

It is well to bring all those who expect to be saved by a righteous life into the presence of God, for in His holy presence self-righteousness fades away. (See Isaiah 6:5 and Job 42:5–6.) But how shall we bring anyone into the presence of God? By opening to them passages that reveal the holiness of God, and by praying the Holy Spirit to carry these passages home. It is also well, whenever possible, to get the inquirer to pray. Many who are stoutly maintaining excellence before God have given way when they have been brought to their knees in God's very presence.

II. "GOD IS TOO GOOD TO DAMN ANYONE."

A. The Bible defines God's goodness.

When anyone says this, you can reply, "We know nothing about God's goodness except what we learn from this Bible. If we give up the Bible, we have no conclusive proof that God is love, and can therefore build no hopes upon His goodness. But if we accept the Bible statement that God is love, we must also accept the Bible representations of the goodness of God. Let us then go to the Bible and find out the character of God's goodness." Then turn the inquirer to Romans 2:4–5: "Or do you despise the riches of His goodness, forbearance, and longsuffering, not knowing that the goodness of God leads you to repentance? But in accordance with your hardness and your impenitent heart you are treasuring up for yourself wrath in the day of wrath and revelation of the righteous judgment of God." When one has read the verse, you can say, "This verse tells us what the purpose of God's goodness is; what is it?" "To lead us to repentance." "And what does this verse tell us will be the result if we do not permit the goodness of God to lead us to repentance, but trample it underfoot and make it an excuse for sin?" One will find the answer to this question in verse 5; hold to it until it is seen, that if we despise the riches of His goodness, then we are treasuring up unto ourselves "wrath against the day of wrath and revelation of the righteous judgment of God." You can also use John 8:21, 24 and John 3:36 to show that however good we may be, if we do not believe in Jesus with a living faith, we shall die in our sins, and not go where Jesus is, and that we shall not see life, but that the wrath of God abides upon us.

B. We choose not to repent.

Still another way to deal with this is to show that it is not so much God who damns, as we who damn ourselves in spite of God's goodness, because we will not repent and come to Christ and accept the life freely offered. For this purpose, use 2 Peter 3:9–11 or John 5:40. Press the thought of this text, that if anyone does not obtain life, it is because he will not come to Christ, and therefore a person is damned in spite of God's goodness if he will not come to Christ and accept life. In much the same way, one can use Ezekiel 33:11. It is sometimes well to say, "You are right in thinking that God is not willing to damn anyone; furthermore, He offers life freely to you, but there is one difficulty in the way. Let us turn to John 5:40 and see what the difficulty is." When it has been read, say, "You see now that the difficulty is not that God wishes to damn you, but that you will not come to Christ that you might have life."

C. Look at what God has already done.

If these methods do not succeed, 2 Peter 2:4–6, 9 may prove effectual. Before using the passage, you can say, "The best way to judge what God will do is not by speculating about it, but by looking at what He has done in the past." Then turn to these passages, let him or her read, and ask, "What did God do with the angels that sinned? What did He do with the world of the ungodly in the days of Noah? What did He do with the wicked in the days of Sodom and Gomorrah? What then may you expect Him to do with you in spite of any theories that you may have about His character and actions?" This should all be done not in a confrontational way, but with great earnestness, tenderness, and solemnity.

You can say still further "God has not left us to speculate as to what He will do with the persistently impenitent; He has told us plainly in Matthew 25:41, 46." You may say still further, that God does bear long with man, but His dealings with man in the past show that at last His day of waiting will end, and in spite of one's doubt of His Word, and doubt of his severity in dealing with the persistently impenitent, He does at last punish. You might use 2 Chronicles 36:11–21 as an illustrative case in point.

D. Unbelievers are already condemned.

It is well sometimes to add to all the other passages, John 3:18–19: "He who believes in Him is not condemned; but he who does not believe is condemned already, because he has not believed in the name of the only begotten Son of God. And this is the condemnation, that the light has come into the world, and men loved darkness rather than light, because their deeds were evil." Before having the inquirer read the verses, you can say, "You say God is too good to damn anyone, but the truth is that you are condemned already. It is not a question of what is going to happen to you in the future, but a question of your present position before God." When the passage has been read, ask, "When is it that the one who does not believe is condemned?" "Already." "Why is it that one is condemned?" "Because light is come into the world, and that one loves darkness rather than light."

E. God addresses this directly.

Luke 13:3 is very effective in some case, for it shows how the "good" God deals with persons who persist in sin. The passage can be used in this way: "You say God is too good to damn anyone, but let us see what God Himself says in His Word." Then turn to the passage and read, "Unless you repent you will all likewise perish." Repeat the passage over and over again until it has been driven home.

An earnest missionary in the western part of New York was once holding meetings in a country village. The Universalist minister of the place was very anxious to engage the missionary in a controversy, but the missionary always said that he was too busy for controversy. One day the Universalist minister came into the house where the missionary was calling; the Universalist was delighted to see him, for he thought that his opportunity for a discussion had come at last. He began the customary universalist argument about God being too good to damn anyone.

Universalism refers to the belief that all people are saved, even though all may "come to God" in their own ways. This movement was gaining momentum at the time of Torrey's ministry and accompanied the development of liberal theology that denied the uniqueness of Christianity and the truth of Scripture.

After the Universalist had gone through the usual volume of words, the missionary simply replied, "I am too busy for argument, but I just want to say to you, that except you repent, you shall likewise perish." The Universalist was somewhat angry, but replied sneeringly, "That is not argument; it is simply a quotation from the Bible," and then ran on with another stream of words. When he had finished his second speech, the missionary simply replied, "I have no time for argument, but I just want to say to you, except you repent, you shall likewise perish." Again the Universalist sneered and poured forth another torrent of what he called argument. When he had finished this time, the missionary again said, "I have no time for controversy; I simply want to say to you that except you repent, you shall likewise perish. Now I must go, but let me say, you will not be able to forget what I have said." The Universalist preacher laughed, and said he guessed he would forget it quick enough, that the missionary had used no argument whatever, but had simply quoted the Bible.

The following day there was a knock at the missionary's door, and when it was opened, the Universalist preacher came in. The missionary said, "I have no time for argument." "Oh sir!" said the other, "I have not come to argue with you. You were right yesterday when you told me there was one thing I would not be able to forget. I feel that it is true, that except I repent I must perish, and I have come to ask you what I must do to be saved." The missionary showed the man the way of life, and the result was that the Universalist became a real believer in Christ and a preacher of the truth he had previously labored to pull down.

III. "I AM TRYING TO BE A CHRISTIAN."

A. Show the inquirer that it is trusting and not trying that saves.

For this purpose, use Isaiah 12:2: "Behold, God is my salvation, I will trust and not be afraid; for Yah, the Lord, is my strength and song; he also has become my salvation." When it has been read, ask what it is the prophet says. Is it "I will try"? No, "I will trust." Another verse that can also be used to show that it is not trying to be a Christian, but believing on Christ, that saves is Acts 16:31: "So they said, 'Believe on the Lord Jesus Christ, and you will be saved, you and your household." John 1:12 is very useful. Before using it, you can say, "What God asks of you is not to try to be a Christian, or to try to live a better life, or to try to do anything but simply to receive Jesus Christ who did it all." Then have the passage read and say to the inquirer, "Will you now stop your trying and simply receive Jesus as Savior?" Make it very clear what this means, and hold the inquirer to this point.

B. Show that it is not trying what we can do, but trusting what Jesus has done that saves from guilt.

Use for this purpose Romans 3:23–26. When the inquirer has read the passage, ask if this teaches us that we are justified by trying to do something. "No." "Then how are we justified?" Hold to it until the response is, "Freely by His grace, through the redemption that is in Christ Jesus," and the person sees that it is on the simple condition of faith. Another very effective passage to use in the same way is Romans 4:3–5. This makes it clear as day that it is not our trying, but our believing on Him that justifies us. Acts 10:43 and 13:38 can be used in a similar way.

C. Show that it is not our trying in our own strength, but our trusting in Christ's strength, that saves from the power of sin.

To make this clear, use the following passages: Jude 24, 1 John 5:4–5, 2 Timothy 1:12, and 1 Peter 1:5. Do not let this class of inquirers go until they are perfectly clear that they are saved and are no longer merely "trying to be Christians."

IV. "I FEEL SAVED," OR "I FEEL THAT I AM GOING TO HEAVEN."

A. Show the utter unreliability of our feeling as a ground of hope.

An excellent passage for this purpose is Jeremiah 17:9: "The heart is deceitful above all things, and desperately wicked; who can know it?" Follow this with Proverbs 14:12. After reading the latter passage, you can say to the inquirer, "The way you are going seems to be right, it seems to you as if it would lead to heaven, but what does this passage tell us about a way that seems to be right?" "The end is the way of death." Then drive the thought home that it will not do to rest our hope upon anything less sure than the Word of God. Luke 18:9–14 may be used in this way. You can say, "We are told in the Bible about a man who felt saved, and felt sure of going to heaven; let us read about him." Then let him read the story of the Pharisee, and show how he was not saved for all his self-confidence. Isaiah 55:8 can also be used to enforce the thought that God's thoughts are not our thoughts, and while we may think we are saved, God may clearly see that we are not.

B. Show the true ground of hope, namely God's Word.

Use for this purpose Titus 1:2: "In hope of eternal life which God, who cannot lie, promised before time began." You can say, "Paul had a hope of eternal life. Upon what was that hope built?" "The Word of God that 'cannot lie.'" Then say to the person, "Do you want a hope built upon that sure ground?" Take him then to John 3:36. That verse tells clearly how to get such a hope.

One afternoon I was speaking to a woman who, a few weeks before, had lost her only child. At the time of the child's death, she had been especially interested, but her serious impressions had largely left her. After a time I put to her the question, "Do you not wish to go where your little one has gone?" She replied, "I expect to." "What makes you think that you will?" I asked. She answered, "I feel so; I feel that I will go to heaven when I die." I then asked her if there was anything she could point to in the Word of God which gave her a reason for believing that she was going to heaven when she died. She replied that there was not. She then turned to me and began to question me: "Do you expect to go to heaven when you die?" "Yes, I know I shall." "How do you know it? Have you any word from God for it?" "Yes," I answered, and turned to John 3:36. She was then led to see the difference between a faith that depended upon her feeling and a faith that depended upon the Word of God.

V. THE HOPE OF BEING SAVED BY A MERE PROFESSION OF RELIGION, OR BY A FAITH THAT DOES NOT SAVE FROM SIN AND LEAD TO REPENTANCE

In many communities, it is very common to meet men and women who believe they are saved because they hold to an orthodox creed, or because they have been baptized or made a profession of religion. This is one of the most dangerous of all false hopes, but it can be readily dealt with.

——ᏅᎦ *Orthodox creed refers to the statements of belief that are common in churches with roots in Europe and the Reformation.*

A. Not all who profess are saved.

A good passage to begin with is Titus 1:16: "They profess to know God, but in works they deny Him, being abominable, disobedient, and disqualified for every good work." You can say to the person, "You profess to know God, but God Himself tells us that many who profess to know Him are lost; let me show it to you in His Word." When he or she has read the verse, you can say, "Now if one professes to know God, but denies Him in his life, what does God Himself say that such a one is?" "Abominable, disobedient, and disqualified for every good work." Another passage that can be used in very much the same way is Matthew 7:21–23. You might say, "God tells us plainly in His Word that one may make a profession of religion, may be active even in Christian work, and yet be lost, after all." Then read the verses and say, "According to these verses, will a mere profession of religion save anyone?" "No, only doing the will of the Father who is in heaven." "Are you doing His will?"

B. To be saved, we must be born again.

A second way of dealing with this class is to say, "God tells us plainly that in order to be saved we must be born again." Then show them John 3:3–5: "Jesus answered and said to him, 'Most assuredly, I say to you, unless one is born again, he cannot see the kingdom of God.' Nicodemus said to Him, 'How can a man be born when he is old? Can he enter a second time into his mother's womb and be born?' Jesus answered, 'Most assuredly, I say to you, unless one is born of water and the Spirit, he cannot enter the kingdom of God.'" When these verses are read, you can say, "Now these verses make it clear that in order to enter the kingdom of God, one must be born again. Now let us turn to other parts of the Bible and see what it is to be born again." For this purpose, use 2 Corinthians 5:17.

C. It is a certain kind of faith that saves.

A third method of dealing with this class is by saying, "Yes, faith does indeed save, but it is a certain kind of faith that saves." To show what the faith that saves is, turn to Galatians 5:6: "For in Christ Jesus neither circumcision nor un-circumcision avails anything, but faith working through love."

This passage says that it is faith which works by love. Romans 10:9–10 says that it is a faith of the heart, while James 2:14 tells us that it is faith that shows itself in works.

D. Saving faith overcomes the world.

First John 5:4–5 is also very useful as showing that one who really has faith in Jesus as the Son of God, and is born of God, overcomes the world. The fact that one is living in sin and not overcoming the world, but being overcome by it, is conclusive proof that he really has not faith that Jesus is the Son of God, and he has not been born of God.

LEARNING ACTIVITIES

1. Are you able to identify folks in your life who fall into any of the categories of those having false hope? Have you ever approached them in the manner suggested in this lesson? How did they respond (or how do you expect them to respond)?

2. What other ways might people use to express false hope regarding their own need for salvation? What verses would you use to respond to them?

3. Ask several people in your church or community about their own testimonies in order to find some who have overcome false hopes. What brought them to the true hope of salvation in Christ? How do their experiences compare to the material in this lesson?

HOW TO DEAL WITH THOSE WHO LACK ASSURANCE

*I*T IS NOT ENOUGH THAT ONE BE SAVED. To be of the most use to God, one must know that he or she is saved, and no small part of our work as personal workers will be to lead into assurance of salvation those men and women who do not as yet know that they are saved. There are two classes of those who lack assurance.

I. THOSE WHO LACK ASSURANCE BECAUSE OF IGNORANCE

A. Many lack assurance because they do not know that it is anyone's privilege to know that he has eternal life.

Oftentimes, if you ask people if they know that they are saved, or if they know that their sins are forgiven, they reply, "Why, no, no one knows that." You can say, "Yes, the Bible says that all who believe may know it," and then show them 1 John 5:13: "These things I have written to you who believe in the name of the Son of God, that you may know that you have eternal life, and that you may continue to believe in the name of the Son of God." It is well to begin with this passage, and not to leave it until it becomes very clear that it is every believer's privilege to know that he or she has everlasting life. Follow this up with John 1:12. This verse shows that Christ gives to as many as receive Him power to become the sons of God. A good way to use this verse is to ask the inquirer questions regarding it. "What does everyone who receives Him receive power to become?" "A child of God." "Are you sure that everyone who receives Jesus obtains power to become a child of God?" "Yes." "What makes you sure?" "God says so here." "Have you received Jesus?" "Yes." "What then have you received the right to become?" Just hold the inquirer to the point that it is not what he feels he has power to become, but what God here in His Word says he has power to become. It will usually be necessary to go through it again and again and again.

John 3:36 can be used in a similar way. "He who believes in the Son has everlasting life." Ask the inquirer, "Who does this verse say has everlasting life? How many who believe on the Son have everlasting life? Does God merely say that those who believe on the Son 'shall have' everlasting life? Do you believe on the Son? What then does God say you have?" In a little while, he or she will see it and say, "Everlasting life." Have him or her stand by it because God says so, and then have the person kneel down and thank God for giving everlasting life. Do not let the inquirer go while continuing to say, "I hope I have everlasting life." Insist upon resting absolutely upon what God says.

One night I found a young man upon his knees in great distress at the close of an evening service. I showed him from the Bible how Jesus Christ had borne his sins, and asked him if he would accept Christ as his Savior. He said he would, and seemed to do it; but he seemed to get no light, and went out of the meeting in deep distress still. The next night he was there again, professing to accept Christ, but with no assurance that his sins were forgiven. I tried to show him from John 3:36 what God said of those who believed on the Son, but the light did not come. Finally he rose to leave the room. As he turned to leave me, he said, " Will you pray for me?" I said, "Yes." He walked a few steps down the aisle, and I called after him, "Do you believe I will pray for you?" He turned toward me with a look of astonishment, and said, "Yes, of course." I said, "Why do you think I will pray for you?" "Because you said so." I said, "Is not God's word as good as mine?" He saw it at once, that while he was willing to believe my word, he was not willing to believe God's Word. He received assurance on the spot and knew that he had everlasting life.

Other verses that can be used to advantage are John 5:24 and 1 John 5:12.

Acts 13:39 has been greatly used of God in dealing with this class. I was dealing one night with a young woman who was in great distress of soul because she could not see that she had forgiveness of sin. I went carefully over the ground to find if she really had accepted Christ, and it appeared clear that she had. Then I had her read this passage, "By Him everyone who believes is justified from all things." "Now," I said, "who does God say in this verse is justified from all things?" "Everyone who believes." "Believe on whom?" "Believe on Christ." "Do you believe on Christ?" "I do." "Have you really accepted Him as your Savior and Lord and Master?" "Yes." "Then you are sure you believe on Him?" "Yes." "And what does this verse say that all who believe are?" "Justified." "What then are you?" She would not say, "I am justified," but wept over the thought that her sins were not forgiven. I went over it again and again and again. At last, the simple meaning of the words seemed to dawn upon her darkened mind. I asked her as before, "Who does God say are justified?" "Everyone who believes." "From what are they justified?" "From all things." "Who is justified from all things?" "Everyone who believes." "Who says so?" "God says so." "Do you believe?" "I do." "What are you then?" A joyous light spread over her countenance, and she said, "Why, I am justified from all things," and immediately she turned toward her friend standing near and said to me, "Now won't you speak to my friend about Christ?"

B. Many inquirers of this class stumble over the fact that they have not the witness of the Holy Spirit.

Show them that the witness of the Word to their acceptance is sufficient, from 1 John 5:10: "He who believes in the Son of God has the witness in himself; he who does not believe God has made Him a liar, because he has not believed the testimony that God has given of his Son." This verse tells us that if we believe not the witness of God, in His Word, we make Him a liar. I was once dealing with a very intelligent young man along this line. He professed that he had accepted Jesus Christ, but that he did not know that he had eternal life. I showed him God's testimony that "he who has the Son has life" (1 John 5:12). "Now," I said, "you have the Son." "Yes." "And God says that he who has the Son has what?" "Life." Then I read the tenth verse, "He who does not believe God has made Him a liar, because he has not believed the testimony that God has given of his Son." "Now," I said, "God's record concerning His Son is that eternal life is in Him" (verse 11), "and that he who has the Son has life" (verse 12). "Now this is God's record. If you do not believe it, no matter what your feelings are, what are you doing?" In a little while, the man replied, "I am making God a liar, but I never saw it before." Then and there he trusted the naked Word of God, and went out with the knowledge that his sins were forgiven, and that God had given him eternal life.

Also show those who are waiting for the witness of the Holy Spirit that it is after we believe the testimony of the Word that we are sealed with the Holy

Spirit of promise, using Ephesians 1:13 for this purpose. The natural order in assurance is this: First, assurance of our justification, resting upon the naked Word of God (such passages as Acts 13:39); second, public confession of Christ with the mouth (Romans 10:10); and third, the witness of the Holy Spirit (Ephesians 1:13; Romans 8:16). The trouble with many is that they wish to invert this order and have the witness of the Holy Spirit before they confess Christ with the mouth.

It is very important in using these texts to make clear what saving faith is, because many say that they believe when they do not in the sense of these texts, and so get a false assurance, and entertain false hopes, and never get deliverance. There is a good deal of careless dealing with those who lack assurance. Workers are so anxious to have inquirers come out clearly that they urge them on to assurance when they have no right to assurance because they have not really accepted Christ. It is better not to have assurance of salvation than to have assurance that is false. John 1:12, 2 Timothy 1:12, and Romans 10:10 make very clear what the character of saving faith is.

II. THOSE WHO LACK ASSURANCE BECAUSE OF SIN

Oftentimes, the trouble with those who lack assurance is that there is some sin or questionable practice in their lives that they ought to confess and give up. When this is the case, it will not do to deal with the inquirer along the lines mentioned above. Go to passages such as John 8:12: "Then Jesus spoke to them again, saying, 'I am the light of the world. He who follows Me shall not walk in darkness, but have the light of life." When the person has read the passage, you can tell that Jesus' promise was that if we follow Him we shall have the light of life. "You do not have the light of life, so the probability is that you are not following Him. Are you following Him?" Push the inquirer along this line to find if there is not some point in which he or she is untrue to Christ, or to the leading of the Holy Spirit.

One night in an after meeting, I was walking around here and there asking different ones about their Christian experience. A gentleman and his wife, friends from another church, had come down to the meeting. I noticed the gentleman looked at his wife as much as to say, "Speak to her." In a little while I came around to her, and asked her how she was getting on in her Christian life. She replied that she was all in the dark. I simply quoted John 8:12 and passed on to speak to others. She and her husband stayed after everyone else had gone, and I had a private conversation with her. I asked her if she was rebelling against the will of God at any place. She confessed that she was, that her husband had received a great anointing of the Holy Spirit and she had not, and what was more, she was afraid her husband would go into Christian work and she did not want him to, and so she had gotten utterly in the dark. After some conversation and prayer, she surrendered wholly to the will of God, and the next morning received a wonderful empowerment from the Holy Spirit.

—Ↄ An after meeting is an event held after a church service or evangelistic service in which those who have further questions or matters to deal with are handled.

Isaiah 55:7 is a good passage to use with those who lack assurance because of sin. Proverbs 28:13 and Psalm 32:1–5 are good passages to use with those who have some unconfessed sin that is keeping them out of the enjoyment of fellowship with God. These passages show that when sin is forsaken and confessed we receive pardon and light and assurance.

Oftentimes, it is well when one lacks assurance, first, to put the question clearly, "Do you know of any sin that you are cherishing, or anything in your life that your conscience troubles you about?"

1. Before you put too much attention on the lack of assurance of others, it might be good for you to reflect on your own assurance of salvation. Are you able to express clearly why you can be certain of your salvation? Do you have a confident assurance? If not, is it because of ignorance, sin, or some other reason? You would be wise to seek out a trusted Christian who can help you come to the place of assurance in your own life.

2. Can you think of any other reasons, other than ignorance or sin, why someone might not have assurance of salvation? What Scripture passages address these reasons? How would you lead someone in these conditions to assurance?

3. What are the key verses that you would want to use in a discussion about assurance? Memorize them (or copy them down and take them with you) so that you are always ready to put them to use.

CHAPTER FIVE

DEALING WITH THE RESISTANT

ANYONE WHO SPENDS MUCH TIME in personal work will have many encounters with those who have come to Christ in faith, but have fallen away in their own fleshly pursuits. Much personal work is spent in helping these people return to a close walk with the Lord. Although it would be nice if progress in the Christian life were a straight line upward, it is more often a path of three steps forward, two steps back. In this sense, we are all backsliders, in constant need of help moving forward and staying pure in our relationship with God and each other. Ministering to backsliders is closely related to our everyday walk with the Lord, acknowledging our need and learning to depend more on God. This chapter includes special guidance for how to deal with people whose lives are characterized by falling away from their Christian walk.

The lessons on skeptics and unbelievers deal with some of the same issues as the lesson on those with difficulties, but the difficulties here are much stronger and more developed. Often the positions are very firmly held and poised in the context of intellectual superiority. It is easy for the child of God to be timid or fearful in these settings. Torrey equips us for using the Scripture in these situations, not our personal disposition or intellectual prowess. His stories of how God blessed the simple repetition of appropriate Scripture illustrates that the power is from God, not us. God calls us to use our abilities, but subject to His Word and His Holy Spirit. In this way, dealing with skeptics and unbelievers is "easy." They are very forthright with the issues and can be addressed plainly with the statements of the Word of God.

In some ways, Torrey seems odd to the current age because of his clear distinction between right and wrong. He believes in absolute truth and thinks that the Scriptures speak plainly and clearly. Postmodern thought is not comfortable with such rigid morality. Torrey does not address this cultural shift, but he clearly believes that the Bible's meaning can be clearly found and that it is relevant for all eras. Other resources will help you learn how to build relationships and communicate with those influenced heavily by postmodernism. Yet Torrey's lessons will help you know what parts of God's Word to use. There is a desperate hunger in the contemporary world for truth and the fulfillment that it brings.

In other ways, it is striking how contemporary Torrey is. His references to the evidence of an intelligent Maker of the universe is startlingly similar to the current intelligent design movement in the argumentation about creation. He also recognizes our tendencies to look down on those who don't share our beliefs. Although we have truth on our side, we must never treat even the worst skeptic or atheist with disrespect. Torrey has also addressed the temptation to put off doing personal work, but reminds us of its importance and urgency.

Torrey uses the politically incorrect term "deluded" to refer to people of other faiths. In this section, he specifically addresses Catholics, Jews, Spiritists, and Christian Scientists. Although there may be individual people associated with these groups who are true believers, Torrey draws our attention to the fact that these religious organizations are not proclaiming the truth of the Gospel. Our personal work is very likely going to involve dealing with religious people, and it requires great sensitivity. However, if Jesus is the Way, the Truth, and the Life, and no one comes to the Father but by Him, then we must be prepared to deal with those who have misplaced their faith in other religions.

HOW TO
DEAL WITH
BACKSLIDERS

ONE OF THE LARGEST CLASSES FOUND in the inquiry room, and in all personal work in our day, are those who are or call themselves backsliders. They are not all alike by any means, and they ought not all to have the same treatment. There are two classes of backsliders:

I. CARELESS BACKSLIDERS, THOSE WHO HAVE NO GREAT DESIRE TO COME BACK TO THE SAVIOR

A. Use Jeremiah 2:5.

There is perhaps no better passage to use with such than Jeremiah 2:5: "Thus says the Lord: 'What injustice have your fathers found in Me, that they have gone far from Me, have followed idols, and have become idolaters?'" Drive God's question contained in the text right home to their hearts, "What injustice have you found in the Lord?" Dwell upon God's wonderful love to them, and show them the base ingratitude and folly of forsaking such a Savior and Friend. Very likely, they have wandered away because of the unkind treatment of some professed Christian, or of some minister, but hold them right to the point of how the Lord treated them and how they are now treating Him.

Use also Jeremiah 2:13. Have the inquirer read the verse, and ask, "Is not that verse true? What does the Lord say that you forsook when you forsook Him?" "The fountain of living waters." "And to what does He say you turned?" "Broken cisterns that can hold no water." "Is not that true in your experience? Did you not forsake the fountain of living waters, and have you not found the world to be broken cisterns that can hold no water?" I have yet to find the first backslider of whom this is not true, and I have used it with many. Then illustrate the text by showing how foolish it would be to turn from a fountain of living water to broken cisterns or muddy pools. If this verse does not accomplish the desired result, use Jeremiah 2:19. When they have read it, ask them if they have not found it an "evil and bitter thing" that they have forsaken the Lord their God. It is well sometimes to go over the misfortunes and troubles that have come since they forsook the Lord, for it is a fact, as every experienced worker knows, that when one who has had a real knowledge of Christ backslides, misfortune after misfortune is likely to overtake him. Proverbs 14:14, the first half of the verse, is also a good passage to use, as is 1 Kings 11:9. One of the best passages to show the folly and evil results of backsliding is Luke 15:13–17. Go into detail in bringing out the point of the picture here given of the miseries that came to the backslider in the far country.

B. Sometimes use Amos 4:11–12.

It is well sometimes to use Amos 4:11–12: "'I overthrew some of you, as God overthrew Sodom and Gomorrah, and you were like a firebrand plucked from the burning; yet you have not returned to Me,' says the Lord. 'Therefore thus will I do to you, O Israel; because I will do this to you, prepare to meet your God, O Israel!'"

Before the passage is read, you can say, "There is a passage in the Old Testament that contains a message from God to backsliding Israel, and I believe it is a message for you, also." Then read the passage carefully and ask what the message of God to backsliding Israel was. "Prepare to meet your God." Then say, "It is God's message to you too, as a backslider tonight, 'prepare to meet your God.' " Go over this again and again until the thought is deeply understood.

II. BACKSLIDERS WHO ARE SICK OF THEIR WANDERING AND SIN, AND DESIRE TO COME BACK TO THE LORD

These are a very different group from those just mentioned, though of course they are related. They are perhaps as easy a class to deal with as we ever find. There are many who once had a knowledge of the Lord who have wandered into sin and who are now sick and tired of sin, and are longing to come back, but think that there is no acceptance for them. Point them to Jeremiah 3:12–13, 22: "'Go and proclaim these words toward the north, and say: "Return, backsliding Israel," says the Lord; "I will not cause My anger to fall on you. For I am merciful," says the Lord; "I will not remain angry forever. Only acknowledge your iniquity, that you have transgressed against the Lord your God, and have scattered your charms to alien deities under every green tree, and you have not obeyed My voice," says the Lord. . . . Return, you backsliding children, and I will heal your backslidings.' 'Indeed we do come to You, for You are the Lord our God.'" This will show them how ready the Lord is to receive them back, and that all He asks of them is that they acknowledge their sin and return to Him.

Hosea 14:1–4 is full of tender invitation to penitent backsliders, and it also shows the way back to God. I use this passage more frequently than almost any other with the class of whom we are speaking, especially the first and fourth verses. I show them first of all that God is inviting the backslider to Himself, and second that He promises to heal their backsliding and love them freely, and third that all that He asks is that they take words of confession and return to Him (verse 2).

The following verses all set forth God's unfailing love for the backslider and His willingness to receive him back: Isaiah 43:22–25; 44:20–22; Jeremiah 29:11–13; Deuteronomy 4:28, 31; and 2 Chronicles 7:14. One of the most useful verses in dealing with an intelligent backslider who wishes to return to the Lord is 1 John 1:9: "If we confess our sins, He is faithful and just to forgive us our sins and to cleanse us from all unrighteousness." It is well sometimes to follow this up with 1 John 2:1–2. Often it is helpful to give illustrations of great backsliders who returned to the Lord, and how lovingly He received them. For this purpose, you can use Mark 16:7. This tells of Christ's loving message to Peter after he had so grievously sinned and deliberately denied his Master. Second Chronicles 15:4 and 33:1–9, 12–13 give illustrations of great backsliders who returned to the Lord and how lovingly He received them. Luke 15:11–24 is perhaps the most useful passage of all in dealing with a backslider who wishes to return, for it has both the steps that the backslider must take, and also a picture of the loving reception from God that awaits him.

LEARNING ACTIVITIES

1. Pause and examine your own life. Are you harboring sin? If so, you first need to apply the teaching of this lesson to yourself. How have you taken three steps forward and two steps back, even today? Don't let your own sinfulness keep you from doing personal work with backsliders, but use personal work with backsliders as an opportunity to make sure that you are dealing with the sin in your own life.

2. Identify people in your life who fit into each of the two main categories of backsliders. Consider how differently you will need to approach the two types. Pray for God to use you this week to help them come back to the Lord.

HOW TO DEAL WITH PROFESSED SKEPTICS AND UNBELIEVERS

THERE ARE VARIOUS CLASSES OF SKEPTICS, and it is not wise to use the same methods in dealing with all.

I. SKEPTICS WHO ARE MERE TRIFLERS

A very large share of the skeptics of our day belong to this class. Their professed skepticism is only an excuse for sin and a salve for their own consciences. As a rule, it is not wise to spend much time on an individual of this class, but rather give him something that will sting his conscience and arouse him out of his shallowness. A good passage for this purpose is 1 Corinthians 1:18: "For the message of the cross is foolishness to those who are perishing, but to us who are being saved it is the power of God." Very likely the skeptic will say, "The Gospel and the whole Bible is all foolishness to me." You can reply by saying, "Yes, that is exactly what God says." Curiosity will be piqued, and his or her mind opened by his curiosity to receive a word of truth when he is off his guard. Read 1 Corinthians 1:18. Then you can say, "You said that the Gospel was foolishness to you, and God Himself says that 'the message of the cross is foolishness to those who are perishing,' and it is foolishness to you because you are perishing; 'but to us who are being saved it is the power of God.' " Oftentimes, it will be well to leave without another word of comment. Be careful not to laugh at him and not to produce the impression that you are joking; but leave the person with the thought of perishing.

Second Corinthians 4:3–4 can be used in much the same way. Before the passage is read, you can say to the person, "You are a skeptic because the Gospel is hidden to you, but God Himself has told us in His Word to whom the Gospel is hidden, and why it is hidden to them." When it has been read, you can say, "That verse explains to you the secret of your difficulty. The Gospel is hidden to you because you are lost, and the reason it is hidden is because the god of this age, Satan, has blinded your mind, lest the light of the glorious Gospel of Christ, who is the image of God, should shine upon you."

I have also found 1 Corinthians 2:14 useful. I have used it to show that it was no more than was to be expected that the things of the Spirit of God would be foolishness to him, because they are spiritually discerned. I was dealing one night with a very bright student. He could hardly be called altogether a trifler, for he was a young man of a good deal of intellectual earnestness. He said to me, "This is all foolishness to me." I replied by saying, "That is exactly what the Bible says." He looked very much astonished and protested that I did not understand him, that he had said it was all foolishness to him. "Yes," I replied, "that is what the Bible says. Let me show it to you." I opened my Bible to the passage and let him read. When he had read it, I said, "That explains why it is foolishness to you; 'the natural man does not receive the things of the Spirit of God, for they are foolishness to him.' " "Why," he said, "I never thought of that before." The Spirit of God carried it home to his heart, and the man was led to an honest acceptance of Christ.

Second Thessalonians 1:7–9 can be used with good results with a trifling skeptic or agnostic. If he or she says in an uppish way, "I am an agnostic," you can say, "Well, God has told us a good deal about agnostics and their destiny; let us see what He has said." When it is read, you can say, "Now an agnostic is one who knows not God; and this verse tells us exactly what is the destiny of an agnostic and all those who know not God. This is God's own declaration of their destiny." Then have him or her read it again if possible. You may be laughed at, but the Word of God often sinks deeply into the heart, even when it is treated with a sneer.

Mark 16:16 has been found very useful in dealing with trifling skeptics. When one says to you that he or she is a skeptic or an atheist, it is well sometimes to say, "God has said some very plain words about those who do not believe." Then give the passage, "He who believes and is baptized will be saved; but he who does not believe will be condemned" and say, "I simply want to leave that message of God with you." John 3:36 can be used in a similar way.

Sometimes it is well to say to the trifling skeptic, "I can tell you the origin of your skepticism, but I can do better—I can tell you what God says of the origin of your skepticism." Then show John 8:47: "He who is of God hears God's words: therefore you do not hear, because you are not of God." Second Thessalonians 2:10–12 can be used in extreme cases. You can say, "There is a very interesting passage in the Bible regarding skeptics. It tells what is the origin of their skepticism and what is the outcome of it." Then read the passage and say, "Now what does this passage say about the origin of skepticism?" It is "because they did not receive the love of the truth, that they might be saved." "What is the result of their refusal to receive the truth?" "God will send them strong delusion, that they should believe the lie." "And what is the outcome of it all?" "That they all may be condemned who did not believe the truth but had pleasure in unrighteousness."

Psalm 14:1 is useful in some cases, though it needs to be used with discretion and kindness. Before giving it to be read, you can say, "I do not wish to say anything unkind to you, but God Himself has said a very plain word about those who say there is no God; let me show it to you." Then let him or her read: "The fool has said in his heart, 'There is no God.'" When it has been read, say, "I am not saying that, but God has said it. Now it is a matter between you and God, but I would advise you not to forget what God has said." Of course, this applies especially to one who is skeptical about, or denies, the existence of God.

In dealing with a skeptic who is a trifler, and in fact with all skeptics, don't argue, don't get angry; be very gentle but very solemn, and be very much in prayer, depending upon the Holy Spirit to give you words to say and to make them effective.

II. AN EARNEST-MINDED SKEPTIC

Many skeptics are not triflers. There are very many men and women in our day who are really very desirous of knowing the truth, but who are in an utter maze of skepticism. There is no more interesting class of people to deal with than this. In beginning work with them, it is well to ask them the following preliminary questions:

A. "*What* can't you believe?"

Get as full an answer as possible to this question, for many think they are skeptics when really they do believe the great fundamental truths. Furthermore, in finding out what one does believe, no matter how little it is, you have a starting point to lead to further faith.

B. *"Why* can't you believe?"

This will oftentimes show how utterly without foundation are the grounds for unbelief.

C. "Do you live up to what you do believe?"

This will give you an opportunity in many cases to show that the trouble is not so much what is not believed as failure to live up to what is believed.

D. "What do you believe?"

A few important lines along which to carry out this inquiry are, "Do you believe that there is an absolute difference between right and wrong?" "Do you believe that there is a God?" "Do you believe in prayer?" "Do you believe any part of the Bible; if so, what part?"

Having asked some of these preliminary questions, proceed at once to show how to believe. I have found no passage in the Bible equal to John 7:17 in dealing with an honest skeptic: "If anyone wills to do His will, he shall know concerning the doctrine, whether it is from God or whether I speak on My own authority." It shows the way out of skepticism to faith, and it has been used of God to the salvation of countless skeptics and infidels. You can say to the skeptic, "Now Jesus Christ makes a fair proposition. He does not ask you to believe without evidence, but He asks you to do a thing that your own conscience approves, and promises that if you do it, you will come out of skepticism into knowledge. What Jesus asks in this verse is that you will to do God's will; that is, that you surrender your will to God. Will you do it?"

—⌒ *Infidels do not accept Christianity (or sometimes religion in general). In some places we have changed the word to "atheist" or "unbeliever." Skeptics question the truth of Christianity (or other apparent truths).*

When this point has been settled, next say, "Will you make an honest search to find out what the will of God is, that you may do it?" When this point has been settled, ask, "Do you believe that God answers prayer?" Very likely the skeptic will reply that he or she does not. You can say, "Well, I know that He does, but of course I don't expect you to accept my opinion, but here is a possible clue to knowledge. Now the method of modern science is to follow out any possible clue to see what there is in it. You have given me a promise to make an honest search to find the will of God, and here is a possible clue and if your promise was honest, you will follow it. Will you pray this prayer? 'O God, show me whether Jesus is Your Son or not; and if You show me that He is, I promise to accept Him as my Savior and confess Him as such before the world.'" It is well to make his promise definite by putting it in writing.

After this is done, show still another step by going to John 20:31: Here we are told that the gospel of John was written that we might believe that Jesus is the Christ, the Son of God. Tell him, "Now this gospel is given for this purpose, to show that Jesus is the Christ the Son of God. Will you take this gospel and read it, honestly and carefully?" Very likely he will say, "I have read it often before." You can say, "I want you to read it in a new way. Will you read it this way? Read a few verses at a time, and each time before you read, will you ask God to give you light on the passage that you are about to read, and promise that if He does, you will follow as much as you see to be true? Now when you have read the gospel through, come back to me and tell me the result." I would again carefully go over all the points as to what he is to do. It would be well also to ask him to especially notice the following verses in the gospel: 1:34; 3:2–3, 16–19, 32–36; 4:10, 14, 52–53; 5:8–9, 22–24, 28–29, 44; 6:8–14, 19, 27–29, 35, 40, 66–69; 7:17, 37–39, 45–46; 8:12, 18, 21, 24, 31–38, 42, 47; 9:17, 24–25, 35–39; 10:9–11, 27–30; 11:25–26, 43–45; 12:26, 42–46, 48–50; 13:13; 14:3, 6, 9, 21, 24, 27; 15:5–6, 9–11, 23–26; 16:7–14, 24; 17:3–5, 22–26; 18:37; 19:6–8; 20:8, 13–19, 24–31.

This method of treatment, if it is honestly followed by the skeptic, will never fail.

If the skeptic does not believe even in the existence of God, you will have to begin one step further back. Ask if he or she believes there is an absolute difference between right and wrong. If not, which will be very rarely the case, it is just as well to tell him then and there that he is a mere trifler. If so, ask if he or she will take his stand upon the right and follow it wherever it goes. If you are put off by the question, "What is right?" you can say that you do not ask him to take your conception of right, but will he take his stand upon the right and follow it wherever it goes and make an honest attempt to find out what the right is?

Next say, "You do not know whether there is a God and whether He answers prayer or not. I know that there is a God and that He answers prayer; but I do not ask you to accept my opinion, but here is a possible clue to knowledge. Will you follow it?" If he or she refuses, of course you will know at once that you are not dealing with an honest skeptic. If willing to try, have him or her offer this prayer, "O God, if there is any God, show me whether Jesus Christ is Your Son or not, and if You show me that He is, I promise to accept Him as my Savior and confess Him as such before the world." Then have him or her proceed by reading the gospel of John, etc., as in the former case.

If the person is not an honest skeptic, this course of treatment will reveal the fact, and you can tell that the difficulty is not with skepticism, but with a rebellious and wicked heart. If a person says he does not know whether there is an absolute difference between right and wrong, you can set it down at once that he or she is bad and say frankly but kindly, "My friend, there is something wrong in your life. No one who is living a right life will doubt that there is an absolute difference between right and wrong. You probably know what the wrong is, and the trouble is not with your skepticism but with your sin."

A man who was a thoroughgoing agnostic once came to me and stated his difficulties. The man had had a very remarkable experience. He had dabbled in Unitarianism, Spiritualism, Buddhism, Theosophy, and many other "isms." He was in a state of absolute agnosticism. He neither affirmed nor denied the existence of God. He told me that I could not help him, for his case was "very peculiar," as indeed it was, but I had John 7:17 to build my hope upon, and the man seemed honest. I asked him if he believed there was an absolute difference between right and wrong, and he said that he did. I asked him if he was willing to take his stand upon the right and follow it wherever it carried him. He said that he was. I called out my stenographer and dictated a pledge somewhat as follows: "I believe that there is an absolute difference between right and wrong, and I hereby take my stand upon the right to follow it wherever it carries me. I promise to make an honest search to find if Jesus Christ is the Son of God, and if I find that He is, I promise to accept Him as my Savior and confess Him as such before the world." I handed the pledge to the man and asked him if he was willing to sign it. He read it carefully and then signed it. I then said to him, "You don't know there is not a God?" "No," he said, "I don't know that there is no God. Any man is a fool to say that he knows there is not a God. I neither affirm nor deny." "Well," I said, "I know there is a God, but that will do you no good."

—◌ Unitarians deny the Trinity and believe only in God the Father; Spiritualism is focused on witchcraft and the evil spirit world; Buddhism teaches that right living leads to nirvana (a state of freedom from desire or pain); and Theosophy claims to provide spiritual self-development. Agnostics do not believe that anything can be known about God.

I said further, "You do not know that God does not answer prayer." "No," he said, "I do not know that God does not answer prayer, but I do not believe that

He does." I said, "I know that He does, but that will not do you any good. Here is a possible clue to knowledge. Now you are a graduate of a British university. You know that the method of modern science is to follow out a possible clue to see what there is in it. Will you follow out this clue? Will you pray this prayer: 'O God, if there is any God, show me whether Jesus Christ is Your Son or not, and if You show me that He is, I promise to accept Him as my Savior and confess Him as such before the world'?" "Yes," he said, " I am willing to do that, but there is nothing in it; my case is very peculiar." I then turned to John 20:31 and read, "These are written that you may believe that Jesus is the Christ, the Son of God, and that believing you may have life in His name." After reading the verse, I said, "John wrote this gospel that 'you may believe that Jesus is the Christ, the Son of God.' Will you take this gospel and read it, not trying to believe it, but simply with a fair mind, willing to believe it if it approves itself to you as true?" He said, "I have read it time and time again, and could quote a good deal of it." I said, "I want you to read it in a new way; read a few verses at a time, ask God for light each time you read, and promise to act upon so much as you see to be true." This the man promised to do, but closed by saying, "There is nothing in it; my case is very peculiar." I went over again the various points and bade the man good-bye.

A short time after, I met him again. He hurried up to me, and almost the first words he said were, "There is something in that." I replied, "I knew that before." "Why," he said, "ever since I have done what I promised you to do, it is just as if I had been taken up to the Niagara River and was being carried along." Some weeks after, I met the man again; his doubts had all gone. The teachings of the men he had formerly listened to with delight had become utter foolishness to him. He had put himself in a way to find out the truth of God, and God had made it known to him, and he had become a believer in Jesus Christ as God's Son, and the Bible as God's Word.

There is no more interesting class, and no easier class to deal with, than honest skeptics. Many are afraid to tackle them, but there is no need of this. There is a way out of skepticism into faith laid down in the Bible that is absolutely sure if anyone will take it. As for skeptics who are triflers, it is not best to spend much time on them, but simply to give them some searching passages of Scripture, and to look to the Spirit of God to carry the Word home.

III. SPECIAL CLASSES OF SKEPTICS

A. Those who doubt the existence of God

The passages given previously in this lesson may be used with this class of skeptics, and usually it is wise to use them before the specific passages given under this heading.

1. *The evidence of nature*

An excellent passage to use with those who claim to doubt the existence of God is Romans 1:19–22. Ask the doubter to read this passage carefully. When done, you can say, "Of course you never saw God, but this verse tells us how the invisible things of Him whom we have never seen can be known, and how is it?" "By the things that are made." "What does Paul say we can understand by the things that are made?" "His eternal power and Godhead." "Is not this true? Do not the facts of nature prove an intelligent Creator?" It is well sometimes to illustrate by a watch or something of that sort. Show the inquirer a watch and ask if he or she believes it had an intelligent maker, and why; then ask about the eye, which shows more marks of intelligence in its construction than a watch, or anything a human ever made. Having dealt this argument and made it clear, ask what God says those are who do not believe in God as revealed in His works. Bring out the fact that God says they are "without excuse." Then you can say, "The twenty-first verse tells us why people get in the dark about God. According to this verse, why is it that people get in the dark about God?" "Because, although they knew God, they did not glorify Him as God, nor were thankful." "Is not this true about you? Was there not a time when you knew God, believed that there was a God, but did not glorify Him as God, neither returned thanks to Him? What does God say is the result of this course?" "They became futile in their thoughts, and their foolish hearts were darkened." "Now is this not precisely your case? Has not your foolish heart been darkened by not glorifying God when you knew Him? Now the twenty-second verse describes such persons. Exactly what does it say about them?" "Professing to be wise, they became fools."

In something the same way, you can use Psalm 19:1–2. "According to this passage, what declares to us the glory of God?" "The heavens." "What shows His handiwork?" "The firmament." "Do you know anything about the stars?" Let the skeptic tell what he or she knows about the stars. If nothing, tell something about their greatness, their magnitude, and their wonderful movements, and then ask if it does not indicate a wonderful Creator. Endeavor to show that he or she is not honest in the denial of God.

2. *The foolishness of unbelief*

There is still one verse that you should give. Tell the skeptic that you hope he or she will bear in mind that it is not you who says it, but God; and that it applies to his or her case exactly. Then read the first half of Psalm 14:1: "The fool has said in his heart, 'There is no God.'" Ask who it is, according to this verse, who says "there is no God." "The fool." "Where is it that the fool says there is no God?" "In his heart." "Why is it then that the fool says there is no God—is it because the fool cannot believe in God, or because the fool does not wish to believe in God?" You can add that the folly of saying in one's heart there is no God is seen in two points: first, because there is a God, and it is folly to say there is not one when there is; and second, because the doctrine that there is not a God always brings misery and wretchedness. Ask if he or she ever knew a happy atheist. Before leaving, you can state that he or she is losing the greatest blessing for time and for eternity, by doubting the existence of God.

Turn to Romans 6:23 and show that this is so. "This verse tells us that we have our choice between eternal death, which is the wages that we have earned by sin, and eternal life, which is the gift of God; but of course if we do not believe in God, we cannot look to Him for this gift." You can further tell that in his present state of mind it is impossible to do anything that pleases God, and show Hebrews 11:6.

B. Those who doubt that the Bible is the Word of God

The method of dealing with honest skeptics described above is as a rule the best method of dealing with this class, but other plans will be useful with some.

1. *Oftentimes skeptics say, "I do not believe the Bible as a whole is the Word of God, but I accept what Jesus Christ says."*

If one says this, get him or her to take a stand clearly and definitely upon the statement of accepting the authority of Jesus Christ. Then say, "Well, if you accept the authority of Jesus Christ, you must accept the authority of the whole Old Testament, for Jesus Christ has set the seal of His authority to the entire book." Turn to Mark 7:13; show the context, thereby proving that Jesus here calls the Law of Moses the Word of God. Then say, "If you accept the authority of Jesus, you must accept the authority of at least the first five books of the Bible as being the Word of God." You can follow this up by Matthew 5:18 to show how Jesus sets His authority to the absolute inerrancy of the Old Testament law. Then turn to John 10:34–35 and show that Jesus quotes a passage from the Psalms (Psalm 82:6) and says that the Scripture cannot be broken, and hereby sets the stamp of His authority to the absolute inerrancy of the entire Old Testament Scriptures.

―⌒ *Inerrancy is the belief that the Bible is without errors.*

Turn next to Luke 24:27 and show from this passage how Jesus quoted the entire Old Testament Scriptures, Moses and the Prophets, as being of conclusive authority. Then go on to verse 44, and call attention to the fact that Jesus said that "all things must be fulfilled which were written in the Law of Moses and the Prophets and the Psalms concerning Me." The Jews divided their Bible, the present Old Testament Scriptures, into three parts, the Law, the Prophets and the Psalms, and Jesus took up each one of these parts in detail, and set the stamp of His authority upon the whole. Therefore, if one accepts the authority of Christ, one must accept the authority of the whole Old Testament.

To prove that Christ set the stamp of His authority to the New Testament, take him to John 14:26. Here Jesus plainly declares that not only would the teaching of the apostles be true, but that it would contain all the truth, and furthermore, that their recollection of what He Himself said would not be their own recollection, but the recollection of the Holy Ghost. Follow this up with John 16:12–13 and show that Jesus Himself said, "I still have many things to say to you, but you cannot bear them now. However, when He, the Spirit of truth, has come, He will guide you into all truth." Therefore, tell the skeptic that Jesus said the apostles would be taught of the Holy Spirit, that the Holy Spirit would guide them into all the truth, and that their teaching would be more complete than His own. "Therefore, if you accept the authority of Jesus, you must accept the authority of the entire New Testament."

2. *If the objector says that Paul never claimed that his teachings were the Word of God, turn him to 1 Thessalonians 2:13.*

3. *A passage that is useful as describing the character of Bible inspiration is 2 Peter 1:21. First Corinthians 2:14 is useful as proving verbal inspiration.*

—◌⟩ *Verbal inspiration refers to the actual words of the Bible being inspired by God.*

4. *Sometimes it is well to say to the doubter, "The Bible itself explains why it is that you do not believe the Bible is the Word of God."*

Then show John 8:47. Follow this up by saying, "That you do not believe the Bible is God's Word does not alter the fact," and show Romans 3:3–4. You can go further yet and say that God Himself tells us that there is awful guilt attaching to the one who will not believe the record that He has given, and then show 1 John

5:10. Ask, "What does God say here of the one who does not believe the record that He has given of His Son?" and show that God says this declares God a liar.

5. *Finally, you may use Luke 16:30–31.*

Before reading it, say, "Well, God says that the case of one who will not listen to the Bible is very desperate. Just read and see what He says upon this point," and then read the verses.

C. Those who doubt the divinity of Christ

It is very common in our day to have people say that they believe in God, but they do not believe that Jesus Christ was the Son of God. The best way, as a rule, to deal with such is along the line described in sections I and II, especially under II; but sometimes there is someone who has real difficulties on this point, and it is well to meet this person directly.

1. *In the first place, show that we find several divine titles applied to Christ, the same titles being applied to Christ in the New Testament that are applied to Jehovah in the Old: Acts 10:36 and 1 Corinthians 2:8 (compare Psalm 24:8–10).*

Read Hebrews 1:8, John 20:28, Romans 9:5, and Revelation 1:17 (compare Isaiah 44:6).

2. *Show further that offices are ascribed to Christ that only God could fill.*

For this purpose use Hebrews 1:3, 10.

3. *Show that the Bible expressly declares that Jesus Christ should be worshiped as God.*

Use for this purpose Hebrews 1:6, Philippians 2:10, and John 5:22–23 (compare Revelation 5:13).

4. *Show that Jesus claimed the same honor as His Father, and either He was divine or the most blasphemous impostor who ever lived.*

For this purpose, use John 5:22–23. Drive home the truth that the one who denies Christ's divinity puts Him in the place of a blasphemous impostor (Mark 14:61–62).

5. *Show that the Bible says the one who denies the divinity of Christ, no matter who he or she may be, is a liar and an antichrist.*

For this purpose, use 1 John 2:22–23, compared with 1 John 5:1, 5. First John

5:10–12 shows that the one who does not believe that Jesus is divine makes God a liar, "because he has not believed the testimony that God has given of His Son."

6. *Make it clear to the inquirer that God regards it as a matter of awful folly and guilt, deserving the worst punishment, to reject Christ as the Son of God.*

For this purpose, use Hebrews 10:28–29. Follow this up with John 8:24, which shows beyond a question that one who does not believe in the divinity of Christ cannot be saved, and John 20:31, which shows that we obtain life through believing that Jesus is the Christ the Son of God.

7. *I have found that making clear the fact that Christ rose from the dead, and that this was God's seal to His claim to be divine, is very helpful in dealing with many who have doubts as to His divinity.*

I have also found Acts 9:20 very helpful. I call attention to who it was in this verse that declared Jesus to be the Son of God, namely, Saul of Tarsus. I then bring out what it was that led Paul to say this; that is, his actually seeing Jesus in the glory, and hearing the words that He spoke to him. Then I make it clear that one of three things is true: Either Saul actually saw Jesus in the glory, or else he lied about it, or else he was deceived, being in a heated state of imagination or something of that kind. Then I show how he could not have lied about it, for men do not manufacture a lie for the sake of suffering for it thirty or thirty-five years.

Second, I show that the circumstances were such as to preclude the possibility of an optical delusion, or an overheated state of the imagination, for not only did Paul see the light, but those who were with him, and those who were with him also heard the voice speaking, though they did not hear what the voice said. Furthermore, there was a second man, Ananias, who received a commission independently, to go to Saul and lay hands upon him and his eyes would be opened; and Saul's eyes were opened, which of course could not be the result of imagination. So Saul of Tarsus must actually have seen Christ in the glory, and if he did, in the way described, it settles it beyond question that Jesus is the Son of God; so the divinity of Christ is not a theological speculation, but an established fact.

D. Those who doubt the doctrine of future punishment or the conscious, endless suffering of the lost

As a rule, it is not wise to discuss this difficulty with one who is not clearly a Christian. No one who has not surrendered his will and his mind to Jesus Christ is in a position to discuss the details of future punishment, but if one is skeptical on this point, though a Christian, it is well to show the teaching of God's Word. A great deal is made by those who deny the conscious, endless suffering of the lost, of the words "death" and "destruction," which are said to mean annihilation, or at least nonconscious existence. Say to such a one, "Let us see how the Bible defines its own terms." Revelation 21:8 defines what death means when used in the Scriptures as the punishment of the wicked. Revelation 17:8 tells us that the beast was to go into "perdition" (destruction). Revelation 19:20 tells us just where the beast went, "into the lake of fire burning with brimstone." This then is "perdition." But Revelation 20:10 shows us the beast still there at the end of one thousand years, and being still consciously tormented, and to be tormented "day and night forever and ever." This then is what the Bible means by "perdition" or "destruction," conscious torment forever and ever in a lake of fire. Revelation 20:15 shows that those who are subjected to the terrible retribution here described are those who are not found written in the Book of Life.

Annihilationism holds that souls of wicked people don't suffer eternally, but are annihilated. Restorationism holds that souls are restored in some manner rather than punished eternally.

Matthew 10:28 shows that there is a destruction for the soul apart from the destruction for the body. Luke 12:5 shows that after one is killed (and is, of course, dead), there is still punishment in hell. Mark 3:28–29 shows that there is such a thing as an eternal sin. Luke 16:23–26 shows that the condition of the wicked dead is one of conscious torment. Mark 14:21 shows that the retribution visited upon the wicked is of so terrible a character that it would be better for the ones upon whom it is visited if they had never been born. Second Peter 2:4 and Jude 6 show that hell is not a place where the inhabitants cease to exist, but where they are reserved alive for the purposes of God. Hebrews 10:28–29 shows that while the punishment for the transgression of the Mosaic Law was death, even worse punishment awaits those who have trodden underfoot the Son of God. Matthew 25:41 shows that the wicked go to the place prepared for the devil and his angels and share the same endless, conscious torment. The character of this place and the duration of its punishment are very clearly stated in Revelation 19:20 and 20:10.

LEARNING ACTIVITIES

1. If you have opportunities to deal with skeptics and infidels, it is important to begin with special prayer. If you are timid or not confident of your own intellectual abilities, you will want to ask God for boldness. If you are bold or confident, you will want to ask God for compassion and sensitivity. Examine your own attitude to make sure that you are a fit vessel for God to use in this aspect of personal work.

2. Reflect on all of the verses and arguments that can be used with skeptics. Are there two or three verses (or main points) that stand out to you? Make sure that you have memorized these verses or copied them so that you will always have them with you.

3. If you have frequent opportunities to deal with skeptics, you will want to consult a Christian bookseller regarding other resources that will help you. However, you need to remember that the power is in the Word of God and the presence of the Holy Spirit, not in the arguments themselves.

HOW TO DEAL WITH THOSE WHO WISH TO PUT OFF A DECISION UNTIL SOME OTHER TIME

OFTENTIMES WHEN YOU HAVE SWEPT AWAY every difficulty and the way of salvation is made as clear as day, still the inquirer is not ready to decide then and there, but wishes to put off a decision until some future time. There are several classes of those who wish to put off a decision:

I. THOSE WHO SAY, "I WANT TO WAIT."

One of the largest classes is composed of those who say, "I want to wait," or "Not tonight," or "I will think about it," or "I will come tomorrow night," or some other such thing. Give to such a person Isaiah 55:6: "Seek the Lord while He may be found, call upon Him while He is near." When the inquirer has read the passage, ask when it is that one is to seek the Lord. "While He may be found." Ask when that is, and make it clear that the only time when one can be absolutely sure of finding the Lord is right now. Ask if one can be sure of finding the Lord tomorrow if he or she does not seek Him today. Sometimes it is well to give illustrations from life concerning those who put off seeking the Lord, and when the next day came it was too late.

Proverbs 27:1 is also a good verse to use. Proverbs 29:1 has often been used of the Holy Spirit to bring an immediate decision. Other passages are Matthew 25:10–12 and Luke 12:19–20. A passage especially effective in dealing with those who say, "I am not ready" is Matthew 24:44.

A passage that can also be used with good effect in extreme cases is 1 Kings 18:21: "And Elijah came to all the people, and said, 'How long will you falter between two opinions? If the Lord is God, follow Him; but if Baal, follow him.'" An excellent way to use this verse is by asking the person whether he or she would be willing to wait a year and not have an opportunity under any circumstances, no matter what came up, of accepting Christ. If the answer is, "No, I might die within a year," ask if he or she would be willing to wait a month, a week, a day. Ask if he or she would like God, the Holy Spirit, and all Christians to leave him or her alone for a day, and not have the opportunity under any circumstances of accepting Christ. Almost any thoughtful person will say "No." Then tell the person if that is the case, he or she had better accept Christ at once. Dr. Chalmers was the first one to use this method, and it has been followed by many others with great success.

Other passages that can be used with this class are James 4:13–14, Job 36:18, Luke 13:24–28, John 8:21, 12:35, 7:33–34.

II. THOSE WHO SAY, "I MUST GET FIXED IN BUSINESS FIRST, AND THEN I WILL BECOME A CHRISTIAN."

With such persons use Matthew 6:33: "But seek first the kingdom of God and His righteousness, and all these things shall be added to you." This verse makes it very clear that we must seek the kingdom of God first, and everything else must be made secondary.

III. THOSE WHO SAY, "I AM WAITING FOR GOD'S TIME."

Quite frequently this is said in all honesty. Many people have an idea that God has a certain time for saving people, and we must wait until this time comes. If anyone says this, ask if he or she will accept Christ in God's time if you will show just when God's time is. Turn to 2 Corinthians 6:2: "For He says: 'In an acceptable time I have heard you, and in the day of salvation I have helped you.' Behold, now is the accepted time; behold, now is the day of salvation." This verse shows that God's time is now. Or turn to Hebrews 3:15: "While it is said: 'Today, if you will hear His voice, do not harden your hearts as in the rebellion.'"

IV. THOSE WHO SAY, "I AM TOO YOUNG TO BE A CHRISTIAN," OR "I WANT TO WAIT UNTIL I AM OLDER."

With such a person, open your Bible to Ecclesiastes 12:1 and read: "Remember now your Creator in the days of your youth, before the difficult days come, and the years draw near when you say, 'I have no pleasure in them.'" Matthew 18:3 and 19:14 are also good passages to use, as they show that youth is the best time to come to Christ, and that all must become as children, even if they are old, before they can enter into the kingdom of heaven.

It is oftentimes wise in dealing with persons who wish to put off a decision until sometime in the future, to use the passages given for dealing with those who have little or no concern about their salvation, until such a deep impression is made of their need of Christ that they will not be willing to postpone accepting Him. As a rule in dealing with those who want to wait, it is best to use only one passage and drive that home by constant repetition.

One night I was dealing with a man who was quite excited, but kept saying, "I cannot decide tonight." Over and over again I quoted Proverbs 29:1. In reply to every answer he made, I would give this passage. I must have repeated it a great many times in the course of the conversation, until the man was made to feel not only his need of Christ, but the danger of delay, and the necessity of a prompt decision. He tried to get away from the passage, but I held him to this one point. The passage remained with him, and it was carried home by the providence of God, for he came nearly being destroyed on the street that night; he was assaulted. He came back to the meeting the next night with his head all bandaged, and then and there accepted Christ. The pounding he received from his assailant would probably have done him little good if the text of the Scripture had not been previously pounded into his head.

LEARNING ACTIVITIES

1. Many Christians struggle with wanting to put off their own involvement in personal work. Are you using any of the excuses in this lesson to keep from doing what you should be doing for Christ?

2. Why is it that so many people are willing to postpone dealing with matters of eternity? Why is it so important that Christians be aggressive and intentional in trying to reach them with the Gospel?

3. Find a Christian friend again and try to role-play these common interactions. Take turns being the one trying to delay a decision and being the one who is presenting the Gospel. Make sure to encourage each other in what is done well, and give positive suggestions for what might be done even better.

HOW TO DEAL WITH THOSE OF OTHER FAITHS

I. ROMAN CATHOLICS

A. Show that we can know our sins are forgiven.

Very few Roman Catholics have assurance of salvation; indeed, very few understand that it is our privilege to know that we have forgiveness of sins and eternal life. A good way then to deal with a Roman Catholic is to ask if he or she knows that sins are forgiven. Very likely he or she will not, and may claim that no one else knows it either. Then you can show that it is the believer's privilege to know forgiveness of sins. For this purpose use Acts 13:39, "By Him, everyone who believes is justified" and Ephesians 1:7, "In Him we have redemption through His blood, the forgiveness of sins, according to the riches of His grace."

In a similar way, you can show that it is our privilege to know that we have eternal life. For this purpose, use 1 John 5:13. Oftentimes, when brought to see that it is our privilege to know that we have forgiveness of sins and eternal life, a Catholic will desire to know it too, and will begin to see that we have something he or she does not possess. There is one point at which we always have the advantage in dealing with a Roman Catholic, namely, there is a peace and power in Christianity as we know it that there is not in Christianity as a Catholic knows it.

B. Show the need for the new birth.

Another good way to deal with a Roman Catholic is to show the necessity of the new birth, and what the new birth is. When the one with whom you are dealing claims to be a Roman Catholic, it is well to ask if he or she has been born again. Very likely the person will not know what that means. Show John 3:3–7, and emphasize what Jesus says, that we must be born again. Other passages are 2 Corinthians 5:17, 2 Peter 1:4, and Ezekiel 36:25–27.

Many Roman Catholics understand the new birth to mean baptism. Oftentimes, if you ask a Roman Catholic when he or she was born again, you will be told, "When I was baptized as a baby." It will then be necessary to show that baptism is not the new birth. For this purpose, use 1 Corinthians 4:15. Here Paul tells the believers in Corinth that in Christ Jesus, he had begotten them through the Gospel. If the new birth meant baptism, he must have baptized them, but in 1 Corinthians 1:14 he declares he had not baptized them. It is well to go a step further and show the inquirer what the biblical evidences of the new birth are. For this purpose, use the following passages: 1 John 2:29 and 1 John 3:9, 14, 17.

If the inquirer is sufficiently interested, he or she will now want to know how to be born again. This question is answered in John 1:12, 1 Peter 1:23, and James 1:18.

C. Show the need for repentance.

A third way of dealing with a Roman Catholic is to use Acts 3:19: "Repent therefore and be converted, that your sins may be blotted out, so that times of refreshing may come from the presence of the Lord." This shows the necessity of repentance and conversion in order that our sins may be blotted out. What repentance is will be shown by Isaiah 55:7 and Jonah 3:10. In a similar way, Acts 16:31 can be used to show that the way to be saved is by simply believing on the Lord Jesus Christ; then, to show what it is to believe on the Lord Jesus Christ, use John 1:12 and 2 Timothy 1:12.

D. Show that Christ is the only Mediator.

Another good text to use in dealing with Roman Catholics, and one that comes right at the heart of their difficulties, is 1 Timothy 2:5: "For there is one God and one Mediator between God and men, the Man Christ Jesus." The Roman Catholic, if a true Roman Catholic, is always seeking some mediator besides Jesus Christ, and this verse declares expressly that there is but "one Mediator between God and men, the Man Christ Jesus," and not the priests or saints or the Virgin Mary or anyone else. Sometimes it is well to follow this up with 1 Timothy 4:1–3, but it is not well as a rule to use this passage until one has made some headway.

It is also well to show the advantage of Bible study, for as a rule the Roman Catholic does not study his Bible at all, and in many cases is practically forbidden by the priest to study it. For this purpose, use John 5:39; 1 Peter 2:1–2; 2 Timothy 3:13–17; James 1:21–22; Psalm 1:1–2; Joshua 1:8; Mark 7:7–8, 13; Matthew 22:29. These texts, except the one in 1 Peter 2:1–2, are all practically the same in the Bibles used by Roman Catholics as they are in other Bibles used by Protestants.

E. Show that he is a sinner who needs a Savior.

Still another way to deal with a Roman Catholic is to use the same methods that you would with any sinner who does not realize his need of a Savior, and has no real concern about his salvation, that is, to awaken a sense that he is a sinner and needs Christ. This, as a rule, is the best way if you can get the Roman Catholic to listen to you.

Many people think there is no use talking with Roman Catholics, that they cannot be brought to Christ. This is a great mistake. Many of them are longing for something they do not find in the Roman Catholic Church, and if you can show them from the Word of God how to find it, they come very easily and make some of the best Christians. Always be sure of one thing: Do not attack the Roman Catholic Church. This only awakens their prejudice and puts them in a bad position to be helped. Simply give them the truth, and the errors in time will take care of themselves. Not infrequently our attacks upon the Roman Catholic Church only expose our ignorance, for oftentimes they do not believe just what we suppose they do. It is frequently desirable to use a Roman Catholic Bible in dealing with a Roman Catholic. Of course, if one is going to do that, one should study the texts beforehand in that version. Very many of the texts are, for all practical purposes, the same in the Roman Catholic version of the Bible as in our own.

II. JEWS

A great many Jews today are inquiring into the claims of Jesus the Nazarene, and are open to approach upon this subject. The best way to deal with a Jew is to show him that his own Bible points to Jesus as the Christ. Among the most useful passages for this purpose are Isaiah 53 (the entire chapter). Others are Daniel 9:26, Zechariah 12:10, and Micah 5:2.

If the Jew objects that these passages are different in the Hebrew Bible, do not allow yourself to be put off in this way, for they are not. It may be claimed that Isaiah 53 does not refer to the Messiah. In that case, ask to whom it does refer. If the answer is "suffering Israel," go through the chapter and show that it cannot refer to suffering Israel, because the one who suffers is plainly suffering for the sins of another (Isaiah 53:4–5, 8) and the other for whom he is suffering is God's people Israel. So the sufferer cannot be Israel.

The whole book of Hebrews is excellent to use with a Jew, especially the ninth and tenth chapters, and the seventh chapter, the 25th to the 28th verses. The great difficulty in the way of the Jew coming out as a Christian is the terrific persecution that he must endure if he does. Undoubtedly, it costs a great deal today for a Jew to become a Christian, but show the passages already given for those who are afraid of persecution.

    Good resources for Jewish evangelism can be obtained from Chosen People Ministries or Jews for Jesus.

III. SPIRITUALISTS

Many people who call themselves Spiritualists claim to believe in the Bible. Such persons make a great deal of Samuel's appearing to Saul, 1 Samuel 28:11–20. It is not necessary to deny that Samuel really appeared to Saul, but show the one with whom you are dealing what the result was to Saul of thus consulting one who had a familiar spirit.

Good passages to use in dealing with all Spiritualists are 1 Chronicles 10:13–14 and Isaiah 8:19–20. First John 4:1–3 is also a useful passage, as it brings out how not all spirits are to be believed. Second Thessalonians 2:9–12 is also useful. All these passages can be followed up by Leviticus 19:31, 20:6, Deuteronomy 18:10–12, and 2 Kings 21:1–2, 6. These passages all show how God regards consulting spiritualists and mediums.

    Spiritists focus on witchcraft and the evil spirit world. The spiritists/spiritualists of Torrey's day were a rather narrow and well-defined group. Today, there is a much wider range of groups that espouse spirituality in ways that are not in accordance with biblical teaching. The New Age movement, the growth of Eastern religions in North America, various forms of mysticism, and a growing movement of witchcraft are areas to which Torrey's teaching from the Bible can be applied.

IV. CHRISTIAN SCIENTISTS

Many people in our day are being led astray into Christian Science, and we need to be ready to help them. Most Christian Scientists claim to believe the Bible. Take them to 1 John 4:1–3: "Beloved, do not believe every spirit, but test the spirits, whether they are of God; because many false prophets have gone out into the world. By this you know the Spirit of God: Every spirit that confesses that Jesus Christ has come in the flesh is of God, and every spirit that does not confess that Jesus Christ has come in the flesh is not of God. And this is the spirit of the Antichrist, which you have heard was coming, and is now already in the world."

This passage strikes at the very foundation of Christian Science. Christian Science denies as one of its fundamental postulates the reality of matter and the reality of the body and, of necessity, the reality of the Incarnation. Show them by this passage that the Bible declares that every spirit that confesses not Jesus Christ come in the flesh is not of God, but is the spirit of antichrist. Christian Science also denies the doctrine of substitution. Of course, many Christian Scientists are not aware of this fact, for it is the common practice in leading one into Christian Science not to let one see at once all that is involved in it. Therefore, take the one with whom you are dealing to such passages as 2 Corinthians 5:21, Galatians 3:13, 1 Peter 2:24, and Hebrews 9:22. In these passages the doctrine of substitution is clearly brought out.

The average Christian Scientist, in defending his position, makes a great deal of the fact that the Christian Scientists have physical cures. Of this there can be no question. Many people are better physically because of Christian Science treatment, so it is neither necessary nor wise to deny the reality of all their cures. Admit the cure, and then show that the fact that one cures sickness proves nothing for the truth of the position held, or for acceptance before God. Use for this purpose the following passages: Matthew 7:22–23, 2 Thessalonians 2:8–9, and 2 Corinthians 11:14–15.

Christian Scientists believe that a thorough spiritual understanding can destroy sin and sickness without material aid.

V. FOLLOWERS OF FALSE PROPHETS

New false prophets are constantly rising, and it is impossible to mention them all by name; furthermore, they often disappear as rapidly as they appear, but practically the same method of treatment will serve to help.

A. First show the deluded one Christ's own warning that false Christs and false prophets would arise. For this purpose use Mark 13:22–23.

Dwell upon the point that the fact that they heal the sick and perform other wonders is no proof at all that they are not false prophets, that Christ distinctly foretold that the false Christs and the false prophets would do these things.

B. Then give them the following five rules by which they can escape every snare of the false prophet.

1. *The first rule is found in John 7:17: A will wholly surrendered to God.*

Make this point very clear, for many of these people claim to have wholly surrendered their wills to God, but question them unsparingly on this point, and oftentimes you will find that the will is not surrendered.

2. *The second rule is found in 2 Timothy 3:13–17: A careful study of the Word of God.*

This rule is a careful study of the Word of God and a thorough comparison of anyone's claims to be a prophet or a Christ or the messenger of the covenant or John the Baptist or anything of that sort with the teachings of the Word of God. The followers of false prophets generally make a hobby of some few verses in the Bible, and do not study the Book as a whole.

3. *The third rule is found in James 1:5–7: A prayer to God for wisdom.*

Of course the prayer must be sincere, with a readiness to follow the leading of God. Many pray for guidance and still go on in delusion, but the prayer is not sincere. They ask for guidance, but do not utterly renounce their own wisdom and wait upon God for His wisdom. Very many have been led out of the error of following various false prophets when they in utter self-distrust have gone to God for light and guidance.

4. *The fourth rule is found in Matthew 23:8–10: Call no man master.*

Acknowledge no human as an absolute and final authority; accept the authority of no one and nothing but Christ and the Bible in matters of faith and religion. It is well to dwell upon this point, for this is the very point at which many are led astray. The natural, selfish heart craves someone to do our thinking for us in matters of religion, and this makes some ready to swallow whole the teachings of others. It is this tendency that gives power to the pope, priests, Christian Science, Mormonism, and all similar delusions.

5. The fifth rule is found in Proverbs 29:25: Be afraid of no man.

Many a false prophet keeps power over people through fear. While people do not more than half believe, they are afraid that if they leave the person will in some way bring sickness or some other curse upon them. Very likely, the one with whom you are dealing will be in this very position. Show him how clearly he is in a wrong position, the very fact that he is afraid of a person proving this. Show the deluded one that the Holy Spirit is not "a spirit of fear, but of power and of love and of a sound mind" (2 Timothy 1:7). If the deluded person insists that the false prophet works in the name of Christ and succeeds, and therefore must be accepted of God, turn to Matthew 7:22–23. This shows very clearly that one may even cast out devils in the name of the Lord, and yet be one whom He never knew.

It is well in dealing with those who are under the spell of a false prophet to be able to show them what the marks of a false prophet are. The first and most common of these is a greed for money. To show this, use Titus 1:10–11 and 2 Peter 2:3. Make it very clear if the pretended prophet is trying to get money from the people (as is usually the case), that that in itself is a mark of a false prophet.

A second mark of the false prophet is vaunting one's self. To show the deluded one this, use Jude 16 and 1 Corinthians 13:4.

A third mark of the false prophet is the claim to an authority that Jesus Christ forbade anyone claiming. To show this to some person who is in the snare of the false prophet, use Matthew 23:8, 12.

A fourth mark of a false prophet is a false application of Scripture either to ones self or to places with which one is connected. Thus, for example, the Mormons take passages that apply to Israel and apply them to their own Zion. When any place under the false prophet's control is named for some Bible place, and scriptural promises referring to the literal Bible place are applied to the place under the prophet's control, just show the one who is being deceived by this sort of thing how utterly unwarranted such an application is.

Fifth, there is usually an untrue note somewhere in the doctrine taught by the false prophet. Much may be taught that is biblical and true, but somewhere is betrayed the false prophet's satanic origin. The points at which this false note of doctrine are most likely to be found are on the doctrine of future punishment, the matter of the use of meats, or upon legalism of some form—the observation of the seventh day, the matter of tithes, or something of that sort. In the matter of future punishment, false prophets generally go off sooner or later into either annihilationism or restorationism or a combination of the two.

After all, the most important thing to do in dealing with one who is under a delusion is to bring forward the fundamental, saving truth of the Gospel, salvation through the atoning work and upon the single condition of faith in Jesus Christ. Oftentimes error, like typhoid fever, has to be left to take its course and work itself out. I know many today who are out in a clear Christian experience, who for a while were completely under the control of some of our modern false prophets, even thinking that all who did not agree with them were utterly wrong, and saying so in the most bitter terms; but in answer to prayer, and the study of the Word of God, God has led them out of the darkness into the light.

LEARNING ACTIVITIES

1. Are you comfortable using the term "deluded" to refer to people of other faiths? What makes the religious groups listed in this chapter different from biblical Christianity? What are some of the other groups that exist today that might fall into this category?

2. Reflect on your experience sharing the Gospel with a Catholic or someone from one of these other groups. How did your experience compare to Torrey's explanations? If you have never done so, try to find someone of another faith and use some of the instructions in this lesson.

CHAPTER SIX

PRACTICAL HELP IN PERSONAL WORK

R. A. TORREY IS WELL KNOWN as an evangelist, but this chapter shows his pastoral side. Salvation is not a matter of "easy believism" in which one gets saved and then continues living a life without significant change. Quite the contrary, Torrey provides a comprehensive and deep perspective on what it means to live the Christian life. As always, Torrey roots his advice in Scripture.

He also goes beyond guidelines for specific situations in the latter portion of this chapter. Rather than just provide you with models of how to go about personal work, he now provides a series of rich principles that transcend particular applications. Although written nearly a century ago, these principles have stood the test of time and continue to provide tremendous assistance to Christian workers. In this chapter, Torrey makes clear once again that personal work is for everyone because the need is so pervasive. He provides guidance for serving men, women, and children, as well as all levels of social class.

Dependence on God and His Word is a recurring theme in this book. It is made especially vivid in the story of a personal worker who relies on a single verse. Although a typical personal worker would make use of a wide variety of Scripture according to the circumstances, this story shows the impact of God's Word in the hands of an earnest minister empowered by the Holy Spirit.

Torrey also meets us where we are in this chapter. He knows that many of us struggle with tempers, impatience, discourtesy, lack of prayer, and many other problems. The instruction in this chapter helps us to develop ourselves into well-rounded personal workers able to minister in a wide variety of contexts. It is the rare reader who will not find plenty to work on while studying this chapter.

HOW TO DEAL WITH CHRISTIANS WHO NEED COUNSEL, REBUKE, ENCOURAGEMENT, OR COMFORT

IT IS OFTEN NECESSARY to do personal work with those who are really Christians, but whose Christian experience for one cause or another is unsatisfactory.

I. CHRISTIANS WHO ARE NEGLECTING THE OPEN CONFESSION OF CHRIST

There are many who are professing Christians who are not making an open confession of Christ as they ought. The experience of such is, of course, always unsatisfactory. No one can make satisfactory progress in the Christian life who is not confessing Christ openly before men. One of the best passages of Scripture to use with this class is Matthew 10:32–33. Another excellent passage to use is Romans 10:9–10. According to this passage, our very salvation depends upon our confession of Jesus Christ with the mouth. There are many who say that they are Christians and who believe that they are saved because in their hearts they believe in Jesus and have accepted Him as their Savior. They will tell you that they do not regard a public confession of Christ as necessary. The passage just given will show them how utterly unscriptural is their position. A short time ago, a man who called himself a Christian and who entertained the hope that he really was a child of God, but who lacked joy in his experience, approached me with the question, "Do you think it is necessary to publicly confess Christ in order to be saved?" I replied, " It is a matter of very little moment what I think is necessary; the great question is,

What does God tell us in His own Word?" Then I gave him Romans 10:9–10 to read. " Now," I said, "that is what God says." The meaning and application of the passage were so plain that the man had nothing further to say, but promised to make an open confession of Christ before the world. Another helpful passage to use is John 12:42–43.

> *Torrey doesn't believe that you have to make open confession to be saved. This is made clear in many other sections and other material. Rather, he is stressing the close relationship between salvation and open confession. As an evangelist, it is hard for him to separate the two.*

In many cases, I have found that where these other passages did not seem to lead to decisive action, Mark 8:38 did: "Whoever is ashamed of Me and My words in this adulterous and sinful generation, of him the Son of Man also will be ashamed when He comes in the glory of His Father with the holy angels."

II. CHRISTIANS WHO ARE NEGLECTING THE BIBLE

There are many today who make a profession of faith in Jesus Christ, and of whom doubtless many are saved, who are making little or no progress in the Christian life because of neglect of the Bible. A good passage to use with such is 1 Peter 2:2: "As newborn babes, desire the pure milk of the word, that you may grow thereby."

I was once calling upon a member of the church. I put to her the question, "How are you getting along in your Christian life?" She replied, "I am not getting on at all; my Christian life is a disgrace to me, a disgrace to the church, and a disgrace to Jesus Christ." I then asked, "Are you studying the Word of God daily?" She replied that she was not. "No wonder then that your Christian experience is not satisfactory," said I. A little baby was lying in a carriage close at hand. I pointed to the child and said, "Suppose that you fed this baby every two hours today, once every six hours tomorrow, not at all the next day, three or four times the next day, and then let her go two or three days without feeding at all. How do you think the baby would thrive?" She replied, "I do not think the baby would thrive at all; I think she would die." "Well," I said, "this is the exact way in which you are treating your soul." This point is emphasized by the passage just given.

Another passage to use with this class is Acts 20:32. Other helpful passages are: James 1:21–22; 2 Timothy 3:13–17; Ephesians 6:17; Psalm 1:1–2; 119:9, 11,

130; Joshua 1:8; and Acts 17:11. In urging upon others the daily study of the Scriptures, it is always well to give them a few simple directions as to how to study the Bible.

III. CHRISTIANS WHO ARE NEGLECTING PRAYER

One of the most common causes in our day of an unsatisfactory Christian experience is neglect of prayer. A personal worker will often find those who complain that they are not making satisfactory progress in the Christian life. In such a case, the worker should always inquire whether they make a regular practice of prayer and to what extent. When it is found that prayer is being neglected, the following passages will be found useful: "You lust and do not have. You murder and covet and cannot obtain. You fight and war. Yet you do not have because you do not ask" (James 4:2). Other useful passages are Luke 11:9–13, James 5:13–18, Luke 22:46, and Isaiah 40:31.

A passage that is useful as suggesting the need of regular seasons of prayer is Psalm 55:17: "Evening and morning and at noon I will pray, and cry aloud, and He shall hear my voice." Other passages in this regard are Mark 1:35, Daniel 6:10, Mark 6:46, Luke 6:12, and 1 Thessalonians 5:17.

IV. CHRISTIANS WHO ARE LEADING CARELESS LIVES

There are many whom one would hesitate to say are not Christians at all and are not saved, but whose lives are not out and out for Christ as they should be. In dealing with such, the following passages will be found particularly useful: 2 Corinthians 6:14–7:1; especially emphasize in these verses the words, "Come out from among them and be separate." "No one can serve two masters; for either he will hate the one and love the other, or else he will be loyal to the one and despise the other. You cannot serve God and mammon" (Matthew 6:24). Other verses are 1 John 2:15–17; James 4:4, 6–8; Hebrews 12:14; 1 Peter 1:13–19; 4:17–18; Luke 8:14; 12:35–38; 21:34–36; Romans 12:1–2; 14:23; and 2 Timothy 4:7–8.

V. CHRISTIANS WHO ARE NOT WORKING FOR CHRIST

A large proportion of the professing church today is doing little or nothing for the Master. The personal worker who shall succeed in getting other Christians to work will be accomplishing at least as much for Christ as the one who leads the unsaved to Him. The Bible abounds in passages that can be effectively used for this purpose. The following will be found useful: Mark 13:34–37,

Matthew 24:44–51, and 25:14–30. A verse that is useful in showing idle Christians that every professed follower of Christ ought to be a witness for Him and a soul winner is Acts 8:4. Ephesians 4:14–16 is also useful. In using this passage, point out the words "what every joint supplies," and explain their meaning. Other verses that will be found useful are Ephesians 5:14–21, James 5:20, Daniel 12:3, and Revelation 22:12.

VI. CHRISTIANS WHO ARE UNDERGOING TEMPTATION

There come to all Christians, and especially to all young Christians, times of special temptation and trial. At such times, they need and should have the counsel and encouragement of other Christians. We should "bear one another's burdens, and so fulfill the law of Christ" (Galatians 6:2). Here is a large field of usefulness for the personal worker. The following passages will be found exceedingly useful in strengthening the brethren when under trial and temptation: James 1:2–4, 1 Peter 5:8–10, 1 Corinthians 10:13, 2 Corinthians 12:9–10, 1 Thessalonians 5:17, Philippians 4:13, 1 John 2:14, Psalm 119:9, and Isaiah 40:29–31.

VII. CHRISTIANS WHO ARE UNDERGOING PERSECUTION

Many professed Christians fail in the hour of persecution who would have stood if they could have had a few words of counsel from some fellow Christian. The following passages are useful in giving the needed word of counsel and encouragement: Matthew 5:10–12; 1 Peter 4:12–14, 16; 2:21–23; 3:17–18; 2 Timothy 3:12; Acts 14:22; 5:40–42; Hebrews 12:1–4; Revelation 2:10; Luke 12:32.

VIII. CHRISTIANS WHO ARE PASSING THROUGH AFFLICTION

When times of affliction come to Christians, especially to young Christians, a few words fitly spoken by a fellow Christian are oftentimes of great help. Not infrequently, they save the afflicted ones from years of darkness and barrenness in their Christian experience. There are many today who are of little or no use in the church, who would have been of use if some wise worker had come to them in the hour of affliction and given them good counsel from God's own Word. We should all be constantly on the lookout for opportunities of this kind, and we will find them round about us almost every day of our lives. No thoughts of our own can possibly be of as much help in such an hour as the promises and encouragements of God's Word. The following passages will be found useful and sufficient, if wisely used in the power of the Holy Spirit: Hebrews 12:5–7, 11; 1 Peter 1:4–7; 5:6–7; Psalm 46:1–3; 23:4; 50:15; 34:17; 27:1–6, 13–14; and Matthew 11:28–29. The one who is to use these passages should first read them over and over again by himself and think of their relation to the specific trial of the one who needs help.

IX. CHRISTIANS WHO HAVE LOST LOVED ONES

The ministry of comfort to those whose homes have been invaded by death is one of the most blessed of Christian ministries. It is a ministry that is open to us all, but the attempts of many well-meaning persons in this direction, who try to comfort with their own fancies rather than with the sure Word of God, often-times do more harm than good. But the one who knows the Bible, and what it has to say upon the subject of death and of the future, will be able to bind up many a broken heart. Jesus declared in the synagogue at Nazareth that God had anointed Him to heal the brokenhearted (Luke 4:18), and every follower of Jesus should seek an anointing for the same blessed work. The Bible abounds in passages that are useful for this purpose, but the following are among those that experience proves to be most effective: John 14:1–3, 27; 13:7; Psalm 46:10; Revelation 14:13; 2 Samuel 12:22–23; 1 Thessalonians 4:13–18; Philippians 1:23; and 1 Corinthians 15:42–44, 49, 53–58.

I have found this the most comforting of any single passage in the Word of God: "So we are always confident, knowing that while we are at home in the body we are absent from the Lord. For we walk by faith, not by sight. We are confident, yes, well pleased rather to be absent from the body and to be pres-ent with the Lord" (2 Corinthians 5:6–8).

The worker must make a study of each individual case, and decide which of the passages given above will be most helpful in the specific case. Sometimes it will be found well to use them all. They should not be merely read, but dwelt upon, and their meaning explained and applied, wherever necessary. In all the reading and the explanation and the application, we must depend upon the Holy Spirit for His wisdom and power.

X. CHRISTIANS WHO DON'T HAVE THE POWER OF THE HOLY SPIRIT

There are many professing Christians in our day who have not definitely received the power of the Holy Spirit. They have not entered into the fullness of joy and peace and power that there is for us in Christ. They are practically in the same condition that the disciples in Ephesus were in until Paul came and put to them the question, "Did you receive the Holy Spirit when you believed?" (Acts 19:2) and the position that the believers in Samaria were in until Peter and John came down and "prayed for them that they might receive the Holy Spirit. For as yet He had fallen upon none of them" (Acts 8:15–16). There are many today who are inquiring what they must do that they may receive the power of the Holy Ghost, and there are others that ought to be asking this question. The personal worker should know how to show anyone who has not received the power of the Holy Spirit just what he must do that he may receive it. The following are the steps that should be pointed out:

A. Depend for acceptance before God upon the finished work of Christ alone.

A person cannot depend upon anything he or she has done or can do. To make this point clear, use Galatians 3:2. This passage is often interpreted to mean that we receive the power of the Holy Spirit by simply believing that we are going to receive it. This is not at all the meaning of the passage as found in the context. The Christians in Galatia had been told by certain false teachers who came in among them that in order to be justified it was not enough to simply believe on Jesus Christ and His finished work, but in addition to this they must keep the Mosaic Law regarding circumcision. Paul, in the passage before us, shows them the folly of this position by appealing to their own experience. He calls to mind the fact that they had received the Holy Ghost not by keeping the Mosaic Law, but simply by the hearing of faith, that is, by believing God's testimony regarding Christ and His atoning work, and resting in that for pardon.

The first step is to turn our eyes entirely away from ourselves, and anything we ever have done or can do, and fix them upon Jesus Christ and His atoning work on the cross, and depend upon that finished work of Christ for our pardon and acceptance before God.

B. Put away all sin.

To make this clear to the inquirer, use Acts 2:38. This passage makes it clear that we must repent. Repentance is a change of mind about Christ and a change of mind about sin. It is a change, first of all, from a Christ-rejecting attitude of mind to a Christ-accepting attitude of mind. This is involved in what has been already said regarding the first step, but there must also be a change of mind regarding sin; a change of mind from a sin-loving and sin-indulging attitude of mind to a sin-rejecting attitude of mind; that is, we must renounce all sin. One of the commonest hindrances is holding on to some sin. The worker should deal very faithfully at this point with the inquirer. Find out whether there is not some sin that is not renounced. Find if there is not some sin in the past that has not been confessed and straightened out. Instruct the inquirer to go alone with God and ask God to search his or her heart, and to show anything that is displeasing to Him. If anything is thus brought to light, insist that it must be renounced. Tell the inquirer that every known sin must be given up. Dwell upon the fact that the Holy Spirit is the *holy* Spirit, and that He will not manifest Himself in His fullness in an unholy heart; that is, in a heart that holds on to sin.

C. Surrender one's will absolutely to the will of God.

To show this, use Acts 5:32. This passage shows that God gives the Holy Spirit to them who obey Him. Show that the essential thing about obedience is the attitude of the will, and that real obedience involves the absolute surrender of the will to God. Hold the inquirer to the necessity of such an absolute surrender to God. This is the point of difficulty in very many lives. Perhaps more people are kept out of the blessing of the conscious receiving of the Holy Spirit by a lack of absolute surrender than by any other one thing. In many an instance, the Holy Spirit is given at once in fullness as soon as one is led to an absolute surrender of the will to God. If one will not thus surrender, there is no use of trying to go further; God will accept no compromise at this point.

D. Ask God for this definite gift.

To show this to the inquirer, use Luke 11:13. This tells us plainly that God gives the fullness of the Holy Spirit to them that ask Him. It can be illustrated by the use of Acts 2:1–4 (cf. Acts 1:14; 4:31; and 8:15–16). It is well to pray with the inquirer then and there for this definite gift.

E. Have faith.

There are many who take all the steps mentioned thus far, and yet fail of the blessing simply because they do not believe. Mark 11:24 can be used to make this clear. The inquirer should be instructed not to look to feelings, but to the Word of God, and to believe whether any sensation has been experienced or not, simply because God has promised in His Word. In a very large proportion of cases, people receive the power of the Holy Ghost simply by believing God's Word, and that their prayer is heard, without any feeling; and afterwards what they believe they "have received," they do actually obtain in personal experience as a conscious possession. Great help will be found in showing the inquirer how to receive by faith, in 1 John 5:14–15. Make it very clear to the inquirer by the use of this passage that when we ask anything according to the will of God, we know that He hears us, because the passage says so; and when we know that He hears us, we know that we have the petitions we have asked of Him, whether we feel it or not.

Show the inquirer that when we pray for the empowerment of the Holy Spirit, we pray for something according to the will of God. The following passages make this clear: Luke 11:13, Acts 2:38–39, and Ephesians 5:18. Have the inquirer kneel down and definitely pray for the Holy Spirit's power. When this prayer is offered, ask if he or she has received what was sought. If it is not clear, open your Bible to 1 John 5:14–15, lay it open, and have it read. Then ask if he or she has asked for something according to God's will. Then ask, "What then do you know?" until the answer is, "I know that God has heard me." Then read the fifteenth verse and ask, "If you know that God has heard you, what further do you know?" Hold to it until the answer is, "I know that I have the petition that I asked of Him." Then ask, "What do you know you have received?" and hold to it until, resting upon the simple promise of God's Word, he or she can say, "I know I have received the Holy Ghost's power."

Many are waiting for certain ecstatic experiences of which they have heard others speak. In dealing with an inquirer, do not deny the reality of these experiences, for they doubtless are real in many instances, but show the inquirer that there are no such experiences described in the Bible, that the manifestations of having received the Holy Spirit mentioned in the Bible are a new joy and peace in Christ (Galatians 5:22–23), a new and clearer knowledge of Christ (John 15:26), and especially new power in service for Christ (Acts 1:4–5, 8 and Acts 4:31–33).

Also make it clear to the inquirer that the manifestations that result from receiving the Holy Spirit are to be expected not before we believe, but after we believe, after we take by simple faith God's Word. God's way is not first experience and then faith, but first faith resting upon the naked Word of God, and then experience.

XI. CHRISTIANS WHO DO NOT HAVE VICTORY IN THEIR CHRISTIAN LIVES

There are many professed Christians, and doubtless many who are really saved people, whose lives seem to be lives of constant defeat and discouragement. In dealing with such a person, seek to find out what is the cause of defeat. It will be found in one or more of the following points:

A. Because they have not learned to rest absolutely in the finished work of Christ for pardon and for peace

The church is full of people who are looking to something that they themselves can do to find acceptance before God. No one can have a clear, satisfactory, and victorious Christian experience who has not learned to rest entirely in the finished work of Christ for pardon. If this is found to be the cause of failure, use Isaiah 53:6, Galatians 3:13, 2 Corinthians 5:21, and similar passages, to show that our sins are pardoned not on account of anything that we have done or can do, but on the account of what Jesus Christ did when He bore our sins in His own body on the cross.

Next show the inquirer that the pardon and peace thus purchased by the atoning blood of Christ become ours on the simple condition of our believing on Christ. To show this, use the following passages: Romans 5:1, 4:5, 3:21–26, and Philippians 3:9.

B. Because they have not surrendered absolutely to the will of God

This is the cause of failure in a very large proportion of cases. If this is found to be the cause of failure in any specific case, use Acts 5:32 and Romans 6:13, 19.

C. Because of neglect of the study of the Word

If this is the case, use 1 Peter 2:2, Psalm 119:11, and Ephesians 6:17.

D. Because of neglect of prayer

Where this is the case, use 1 Thessalonians 5:17, Luke 22:40, and Isaiah 40:29–31.

E. Because of failure to constantly confess Christ before others

The one who would lead a victorious Christian life must be constantly witnessing for Christ. Make this very plain, and for this purpose use Matthew 10:32–33.

F. Because of neglect to work for Christ

One who would lead a victorious life must be constantly at work for the Master. If the cause of failure is at this point, use Matthew 25:29. Explain its meaning by the context. The evident meaning of the passage is that one who uses the talents that he or she has in the Master's service will get more, but the one who neglects to use the talents will lose even those.

G. Because they have not received the power of the Holy Spirit

Very many today are leading lives of constant failure where they might be leading lives of constant victory, simply because they do not even so much as know that it is the privilege of the individual believer to be filled with the Holy Spirit. If this is the case, use Ephesians 5:18, the last half of the verse, and Galatians 5:16, 22–23. Then show the inquirer how to receive the power of the Holy Spirit, as explained under the former heading.

LEARNING ACTIVITIES

1. As you read this chapter, you probably were focusing on the needs of those around you. However, you should really pause at this point and identify the areas in your own life where you need counsel. Reread these sections and apply the teaching to yourself. Perhaps you could do this together with the friend who has been helping you role-play.

2. What other issues are likely to come up in your experience that aren't mentioned in this section? Make a list of verses that you might use in these situations.

3. Make a list of the problems in this section (including the ones you have added) and write out one verse for each problem. This will allow you to take a wealth of counsel with you wherever you go.

4. Meet again with a friend who is able to role-play with you. Practice addressing each of the needs presented in this section.

SOME HINTS AND SUGGESTIONS FOR PERSONAL WORK

A FEW GENERAL SUGGESTIONS that will be helpful to the personal worker remain to be made.

I. AS A RULE, CHOOSE PERSONS TO DEAL WITH OF YOUR OWN SEX.

There are, of course, exceptions to this rule. One should always be looking to the Holy Spirit for His guidance as to whom to approach, and He may lead us to one of the opposite sex, but unless there is clear guidance in the matter, it is quite generally agreed among those who have had much experience in Christian work that, on the whole, women usually do the most satisfactory work with women, and men with men; especially is this true of the young. It is always a bad sign when a young man is always looking for women to deal with, and a young woman looking for young men to deal with. Many exceedingly unfortunate complications have risen in actual life from young men trying to lead young women to Christ, and vice versa. Of course, an elderly, motherly woman will oftentimes do excellent work with a young man or boy, and an elderly, fatherly man will sometimes do good work with a young woman or girl.

II. AS A RULE, CHOOSE PERSONS TO DEAL WITH OF ABOUT YOUR OWN AGE.

A young man, as a rule, can get hold of young men better than any one else can, and a man of mature years can handle a man of his own age better than a young man, or better even than an old man. It is not wise, usually, for a young and inexperienced person to approach one very much older and more mature and wiser than himself on such an important subject as this. The older person naturally looks with a good deal of distrust, if not contempt, upon those much younger than himself. There are, of course, exceptions even to this rule. Frequently, a man who has gained wisdom by years and who has the confidence of people can do excellent work with a young man or boy. As a rule, people do the best work with people of their own class—educated men with educated men, business men with businessmen, workingmen with workingmen, women of position with women of similar position to themselves. There are many exceptions to this. Many a laborer has been known to lead an employer to Christ.

III. WHENEVER IT IS POSSIBLE, DEAL WITH A PERSON ALONE.

No one likes to open his heart freely to another on the most personal and sacred of all subjects when there are others present. Many will, from mere pride, defend themselves in a false position when others are present, who would freely admit their error or sin or need if they were alone with you. It is far better for a single worker to deal with a single unconverted person than for several workers to deal with an inquirer or a single worker to deal with several inquirers. Nothing can be more unfortunate than for a number of workers to swarm around one poor individual who is trying to find the way of life. If such an individual is a person of any independence of character, he or she is very likely to feel bothered and, for that very reason, take an attitude of opposition. If you have several to deal with, it is better (if possible) to take them one by one. Workers often find that they have made no headway while talking to several at once, but by taking the individuals off by themselves they soon succeed in leading them one by one to Christ. Where two unsaved people are being dealt with at once, oftentimes, each is afraid of the other, and they bolster each other up in their false position.

IV. LET YOUR RELIANCE BE WHOLLY IN THE SPIRIT OF GOD AND IN THE WORD OF GOD.

Have no confidence in yourself. One of the greatest hindrances to successful personal work is self-confidence. But while there should be no self-confidence, there should be boldness, boldness that comes from believing in the power of the Holy Ghost and in the power of the Word of God. No matter with whom you are dealing or how stubborn the person is, never forget that the Spirit of God and the Word of God have power to break the hardest heart. Be always looking to the Spirit to produce conviction of sin, and expect Him to do it; but let your whole dependence be in Him and in His Word alone.

V. HAVE THE ONE WITH WHOM YOU ARE DEALING READ THE PASSAGES HIMSELF.

Do not content yourself with merely reading passages from the Bible, much less with merely quoting them. It is remarkable how much deeper an impression the Word of God oftentimes makes when it is actually seen with the eyes than it does when it is merely heard with the ears. Sometimes it is well to have a marked Bible with the word that you wish especially to impress marked in some striking way so that it will catch the eye and, thus, the mind and heart of the reader. In this way, the truth finds an entrance into the heart through the eye as well as through the ear.

VI. IT IS OFTENTIMES WELL TO USE BUT A SINGLE PASSAGE OF SCRIPTURE.

One verse of Scripture iterated and reiterated will be burned into the memory and will haunt the one with whom you are dealing long after you have left him. I have known a passage to haunt a man for weeks and finally result in his conversion. Do everything in your power to drive it home and clinch it so that the one with whom you are dealing cannot forget it, but will hear it ring in his memory long after your voice has ceased.

Dr. Ichabod Spencer tells in his "Pastoral Sketches" of how he dealt with a young man who had many difficulties. Dr. Spencer kept continually quoting the passage, "Now is the accepted time; . . . now is the day of salvation." The young man tried to get Dr. Spencer off onto something else, but over and over again he kept saying the words, "Now is the accepted time; . . . now is the day of salvation." The young man returned the next day rejoicing in the Lord, and thanking Dr. Spencer that he had "hammered" him with that text. The words kept ringing in his ears during the night, and he could not rest until he had settled the matter by accepting Christ.

It is a good thing when a person can point to some definite verse in the Word of God and say, "I know on the authority of that verse that my sins are forgiven, and that I am a child of God." Indeed, it is well never to let a person go until he can point you definitely to the verse in God's Word upon which he rests his hope of salvation. Be sure that the person grasps it so that if Satan comes to him when he is alone and asks him how he knows that he is saved, he can open his Bible to that verse and put his finger upon it and defy Satan in all his wiles.

There are times, however, when a powerful effect is produced by piling up passages along some line until the mind is convinced and the heart conquered. Especially is this true in showing people their need of a Savior and showing them Jesus as the Savior that they need.

VII. ALWAYS HOLD THE PERSON WITH WHOM YOU ARE DEALING TO THE MAIN POINT OF ACCEPTING CHRIST.

If he or she wishes to discuss outside questions, such as the claims of various denominations, or the mode of baptism, or theories of future punishment, or fine points about the higher criticism, or any other question than the central one of the need of a Savior, state that these questions are important to take up in their right place and time, but the time to settle them is after settling the fundamental question of accepting or rejecting Christ. Many a case has been lost by an inexperienced and foolish worker who becomes involved in a discussion of some side issue, which it is utter folly to discuss with an unregenerated person.

VIII. BE COURTEOUS.

Many well-meaning but indiscreet Christians, by their rudeness and impertinence, repel those whom they would win to Christ. It is quite possible to be at once perfectly frank and perfectly courteous. You can point out to a man his awful sin and his need of a Savior without insulting him. Your words may be very searching while your manner is very gentle and winning; indeed, the more gentle and winning your manner is, the deeper your words will go, for they will not stir up the opposition of those with whom you are dealing. Some workers approach those with whom they wish to work in such a manner that the latter at once assume the defensive and clothe themselves with an armor that it is impossible to penetrate.

IX. AVOID UNWARRANTED FAMILIARITIES WITH THOSE WITH WHOM YOU DEAL.

I have seen many workers lay their hands upon the shoulders of those with whom they are dealing, or even put their arms around them. Now, there are cases in which that is proper and wise. If a man is dealing with an old, wrecked, and ruined drunkard who thinks he has not a friend in the world, it may be well to place his hand upon the man's shoulder—or over his shoulder—but one needs to be exceedingly cautious about these matters. A person of fine sensitiveness is repelled when a stranger takes any familiarities with him. There is no place where good manners count for more than in personal work.

X. BE EARNEST.

Only the earnest person can make the unsaved person feel the truth of God's Word. It is well to let the passage we would use with others first sink deep into our own souls. I know of a very successful worker who has for a long time used the one passage, "Prepare to meet your God" with everyone with whom she has dealt. But that passage has taken such complete possession of her own heart and mind that she uses it with tremendous effect. A few passages that have thoroughly mastered us are much better than many passages that we have mastered from some textbook.

One of the great needs of the day is men and women who are thoroughly in earnest, who are completely possessed with the great fundamental truths of God's Word. The reader of this book is advised to ponder upon his knees such of the passages suggested in it as he decides to use, until he himself feels their power. We read of Paul that he "did not cease to warn everyone night and day with tears" (Acts 20:31). Genuine earnestness will go further than any skill learned in a training class or from the study of such a book as this.

XI. NEVER LOSE YOUR TEMPER WHEN TRYING TO LEAD A SOUL TO CHRIST.

How many a case has been lost by the worker losing his temper. Some persons are purposely exasperating, but even such may be won by patient perseverance and gentleness. They certainly cannot be won if you lose your temper; nothing delights them more or gives them more comfort in their sin. The more irritating they are in their words and actions, the more impressed they will be if you return their insults with kindness. Oftentimes, the one who has been the most insufferable will break down in penitence. One of the most insulting men I ever met afterward became one of the most patient, persistent, and effective of workers.

XII. NEVER HAVE A HEATED ARGUMENT WITH ONE WHOM YOU WOULD LEAD TO CHRIST.

Heated arguments always come from the flesh and not from the Spirit (Galatians 5:20, 22–23). They arise from pride and unwillingness to let the other person get the best of you in argument. If you care more about winning a person to Christ than you do about winning your case, you will often let the other think that he or she has the best of the argument, absolutely refusing to argue. If the one with whom you are talking has mistaken notions that must be removed before being led to Christ, show the error quietly and pleasantly. If the error is not on an essential point, refuse to discuss it at all, and hold the person to the main question.

XIII. NEVER INTERRUPT ANYONE ELSE WHO IS DEALING WITH A SOUL.

Too much emphasis cannot be laid upon this point. You may not think the other is doing the work in the wisest way, but if you can do any better, bide your time, and you will have the opportunity. Many an unskilled worker has had someone at the very point of decision when some meddler, who thought he or she was wiser, has broken in and upset the work. Do not even stand by one who is talking to another and listen to what is being said. Incalculable mischief may be done in this way. The thought of the one who is being dealt with is distracted, his or her heart is closed up, and a case that might have been won is lost. On the other hand, do not let others interrupt you. Of course, sometimes it is not possible to altogether prevent it, but stop the interruption just as soon as possible. Just a little word plainly but courteously spoken will usually prevent it, but at any cost insist upon being left alone.

XIV. DON'T BE IN A HURRY.

One of the commonest and gravest faults in Christian work today is haste. We are too anxious for immediate results, and so we do superficial work. It is very noticeable how many of those with whom Christ dealt came out slowly: Nicodemus, Joseph, Peter, and even Paul (though the final step in his case seems very sudden) were cases in point. It was three days, even after the personal appearance of Jesus to Paul on the way to Damascus, before the latter came out clearly into the light and openly confessed Christ (Acts 22:16). One with whom slow, but thorough, work has been done and who at last has been brought out clearly for Christ (and who knows just where he or she stands and what to do) is better than a dozen with whom hasty work has been done, who think they have accepted Christ, when in reality they have not. It is often a wise policy to plant a truth in one's heart and leave it to work. The seed on rocky ground springs up quickly, but withers as quickly.

XV. GET THE PERSON WITH WHOM YOU ARE DEALING ON HIS KNEES BEFORE GOD.

This rule has exceptions. Sometimes it is not possible to get the person to kneel, and sometimes it is not wise; but it is wonderful how many difficulties disappear in prayer, and how readily stubborn people yield when they are brought into the very presence of God Himself. I remember talking with a young woman in an inquiry room for about two hours and making no apparent headway, but when at last we knelt in prayer, in less than five minutes she was rejoicing in our Savior. Sometimes it is well to have a few words of prayer before you deal with an individual at all, but of course this is not at all wise in many cases; however, in almost every case it is wise if the person is willing to pray to have a few words of prayer before you close. If the way of life has been made perfectly clear to the inquirer, have him also lead in prayer. There are those who object to getting an unsaved person to pray, but there is clear Bible warrant for it. Cornelius was not a saved man. This is perfectly clear from Acts 11:14; nevertheless, he was sincerely seeking the light, and God sent him word that his prayers had come up for a memorial before Him. Now, anyone who is honestly seeking light, even though he has not as yet that knowledge of Jesus that brings salvation, is in practically the same position as Cornelius, and one of the best things to do is to get that one to pray. It is certainly right for a sinner seeking pardon through the atoning blood to pray (Luke 18:13–14). Some may say, "One who has no faith has no right to pray." But such a one has faith; his prayer is the first evidence of that faith (Romans 10:13–14).

XVI. WHENEVER YOU SEEM TO FAIL IN ANY GIVEN CASE, GO HOME AND PRAY OVER IT AND STUDY IT TO SEE WHY YOU FAILED.

Never give up a case because of one failure. If you have been at a loss to know what Scripture to use, study this book to see the different classes we meet and how to deal with them, find out where this person belongs and how to deal with him, and then go back if you can, and try again. In any case, you will be better prepared for the next case of the same kind. The greatest success in this work comes through many apparent defeats. It will be well to frequently study these hints and suggestions, and see if your failure has come through neglect of them. But be sure to take to God in prayer the case in which you yourself have failed.

XVII. BEFORE PARTING WITH THE ONE WHO HAS ACCEPTED CHRIST, BE SURE TO GIVE DEFINITE INSTRUCTIONS AS TO HOW TO SUCCEED IN THE CHRISTIAN LIFE.

It is well to give these instructions in some permanent form. For this purpose, two tracts have been written by the author of this book, one called "The Christian Life Card," and the other "How to Make a Success of the Christian Life." Either of these can be secured from the Bible Institute Colportage Association, Chicago.

XVIII. WHEN YOU HAVE LED ANYONE TO CHRIST, FOLLOW UP AND HELP IN THE DEVELOPMENT OF THE CHRISTIAN LIFE.

There is nothing sadder in Christian work today than the number who are led to Christ and then neglected. Such are almost certain to get on very poorly. No greater mistake could be possible. The work of following up those who are converted is as important as the work of leading them to Christ and, as a rule, no one can do it so well as the person who has been used in the person's conversion.

LEARNING ACTIVITIES

1. Go back through Torrey's hints and rate yourself on each. On which ones are you strong? On which ones are you weak? This will help you to be prepared to rely on your strengths in personal work and develop your areas of weaknesses.

2. Determine what you consider to be the two or three most important pieces of advice in this chapter, and share them with other Christian workers in your church or community. Show them the list, and ask what they consider to be the most important.

3. Which of the hints in this section seem odd or unnecessary to you? Why do you think it was important enough for Torrey to include? How might you integrate and/or adapt this hint to improve your effectiveness in personal work?

CHAPTER SEVEN

HOME OUTREACHES

TORREY NOW SHIFTS TO THE CONTEXTS in which special outreach programs can be conducted. Most of the previous portions of this book have been focused on one-on-one interaction. Now Torrey helps us to consider the ways in which our personal work can be built into ministry programs. Some of the concepts are used today, while others have been largely dropped. The thoroughness with which Torrey presents these ministries compels us to consider how we might make best use of these special outreaches today.

The first section focuses on the potential for personal work in the homes of others. Most churches don't stress door-to-door ministry anymore, but Torrey challenges us to consider the ministry opportunities that are available in the homes of those in our communities. He has tremendous savvy regarding the systematic organization of the effort and ingenuity of how to make use of the opportunities that exist. Many modern marketing concepts are present in his commonsense guidelines for reaching communities for Christ.

He also focuses our attention on our own homes. Cottage meetings are a means by which we can use our own homes to invite people in and present them with the

Gospel. Again, much of the modern concept of cell groups and "open chair" evangelism is contained in Torrey's detailed instruction. Although many of our ministry efforts are aimed at the middle class and the poor, Torrey includes a section in this chapter on how to use "Parlor Meetings" to reach the upper class and the rich. He is no discriminator on the basis of wealth; even the rich need the Gospel.

It is easy to think about church as something that is done on Sunday at a building. However, the church in China, as well as vast movements of church growth in North America, have shown the impact that can be had for the cause of Christ through the effective use of homes. Torrey's instructions are right on target for modern society.

HOUSE-TO-HOUSE VISITATION

I. ITS IMPORTANCE AND ADVANTAGES

A. It is biblical.

The apostle Paul was a house-to-house visitor. In Acts 20:20 he calls to the minds of the Ephesian elders the fact that he had taught them not only publicly, but also "from house to house." Many of us feel above this work, but the apostle Paul—the prince of preachers—found a great deal of time to do it. We have also the example of Christ Himself. Not a little of His work was done in the home. One of the most touching scenes of His life was in the home at Bethany, with Mary sitting at His feet listening to the words of eternal life (Luke 10:39).

B. It brings you near to the people.

When Mr. Moody was in Glasgow, someone asked him how to reach the masses, and his reply was, "Go for them." There is no better way of going for them, and getting near to them, than by going into their homes. One of the simplest solutions of the problem of how to reach the unchurched in city and country is to go right into their homes.

C. You can get hold of people that you cannot reach in any other way.

There are people who never enter a church, who will not attend a theater service or a mission meeting, who will not even attend an open-air meeting, but there is nobody who does not live somewhere; therefore, you can get hold of everybody by house-to-house visitation. There are special classes who can be reached in this way and in this way alone, for instance, the very poor who are afraid to enter a church because of their shabby dress, or who may be utterly unable to leave home on account of the multiplicity of home duties. The sick also can be reached only in this way.

Then there are in every city many who would not attend church if they could; among these are atheists, the great majority of Roman Catholics, and still other classes of nonchurchgoing people who are never seen within the walls of an evangelical church. Some workers pay no attention to Roman Catholics because they think that they are already Christians; others pay no attention to them because they think that they cannot be reached. Doubtless many Catholics are true Christians, but they have a very perverted kind of Christianity. And a very large proportion of them, moreover, are not Christians at all; they have no saving knowledge of Jesus Christ; they are wrapped in superstition and darkness. A large proportion of the Catholic population will not go into a tent meeting, or a mission hall, or even stop at an open-air meeting. The only way to reach them is to go right into their homes. Many a minister can tell of the large number of Catholics who have been converted and come into the church. When converted they make most faithful church members. They have been trained regarding their duty to the church, and when once shown their duty to the Lord Jesus Christ, they make splendid Christians. There is no better way to reach them than by house-to-house visitation. You may not get them the first time, or the second, or the third, but they are bound to yield at last to simple, genuine kindness.

D. It wins people's confidence and attention.

Many people seem to feel that a great honor has been bestowed upon them when the missionary, minister, or Christian worker calls at their home and takes an interest in them. I once called upon a saloon-keeper, but I did not realize what an honor he considered had been conferred upon him until a neighboring saloon-keeper afterward upbraided me for not calling upon him and asked me if he was not just as good as the other man. Few Christian workers realize how much good it does people to go into their homes, and what a short road it is to their confidence and attention. You first go to them, and they will afterward come to you.

E. It gives you an opportunity to see how the people live.

It thus teaches you how to deal with them. It has been well said that "one-half of the world does not know how the other half lives," and we never will know until we go right into their homes. It is a perfect revelation to see some people on Sunday in their Sunday clothes, and then go on Monday and see them at work in the home. You are forced to say, "Does this woman come from a house like this?" or, "Does this child come from a home like this?"

F. They will open their hearts to you more freely at their homes than else-where.

People feel at home at home. They are always more or less restrained at church, or in an inquiry meeting, or in a mission hall—less probably in a mission hall than in a church and still less in a cottage meeting than either—but when you get them at home, they throw off restraint and talk freely. You never know what is going on in people's hearts until you go to their homes, and they open their hearts to you there.

G. It offers opportunity for close dealing with souls.

You can do close personal dealing far better in a quiet house than anywhere else. People do not like to open their hearts in public, and even an inquiry meeting is more or less public.

H. It affords opportunities for suggestions regarding home life.

The great majority of people need to be taught how to live in this world. They need to be taught plain truths on plain subjects. The ignorance of many poor people on the little affairs of everyday life is perfectly astonishing. One great trouble with many poor people is that they do not know how to live; they do not know what to eat or how to cook what they buy; they do not know how to dress or how to spend their money to the best advantage. They do not know how to train their children. They do not know how to eat properly at the table, nor even how to make a bed.

A family living in Minneapolis were in great poverty and destitution; they were in absolute need of the bare necessities of life. The attention of a friend of mine was called to them, and he sent me money with the request that I should go and look them up, investigate the case and, if I found them in real distress, give them this money. I called and found them in very great need. The mother was sick in bed, the father out of work, the glass out of the window and an old garment stuffed in the place. They were without the commonest necessities of life, and I saw at once that it was a case of real distress. Being quite without experience at the time, I gave the family the money as requested. Thinking it well to follow up the work, I called again. To my astonishment, I found that they had used the money in purchasing a mirror that reached from the floor to the ceiling. It was simple ignorance on their part.

I once gave a man some money to buy groceries for a family in extreme destitution. When he came back I asked him what he had bought. He told me, among other things, that he had bought three pounds of cheese and a lot of loaf sugar. I asked him why he bought the loaf sugar, and he said the father said the children liked to have it to eat. A few instructions as to the most economical food to buy and how to prepare it would save many a family from want without it being necessary to give them a cent.

I. It sanctifies the home.

Let a minister of Jesus Christ go into a home and talk and read the Bible and pray, and that home is a different place ever afterward. If the minister is a person who actually brings God down in prayer to the place, it will make a change in that household. Oftentimes after that, the family will be on the point of doing something wrong when they will think what the messenger of Jesus Christ said in that prayer. They will think hallowed things when they go into that room. Many a home has been changed by the presence of the minister of God. You can set up a family altar for them. When you get people converted who have had religious training, they know what family worship means, but if they have never had family worship, it never occurs to them that they ought to have family worship at home. Tell them to "set up a family altar," and you might as well talk Greek to them, but go into their homes, read the Bible to them and pray, then ask them, "Do you enjoy this?" and when they say "Yes," tell them to keep right on doing it every day, and show them how to keep on.

J. It results in many conversions.

It is a question whether any other form of Christian work results in as many satisfactory conversions as house-to-house visitation. Of course, it is a great deal more gratifying to our pride to stand up before a large audience and speak to them; there is an exhilaration in doing that. But when it comes down to definite results, I do not know of any kind of work that brings larger results in souls won for Christ than patient house-to-house visitation. I have often thought that a person who would devote his whole life to going from house to house week after week would have a far more splendid record at the close of life than the minister who preaches to from one hundred to one thousand every Sunday. Take the London Home Missionary Society. They are doing a magnificent work in many directions, but a very large proportion of it is this kind of work. Many are employed for simple house-to-house visitation, and they are accomplishing great results. In country work I am sure we have been laying comparatively too much stress on the church as a church and the gathering at the central meeting-house and too little on the work in the scattered homes.

A great deal of foreign missionary work, and oftentimes the best part of it, is house-to-house work. Foreign missionaries have been far wiser in their work in this direction than we have at home. Perhaps it is so partly from the necessities of the case.

II. HOW TO DO HOUSE-TO-HOUSE VISITATION

A. Be systematic.

It pays to be systematic in everything. The one who has a plan for doing things and carries out his plan is the one who reaps the largest results. Many, however, spend their whole time in making plans that they never carry out. Better to have a poor plan that you execute, than a perfect plan that you spend your whole time in elaborating.

B. A thorough house-to-house visitation should be made by districts.

What I mean by thorough house-to-house visitation is that every habitation in the district should be visited. This is the true way to begin pastoring a country church. In a town where there are other churches than your own, you can invite the Methodists to the Methodist church, the Congregational people to the Congregational church, etc., but you should not be too sensitive about calling on people who do not belong to your own flock. Better to call upon someone who belongs to someone else's flock than to leave someone neglected. Surely if your own church is the only one in the vicinity, you should visit every habitation in that part of the country. It will take time; you will have less time for general reading and for study than if you did not do this work, but you are in the ministry to win souls and not primarily for the glorification of your intellect. You must spend and be spent; you must make full proof of your ministry. Just so in the city; you should yourself visit every family or else get every family visited. It is not the minister who can preach good sermons who succeeds; it is the minister who gets hold of the people. In district visitation, it should be borne in mind that people are constantly moving and need to be visited very frequently.

In an evangelistic campaign, one of the first things that should be done is to have a house-to-house canvass of every house and habitation anywhere within reach of the church, or churches, where the meetings are to be held. Every family in the town or district where you are working should be visited. That means not merely that someone should go to the door with a flier in his hand, which he hastily gives to the first one who comes to the door; it means that someone should go into every house in the town. Visitors should be sent out two and two to go to every house and deal with the people personally about their salvation. If it is a union meeting, it is well that the two should be of different denominations. There should be a thorough house-to-house canvass of every city at least once a year, covering the entire city. This is easily accomplished when the churches unite in the work.

C. Select homes for regular visitation.

In some communities, you must visit every home regularly, and where you cannot do it yourself, you can see that it is done. In other communities, it is wise to visit only part of the homes regularly.

How shall we select the homes?

1. *By a thorough canvass*

As you go around visiting from house to house, you will find some homes that should be visited regularly and others that it will not do to visit regularly. Do not be too hasty in concluding that it is of no use to visit a certain family. For instance, do not conclude because a family is Roman Catholic it is of no use to visit them regularly. Everyone of much experience knows that some of the "hopeless" families are those which turn out best in the long run.

2. *Persons who do not attend church*

Every person who does not attend church should be visited. Not merely the members of your church should be visited regularly and systematically, but those who do not attend at all should be visited.

3. *The parents of the children who attend the Sunday School*

You have a good excuse and a wide opening in visiting the parents of children who attend your Sunday school. Of course there may be exceptions. There are sometimes children attending Sunday school whose parents do not know that they are attending and who would be angry and opposed if they did know. In such cases, the parents should not be visited, or if they are visited nothing should be said to them about the children attending the Sunday school.

4. *Parents of children you get hold of on the street*

Talk with the children as you go about the street, and if you find children who do not attend Sunday school anywhere, go and visit their homes; go and deal with their parents, and gather the whole family into the church of God.

When Mr. Moody was engaged in Sunday school work in Chicago, he was constantly picking up children on the street and getting them into the Sunday school and afterward getting into their homes. One day on the street, he met a little girl with a pail. He asked her if she went to Sunday school. She said she did not. He then gave her a hearty invitation to his school, and she promised to go, but she did not keep her promise. He at once began to watch for that girl. Weeks after, he saw her on the street. He started for her, and she broke into a dead run and he ran in pursuit. Down one street and up another she went, the eager missionary running behind her. Finally she shot into a saloon and he followed. On she went up a back flight of stairs with Mr. Moody still in close pursuit. She dashed into a room and under a bed. He followed and pulled her out by the foot and had a talk with her. Her mother was a widow with several children; her father had been a drunkard. Mr. Moody had a talk with the mother and called again and again, until at last the whole family was won for Christ and became prominent in the work of the Chicago Avenue Church. There are many families that you can get hold of in no other way than by such persistent pursuit.

⟿ D. L. Moody began as a children's minister and always maintained a strong passion for the care of neglected children. In today's society, one must be very careful to balance outreach to needy children with safeguards against abuse (or even the accusation of abuse). For ideas on how to minister to children today, see Daniel H. Smith, How to Lead a Child to Christ *(Chicago: Moody, 1987) and Cheryl Dunlop,* Follow Me

as I Follow Christ: A Guide for Teaching Children in a Church Setting
(*Chicago: Moody, 2000*).

5. *Funerals afford a good opportunity to get hold of a family.*

Almost everybody wants a minister to conduct a funeral. When you once
get an entrance into a home this way, do not let go of it. I do not know how
many families I have gotten hold of by being invited to conduct a funeral in the
home. Do not consider your work done when the funeral has been conducted;
just consider that an opening for further work.

6. *Weddings also afford good opportunities for getting into homes.*

When you conduct a wedding, do not be satisfied when the fee for services
is safely deposited in your pocket. You have gained an opening into another
family, another opportunity of winning a family for Christ; follow it up.

D. Keep books.

Be just as systematic and thorough as if in business. Have your families classified alphabetically and by streets. Keep an accurate record of when you called
last and the result of your call. If one has a large parish, the card system of
indexing is better than the use of books.

E. Always remember to pray before starting out.

If there is any work that requires wisdom, it is house-to-house visitation, and
God alone can give the wisdom that is necessary.

F. Introduce yourself the best way you can.

It is impossible to lay down rules about this. It often takes almost infinite tact
to get into a home and quite as much tact to keep there after you get in.
Frequently, it is necessary not to let it be known in first coming to the home
that you are there on a religious errand. Proceed to win the confidence of the
people. Be very courteous. Do not notice any rudeness on the part of the people that you are visiting; leave your pride at home, and no matter what insults
are offered you, let them pass unheeded. Remember that you are there not to
serve your own interests, nor to spare your own feelings, but as an ambassador
of Jesus Christ and to win souls to Him. If you keep your eyes open, an opportunity will afford itself for doing some kindly thing that will open the hearts of
the people to you and win their confidence. A young lady got into one home

by offering to do the washing of an overworked woman. It was hard work, but it won that woman and her husband and child to Christ. The woman, who was thoroughly worldly, became a very active Christian, and the husband, who was a drunkard, is now in heaven. The child has grown up into a fine young man.

Take an interest in the things the people you are visiting are interested in. One minister got an entrance into the home of a surly farmer by proving that he could plow. Be sure and notice the children. Children are worth noticing, anyhow, and there is no surer road to the confidence and affection of the parents than by showing attention to the children.

G. As soon as possible, begin to open the Scriptures.

Very frequently, it is not wise to begin this at once. It must be led up to. When the time comes, the Scriptures should be thoroughly applied. Use them to convince of sin, to reveal Christ, to bring to a decision, to lead to entire consecration, and to instruct in the fundamental duties and truths of Christianity. It is astonishing how little the average man or woman really catches of a plain sermon. If there is to be thorough indoctrination in fundamental truths, it must be done largely in the homes.

COTTAGE MEETINGS

I. THEIR IMPORTANCE AND ADVANTAGES

A. You can reach people who cannot be reached in any other way.

1. *People who cannot go to church on account of family duties*

There are a great many people in every city, and still more in the country, for whom it is absolutely impossible to go to church. A mother may have a large family of children and no servant. Many others are detained at home on account of sickness. Few of us realize how many people there are in every place who cannot go to church, either on account of their own physical infirmities or the infirmities of those with whom they have to stay.

A great many cannot go to church on account of age. Who that has ever seen it will forget the joy that lights up the face of these elderly people when you bring a meeting to them? How often such people have asked me if we could not have a meeting in their home. One of the greatest joys in Christian life and service is to hold a cottage meeting for people who cannot go to church.

2. *People who will not go to church*

I recall a family who would not go to church at all through simple indifference. They were an intelligent family—a father and mother, two boys, and two girls. As they would not go to church, we took the church just as near them as we could get it. We held a cottage meeting next door to their home. They came to it out of friendship to the family where the meeting was held. They were interested at once, came to church, and the parents and grown-up children were converted.

Some people will not go to church on account of their clothes. It is all very well for us to say, "Never mind about your clothes," but at the same time it is not very pleasant to go to a place where almost everybody else is better dressed than you are yourself. But one can go to a cottage meeting in the poorest of clothes and not be noticed.

Some people will not go to church because of their positive hatred to the Gospel, and yet the same people can often be induced to attend a cottage meeting.

B. You can hold cottage meetings where you cannot get a large room or rent a hall.

You can always get cottage room. How many sections of the United States today have no church accessible to the population. In the center of the town there will be found two or three churches struggling for supremacy, but three or four miles out in the country there is no church at all. Many churches are trying to maintain possession of "strategic points" where they can glorify the denomination instead of God, while other points are entirely neglected. The only way to reach the people in these faraway and neglected communities is by cottage meetings.

I look back upon my early pastorate in the country with great regret. I fancied I was killing myself with preaching three times on Sunday. I kept it up for three years, and people made me believe I would kill myself. I held these three meetings on Sunday and during the week conducted a class in German, a class in geology, and other things of that sort instead of attending to my proper business, and now I think with bitter regret of the district I could have worked if I had only known how. There was not another church for miles in any direction. Scores and scores of people could never get to church. There was enough work in that pastorate alone to have kept a man busy if it had been done right. A church, which at one time was the largest in that region, had almost died because about the only work done was the ordinary preaching.

Do not be content with preaching your regular sermons on Sunday, but have services all over your parish for miles in every direction, and work the parish for all it is worth. Search out the destitute places, and hold cottage meetings for several nights in the week. Set the other pastors in the district an example of how to work a parish. There is not one parish in fifty today that is worked as it should be. The spiritual destitution of the city is nothing compared with the spiritual destitution of the country. Wherever you get a parish, be sure and work it for all there is in it. If there is any part of that neighborhood where nobody is doing anything, go to work there. Do not be afraid of stepping on someone else's toes, but be sure and go to work.

C. People like the informality of cottage meetings.

There should be nothing stiff about a cottage meeting. Of course, some people turn a cottage meeting into a stiff church service, but that is not necessary. In these meetings you can get people to talk that you could not get to open their mouths in a church prayer meeting, and you can so train them in a cottage meeting that they will soon be able to take part in the church prayer meeting.

D. People are close to the speaker.

In a cottage meeting, if you have worked it up as it should be, you have to pack people together like sardines in a box, while in the church there is a gulf between the minister and the pews, and the people usually get in pews as remote from the minister as possible.

E. Anybody can have a cottage meeting.

It is the simplest thing in the world to hold a cottage meeting, though it is not always the easiest thing in the world to have a good cottage meeting.

F. The cottage meeting sanctifies the home.

It brings religion right into the home. It turns the home into the house of God. The home should be a consecrated place, and the cottage meeting does much to make it so. There is no other place like the place where you have come together for prayer, and where, it may be, you have been brought to the Lord Jesus Christ. The home that has been used for a cottage meeting becomes a hallowed place.

G. Cottage meetings are apostolic.

The first churches were in the homes (1 Corinthians 16:19). We are going back to apostolic times when we return to the homes to hold religious services. A very large share of Paul's work was holding cottage meetings.

H. Cottage meetings take the Gospel to the people.

There are two ways of reaching the people. One way is to invite them to come to you; the other way is to go to them. The latter is God's way; the former is the modern way.

II. HOW TO PREPARE FOR A COTTAGE MEETING

A. Get on your knees before God.

That does not need any amplification, but it needs a good deal of exemplification.

B. Select a place to hold the meeting.

1. *Because of the spaciousness and accessibility of a room*

If you can get a large room, get it unless you are pretty sure you are going to have a small meeting. If you get a large room, it will be an incentive to you to work hard to have a large meeting. If possible, get a room that is accessible. Of course, if you cannot do better, you can get a room where you have to climb two or three flights of stairs, but if a room can be had on the first floor, so much the better. There may be reasons why a room that is quite inaccessible will be better in some special case for your meeting.

2. *Because of someone you wish to reach*

This is an important point in the selection of a room. It may be there is a father you want to get at—the wife and children have been reached, but the father will not come to the meeting. The only way you can get him to a meeting is to have a meeting in his own home. Have the meeting, in that case, in his house. I prayed for one man for fifteen years. I tried to talk with him, but every time I would talk with him he would be worse than ever. I think he used to swear in my presence more than anywhere else just because he knew I was a Christian. But I got him one time where I had him cornered. He was sick for two weeks in a Christian home. He heard the Bible read and heard prayer every day during these two weeks and heard religious conversation constantly. At the end of those two weeks, the day he got up and got out, he took Christ as his Savior and afterward became a preacher of the Gospel. You must be as wise as a serpent in looking for souls.

3. *Because of the popularity of the family*

Avoid as far as possible selecting a home that is unpopular. Many an inexperienced worker tries to hold a meeting and gets for that purpose what appears to be a desirable home, but afterwards wonders why the people will not come to it. Probably the reason is that there is something about the family that makes them unpopular. There may sometimes be reasons for holding the meeting in such a home, but as a rule, if you know a family that everybody likes, that is the place to hold your meeting, other things being equal.

C. Work up the meeting.

Have a great deal of invitation work done, not by yourself only, but by others as well. Be sure and not do it all yourself. Mr. Moody used to say, "It is a great deal better to get ten to work than to do the work of ten." Be careful as to whom you invite. If there is enmity existing between the person at whose house the meeting is to be held and some other person in the vicinity, you would be better to bring about a reconciliation between the two before inviting the latter person to the meeting. A minister should not cater to the prejudices of the people, but should know their prejudices and be governed in actions by knowledge of them. You have to deal with people on the practical basis of what they are and not on the ideal basis of what they ought to be. Oftentimes, it is well to leave the whole matter of invitation to the residents of the house. In some homes they are willing that you should invite everybody, while in others they are particular as to whom you invite. Reaching the poor in the alleys is far easier than reaching the wealthy people up on the avenues. You can go into the homes of the poor and invite them to come and hear the Gospel, but for some reason you do not want to go into the homes of the people living in the elegant houses. But it is quite easy for people who are rich themselves, and who are Christians as well, to invite other rich people to gather at their homes and then have someone there to open up to them the Word of God.

D. Provide for the singing and playing, too, if it is possible.

Instrumental music, however, is not absolutely necessary. We have fallen into the way of depending too much upon instrumental music. The best singing is oftentimes without any musical instrument. It is well to bear in mind that very poor singing goes a good ways in a poor home. As far as possible, you should have the hymns you are going to use selected beforehand, and selected with care.

E. Go early to the place of holding the meeting.

If when you arrive you find the chairs arranged in a most formal way, looking like a funeral, get things a little disarranged. Do not put the chairs in straight lines, but arrange them as for a social gathering.

Another reason for going to the place early is to be ready to welcome people when they come. When they come, do not leave them to take care of themselves; get them to talking, and open the meeting in an informal way before they know it has begun. Make everybody feel as much at home as you can. While people are still talking you can suggest a song, and when that is over have someone lead in prayer. Oftentimes, it is well not to let people know that it is going to be a prayer meeting; call it a social and make it a social, but give it a religious turn.

III. HOW TO CONDUCT THE MEETING

A. Always begin promptly.

That is, if it has been announced as a meeting beginning at a certain time, be sure and begin at that time. In regard to the form of beginning the meeting, it is not necessary to have any particular form.

B. Be as informal as possible.

C. Get everyone to sing.

People like to sing. Oftentimes, the people who have the poorest voices and the least knowledge of music are the ones most fond of singing. Encourage them to sing. This will shock the really musical people present, but not one person in a thousand is really musical, and you can afford to shock them. If necessary, sing the same verse over and over again until the people learn it; do it with enthusiasm. Comment on the hymns. Use for the most part familiar hymns, though a new hymn with a catchy tune will often take well.

Everything about the meeting should be made cheery and bright. There are hosts of people in the world who have very little brightness in their lives, and if you have a bright cottage meeting, they will find it out and come.

D. Make everything brief.

Have no long prayers, no long sermons, and no long testimonies. One man went to a cottage meeting and read a chapter with seventy verses and read the whole chapter. I have heard of a man praying fifteen minutes in a cottage meeting. Those were doubtless extreme cases, but not a few cottage meetings have been killed by long-winded leaders.

E. Take a simple subject to speak upon.

Some foolish workers take the cottage meeting as an opportunity for displaying their profound knowledge of theology. Such people kill the meeting. Do not preach, but talk in an informal, homely way. Do not talk too loud.

F. Draw the people out.

One of the advantages of a cottage meeting is that you can draw the people out. Be sure and use this opportunity of getting people to speak in meeting. To you it may be a very simple matter to speak in meeting, yet most of us can remember when it was a very difficult thing to do; but it is far more difficult for those plain people among whom we hold most of our cottage meetings. It is, however, very easy to draw them out by simply saying, "Now, Mrs. Jones, what do you think about this matter?" "Mr. Brown, what have you to say of this?" Before they know it you have got them to talking on the subject of religion just as they would talk about their sewing or washing or everyday work.

A young lady used to attend a service that I conducted. She warned me beforehand that I must not call upon her to speak, that she had heart trouble, and if she got excited, it was dangerous; at the same time, she was unhappy because she did not take part in meeting. One day when a meeting was going on, quite naturally I turned to her and in an informal way asked her a question upon the subject that was under discussion. Without thinking at all, she got up and expressed her opinion upon it. Afterward I said to her, "You have spoken in meeting; you did not seem to have much trouble about it." She now enjoys speaking in meeting, and her heart trouble has disappeared. Perhaps you could not do this in a church or chapel meeting, but it is the easiest thing in the world in a cottage meeting to get everybody talking on the subject of religion just the same as on any other subject. It is a remarkable fact that when you go into a house and approach the subject of religion after having talked about other things, the people immediately begin to talk in another tone of voice and in a different way. You must break up that sort of thing. Cultivate the habit of gliding into the subject of religion as naturally as into any other subject.

G. Do not have a stereotyped way of conducting a cottage meeting.

It is not well to have a stereotyped way of doing anything. Go to some churches, and they put into your hands an order of service. Every part of the service has its fixed place. It gets to be an abomination in the church service, but it is far more of an abomination in a cottage meeting. One of the greatest advantages of a cottage meeting is its informality. Some get into the habit of uttering stereotyped prayers. When they get to the point of prayer for the Jews, you know that the next prayer will be for the sick of the congregation, etc. That sort of thing is unspeakably tiresome even in church, but it is utterly unendurable in a cottage meeting.

H. Do not let the meeting get away from you.

We have said to draw the people out and get them to talking, but if you are not very careful they will get to talking, and the meeting will run away from you. Let your ideal be perfect freedom and, at the same time, perfect control.

I. Oftentimes have a season of one-sentence prayers.

Sentence prayers are one of the best things that our Young People's Society of Christian Endeavor have introduced into our church life. Of course, sentence prayers can become formal and stereotyped and meaningless. When I first began to go to prayer meeting, there were three or four good old men who monopolized the whole time. To begin with, the minister would give out a hymn, and then make a long prayer, and then sing another hymn, and then read a long chapter and talk fifteen or twenty minutes, and then throw the meeting open. This meant that Brother Brown would grind out a long prayer, and then Brother Jones would grind out another long prayer; they would sing a hymn, and then Brother Smith would pray anywhere from ten to twenty minutes. Another hymn would be sung and the minister would pronounce the benediction, and the affair was over, and all would go home glad the thing was through.

Many people cannot pray five minutes in public, and it is a good thing they cannot; and they fancy that it is impossible for them to pray at all unless they can get off an elaborate address to God. But anybody can ask for what he wants. Make it clear to people that this is real praying, asking God for what we really want. How near God seems to draw during a season of sentence prayers! You can say, "If there is one thing you want today more than anything else, just put that in your sentence prayer. Never forget that prayer is simply asking God for what you want, and expecting to get it."

J. Oftentimes have requests for prayer.

Do not be mechanical about that. I would not always have the same kind of a meeting. I knew a man who was very successful in cottage meeting work who used to have the people get up and move around and talk with one another, and then sit down and go on with the meeting.

K. Have periods of silent prayer.

Oftentimes, the most hallowed moments in a meeting are when all the people are silent before God. Before having these periods of silent prayer, you must be careful to warn people to keep their thoughts fixed upon God, and to keep pouring out their souls before God in prayer. You and I may not need that warning, but many Christians do. If not warned, Mrs. Jones is likely to spend the time thinking about Mrs. Brown's hat, and Mrs. Brown about Mrs. Jones's dress. They would not be thinking about God at all.

L. Do personal work.

A cottage meeting that does not close with personal work has been mismanaged. The cottage meeting offers a very unusual opportunity for this kind of work. The meetings are small; it is rare indeed that there are more than forty people present. You should find out how many of these people are saved. It does not follow that because a person is saved we do not need to do personal work with him. Saved people can get help in these meetings that they cannot get in a large meeting. It is the easiest and simplest thing in the world to get a mother to talking, say, about her children. Draw her away from the crowd, and then lead her on to the subject of her soul's salvation or her spiritual condition. People feel more at home in their own house, and you can get into their hearts as you cannot in a more public gathering.

M. Close promptly.

Be sure to do that. If nine o'clock is understood to be the hour of closing, close promptly at that time, if possible. It is a good thing to establish a reputation for beginning and closing promptly. In this way you will get many people to go to your meeting who would not otherwise go. They can stay to a certain hour, and if they know you will close promptly at the hour appointed, they will go to the meeting. If the interest is so great that you wish to continue the meeting, close the meeting at the appointed time, giving all those who desire to leave an opportunity to do so, and then have a second meeting. You must never forget that a great many people have to get up early in the morning, and in order to do so they must go to bed early. It is very embarrassing for timid people to get up and leave a meeting while it is going on. Then again, the resident of the house where you are holding the meeting may be obliged to get up at five o'clock in the morning, and so must go to bed early. Furthermore, it is far better to close the meeting while there is good interest than to wait until the interest dies out. If you close at high tide, people will want to come again. If people desire to stay around and chat at the close of a meeting, be sure and have them chat on the subject of religion. If people are disposed to hang around after the meeting is over and make themselves a nuisance, you can say pleasantly, "It is getting late; and Mrs. B. wants to shut up her house. I guess we must be going."

As to the time of holding the meeting, the evening is the usual time, but sometimes the afternoon is a good time, especially in country districts.

PARLOR
MEETINGS

PARLOR MEETINGS ARE MUCH THE SAME in thought and in method as cottage meetings, with this difference: that cottage meetings are intended to reach people of the middle classes and the poor, while parlor meetings are intended to reach the rich. There are many who think there is no use trying to reach the rich with the Gospel. This is a great mistake. Some of the most devoted and delightful Christians that I have ever known have been people of much wealth and high position. Indeed, perhaps the dearest Christian friend I ever had—and the one from whom I learned the most by personal contact—was a man who stood very high socially and politically in his country. I think this man more fully realized the meaning of Christ's words, "Unless you are converted and become as little children," than any other person I ever knew. I have known people of much wealth in our own country, and members of the nobility in England, Germany, and Russia who were among the most humble Christians that I have ever met.

I. ADVANTAGES AND IMPORTANCE

The principal advantage in parlor meetings is that they reach many who can be reached in no other way. It may be admitted that the rich are the hardest class to reach of any. It is much easier to bring the Gospel to people who live in the slums than to the people who live in palaces, but many of these latter have been reached by parlor meetings.

II. HOW TO CONDUCT

A. Get some Christians of wealth and position to open their parlors for the meetings.

Rich Christians should make far larger use of their homes than they do to reach people of their own class. Many of them do not open their homes simply because their attention has never been called to the fact that this is a way in which they can do good. Many of them show a great readiness to do this when it is suggested to them.

B. Have the resident of the house invite intimate friends.

Many of them will come out of curiosity; others will come out of friendship. Oftentimes, it gets to be a fad to attend these meetings, and people go scarcely knowing why. It does not matter so much why they go, as long as they go; for if the Gospel is presented in the power of the Holy Spirit after they get there, some of them will be converted.

C. Get an attractive and Spirit-filled speaker.

Sometimes it is well to have the speaker be a person of wealth or position, but there are many who have never known what it means to be rich themselves who still have a peculiar faculty for winning the confidence and esteem of wealthy people.

D. Sometimes take up some line of Bible study.

Bible study under a wise teacher can be made exceedingly interesting for people of wealth and fashion. Indeed, many of these people hardly know how to use their time, and Bible study presents to them a pleasing novelty. Of course, the teacher must be wise and filled with the Holy Spirit. Sometimes it is possible to have a regular class for systematic Bible instruction, extending through many weeks or months.

E. Sometimes have an address on some living religious topic by a Spirit-filled man or woman.

F. It is well oftentimes to interest those who are gathered together for parlor meetings in some missionary work or charity.

Many of them like to give, and it is a blessing to them to give. They should be educated to know just what the crying needs of the wide world are.

G. Aim directly at the conversion of those who attend.

Very little is accomplished, after all, in parlor meetings unless the unsaved ones are brought to Christ. The probability is that they will be brought to Christ at the parlor meeting or else will never be brought to Him. If anyone should have a profound sense that it is "now or never," it is the one who is addressing a company of wealthy men or women gathered together for a parlor meeting in a Christian home.

A woman of wealth once asked a Christian man who called at her home, "Are you a missionary?" "Yes," he replied. "Do you ever speak to people about their souls?" "I do." "Well," she replied, "I wish you would speak to me about my soul." He did, and led her to Christ. When the conversation was over, the lady said, "I have often wished I was poor; missionaries come and talk to my servants about Christ, but they never speak to me. My pastor calls upon me, but he never speaks about my own religious needs, and I have often wished that I was poor so that someone might speak to me about my soul."

Preparation for a parlor meeting need not be elaborate. The principal thing is to teach those who gather together the great fundamental truths of the Gospel in the power of the Holy Spirit. If there is music, it should be of the very best, but should be spiritual rather than classical. The class of people that you are aiming to reach are quite sated with high-class music, but simple Gospel singing in the power of the Holy Ghost is a novelty to them and will touch their hearts and lead to the conversion of many of them. An attractive singer with a sweet voice, a true knowledge of Christ, a burden for souls, and the power of the Holy Spirit will be greatly used of God.

1. How well do you know your neighbors? House-to-house visitation gives you the opportunity to get to know them spiritually. Develop a plan for how you can adapt the instructions in this lesson for use in your neighborhood (or churchwide in your community).

2. Evaluate how effectively you are currently using your home. What have you done in the last week, month, or year that was clearly intended to be an outreach to the spiritually needy? What aspects of Torrey's advice did you follow? Which advice did you not follow?

3. Identify two or three things that you can do in the next week or month in order to use your house for a cottage meeting or parlor meeting. Contact your local Christian bookstore and ask about evangelistic Bible studies and other tools that you can use in the effort.

CHAPTER EIGHT

CHURCH OUTREACHES

*I*N THIS CHAPTER, TORREY PROVIDES instructions on ministries that are usually conducted in the church building itself. The first is not directly an outreach ministry, but it may be the most important ministry of all. Many North American churches have minimized the role of churchwide prayer meetings in favor of emphasis on small-group Bible studies that include prayer. Torrey calls for the kind of church prayer meeting that brings a wide variety of people together and unites them before the Lord. He has said much about prayer throughout this book, but now gives his attention to the priority of organizing the church to pray. His specific, practical instructions are likely to improve the prayer ministry of nearly every church.

Revival meetings were more common during times when evenings were not consumed by busy schedules and perpetual entertainment via television and the Internet. There is much in this section that will help the local church make a greater impact on its community. Torrey calls for creative intentionality in ministry that mobilizes a church's outreach to be as effective as it can be.

Much of the modern church growth emphasis has been on adults. Although this is admirable, Torrey directs our attention to the tremendous importance of outreach to children. He does not relegate this responsibility to specialized ministries within the church or supported by parachurch organizations, but calls for it to be a priority of the whole church. Torrey uses his own expertise as an educator to introduce principles of effective outreach.

CHURCH
PRAYER
MEETINGS

I. IMPORTANCE AND ADVANTAGES

The prayer meeting ought to be the most important meeting in the church. It is the most important meeting if it is rightly conducted. Of course, the church prayer meeting in many churches is more a matter of form than a center of power. The thing to do in such a case is not to give up the prayer meeting, but to make it what it ought to be. There are five reasons why the church prayer meeting is of vital importance.

A. It brings power into all the life and work of the church.

If there is any real power in the church, it is from God, and God has given it in answer to prayer. The prayer meeting is the real expression of the prayer life of the church. Of course, all the living members of the church are praying in private, but it is in the prayer meeting that they come together and pray as a church. God delights to honor the prayers of the church as a whole (Acts 12:5; 1:14). If the prayer meeting of a church runs down, it is practically certain that all the life of the church will run down, and its work prove a failure as far as accomplishing anything real and lasting for God is concerned.

B. It develops the membership of the church.

In the regular services of the church, but few members of the church are developed; the minister plays the leading role; but in the prayer meeting there is an opportunity for the exercise of gifts on the part of the whole body. Altogether too little stress is laid in modern church life on the development of the gifts of the church. The whole organization is conducted on the idea of the work being done by one man or by a few men. It was not so in early church gatherings. Here the people came together for mutual benefit, and every member of the church was allowed to exercise his gifts (1 Corinthians 14:26). About the only place where this is possible in modern church life is in the prayer meeting. A real prayer meeting is one of the most developmental meetings that we have in our modern churches.

C. It results in many conversions.

If a prayer meeting is conducted as it ought to be, many people will be converted in the prayer meeting. In not a few churches, the presence of the Holy Spirit is much more manifest in the prayer meeting than in any other gathering of the church, and unconverted men and women and children coming in there feel His presence and are convicted of sin and oftentimes converted to Christ. Of course, there is nothing in many prayer meetings to convert anyone, but if a prayer meeting is conducted as it ought to be, conversions may be looked for at every meeting.

> *It might strike some readers as odd that unbelievers are present at prayer meetings. However, it was common in Torrey's day for people who considered themselves to be upright to attend such events. This might be compared to the prayer breakfasts of today. Many notable people who may not be believers will attend these events as an act of piety or because it is socially proper. Yet, if the prayer breakfast is handled appropriately, there can be a very powerful presence of God, and unbelievers may find Christ as Savior.*

D. It promotes the life and fellowship of the church.

In a large church, it is quite impossible for people to get very close to one another in the Sunday services. Everything conspires to prevent it, but in the prayer meeting not only do people get in closer physical contact, but heart touches heart in a way that is unknown in the more formal service. People warm up toward one another and come to understand one another in the prayer meeting as in perhaps no other service. Love is increased and multiplied. There has perhaps never been a time in the history of the church when this was more important than today. People belong to the same church and sit under the same minister and look into one another's faces once a week for years and scarcely know one another's names, but in the prayer meeting people learn to know and to love one another.

E. It promotes the home and foreign mission work of the church.

It is very difficult, and in many cases altogether impossible, to keep up a strong missionary interest without a church prayer meeting. Not only does the prayer meeting afford opportunity for missionary intelligence, but it also affords an opportunity for the many in the church to pour out their hearts in prayer for the missionary work. When Jesus wished to promote a missionary interest among His disciples, He set them to praying for missions (Matthew 9:38; 10:1). If we wish to promote the foreign missionary interest in any church, we must get the church to praying for missions.

II. HOW TO CONDUCT

A. Remember that the meeting is primarily for prayer.

Do not transform it into a lecture course or into a Bible class. It would be going too far to say that the prayer meeting should be only a prayer meeting. There are, of course, times when this should be the case, when the whole hour should be given up to prayer, but this is not wise as a universal rule; but at least it ought to be pre-eminently a prayer meeting. Many of our modern prayer meetings are so only in name. There may be a prayer by the minister at the opening of the meeting, and a prayer by someone else in closing, but the meeting is largely given up to talking, and oftentimes very desultory and unprofitable talking at that. Let prayer be the prominent thing in the prayer meeting. It may be that the major part of the time is not taken up by prayer, but see to it that the Bible comment and the testimony has something to do with prayer and leads naturally to prayer.

B. Draw out all the membership of the church in the prayer meeting.

The prayer meeting is the place for the cultivation of the gifts of the membership of the church. In many churches, it is only the chosen few who exercise their gifts and get the fullest measure of blessing. It will not do to say that every member should take part in every prayer meeting. In a large church this is impossible and, furthermore, it leads to a certain mechanical way of taking part that is unprofitable and vain; but the pastor should see to it that all the membership take part sometimes. If there is any attendant at the prayer meeting who never takes part, make a study of that person and find out what his or her gifts are, and give an opportunity for their exercise. Assign reluctant ones something definite to do; it may be nothing more than to read a verse of Scripture. It is not wise, however, to allow people to be content with simply getting up week after week and quoting some passage of Scripture. It is better to give the person some appropriate verse to study during the week, and then let the person bring some thought that has come to him or her in meditating upon that verse.

C. Assign portions of Scripture to study.

For example, one of the most helpful series of prayer meetings I ever conducted took up the book of Psalms. About seven Psalms were given out each week, and the people were requested to read these Psalms over and over again and then to come to the meeting prepared to give some thought that had come to them in the study of these Psalms. When this request was made, one of the most experienced members of the church went to a public library and got down all the leading commentaries on the Psalms and began to study them. He confessed afterward that he had gotten far greater blessing from the comments made by some of the plainest and most uneducated people in the church than he had gotten from all the commentaries that he had studied. A prominent minister who dropped in during these meetings was so impressed by the interest and power of the meeting that he afterward adopted the same plan in his own church. He said that it gave him an entirely new idea of the possibilities of the prayer meeting.

D. Have a well-chosen list of subjects.

It is not always well to have a list of subjects that is followed week after week in the prayer meeting. It is quite possible to get into a stereotyped and formal way in doing this, but lists of subjects are oftentimes helpful. Usually the best list of subjects is the one you make up for yourself. Get as many lists of subjects as you can for suggestion, and then make your own. Usually it is not wise to have a list of subjects that extends over too long a period. A list of subjects extending over an entire year oftentimes gets to be a great nuisance.

E. Have definite requests for prayer.

There is a discouraging vagueness in the prayers at many prayer meetings. When something definite is presented for the meeting, it goes far to give life to the meeting; the prayers no longer wander all over creation, but aim at a definite object. It is well when the requests for prayer are read to have the people bow their heads in silent prayer. Do not read the requests so rapidly as to make it impossible for each one to be remembered definitely. After a few requests have been read, it is well to have someone lead in prayer, then read others and have someone else lead in prayer, and so on through the list. It is well oftentimes to have the requests made verbally from the audience, but there is a great advantage in having them written out. If people are not interested enough to write the request out, it is doubtful if there is much good in asking for the thing desired; furthermore, if the request is written out, it can be read so that everybody in the room hears it.

F. Have a definite opportunity for thanksgiving and praise.

Thanksgiving should always go hand in hand with prayer. The apostle Paul said, "Be anxious for nothing, but in everything by prayer and supplication, with thanksgiving, let your requests be made known to God" (Philippians 4:6). This is a good rule for the conduct of a prayer meeting. Giving definite thanksgiving and praise for blessings already received will increase our faith in asking for new and larger blessings. There is nothing that seems to promote the presence of the Spirit more than true thanksgiving; indeed a large share of the testimony and the talk in prayer meeting should be along the line of thanksgiving and praise.

G. Make much of music in the prayer meeting.

Of course, the prayer meeting ought not to be a song service, but it should be a service in which there is much song. Everyone should be encouraged to sing. See to it that all do sing. The singing should be in the Spirit, but should also be with the understanding. Dwell on the meaning of the words. Have verses sung over and over until they are sung from the heart. A prayer meeting should be one of the brightest, cheeriest gatherings ever held on earth. If it is made so, there will be no need of urging people to come out to the meeting and scolding them for not coming; they will want to come. It will be the brightest spot in the whole life of the week.

H. Train the people to feel the importance of the prayer meeting.

To do this, it is not necessary to scold people for not attending, but often drop a word that emphasizes the importance of the prayer meeting. Let people know of the good time that you are having. Speak to people personally about coming out. Have people go after them and bring them out, and keep after them until they come. Make the meetings so interesting that when they do come once they will want to come again.

I. Make people feet at home.

About the stiffest thing on earth is a stiff prayer meeting, but if the prayer meeting is made a homey place, people will want to come again and again. It is well to stand at the door to welcome people as they come in, having a smile and pleasant word for all who come. It is not at all necessary that the pastor be at the front of the church during the opening moments of the meeting; oftentimes, more good will be done down by the door.

J. Sometimes make the prayer meeting like a social.

Do not have the people sit down in stiff rows, but have them stand up and move around. Then the meeting can be begun in an informal way, and you are in the midst of the meeting almost before you know it.

K. Always aim at, and look for, conversions in the prayer meeting.

If the prayer meeting is conducted as it ought to be, many unconverted people will come, and the whole atmosphere of the place is such as to prepare people for a personal acceptance of Jesus Christ. There is no place where it is so easy to speak to people about their souls as after a good, warm prayer meeting. Oftentimes, when the opportunity is given for requests for prayer, the question should be put, "Is there not someone here tonight who wishes us to pray that they may be saved tonight?" or some question of that character.

L. Stand at the door and shake hands with people and speak to people as they go out.

There is oftentimes untold good in a hearty handshake. I stood one night at the door of our prayer meeting shaking hands with people as they went out, and a lady said to me, "I have been in Chicago for a long time; I have gone to church again and again, but you are the first Christian that has shaken hands with me."

I believe another said that the only reason she went to prayer meeting was to get a good handshake.

M. Make the prayer meeting a matter of prayer.

Ask God to teach you how to conduct the prayer meeting and make it what it ought to be. Ask God definitely to bless every prayer meeting that you conduct or attend; do it expectantly. Always go to the prayer meeting expecting that you are going to have a good time. I always do and am never disappointed.

N. Make the prayer meeting a matter of study.

Do not make it so much a study as to what you will say, but as to how it can be improved. Avoid getting into ruts. It is not well to keep in a rut even if it is a good rut.

III. SOME SUGGESTIONS

A. Don't take up all the time yourself.

The prayer meeting is not so much your meeting as the meeting of the whole church. You have your opportunity to air your views on the Lord's Day; be fair and give the other people an opportunity on the prayer meeting evening.

B. Don't let anyone else take up all the time.

There is liable to be in every community a prayer-meeting killer. This person is given to making long prayers or long speeches that are as stale as they are long. Everybody looks blue as soon as he or she gets up to speak. This must not be permitted, but just how can it be stopped? First of all, look to God to give you wisdom; in the second place, don't lose your temper; in the third place, watch for your opportunity. Something will be said that will enable you to break in with a remark; then ask somebody else his opinion, and someone else hers, and then propose a song. Sometimes it will be necessary to say to the member, publicly and plainly, but kindly, that you are glad for a heart that is so full, but the time is getting very short and there are many who want to speak. Sometimes it will be wisest to go privately and explain that it is not wise for one person to take up so much time in the meeting. If you have tact, you can generally do this without hurting feelings, but at any cost it must be stopped.

C. Don't begin late.

If a prayer meeting is announced to begin at a certain hour, begin at the very tick of the clock. This encourages more people to attend than most people suspect.

D. Don't run over time.

If the prayer meeting is announced to close at a certain time, close at that time. It may be wise to have a second prayer meeting, but close the meeting at the time announced.

E. Don't let the meeting drag.

If it begins to drag, ask someone a question that will draw him out, or say something yourself that will set other people to thinking and talking. Oftentimes, the best thing to do is to propose a season of silent prayer, but do not urge people to "fill up the time." That leads to unprofitable talking. People ought not to speak merely to fill up time; they ought not to speak unless they have something to say that is worth listening to. Far better a season of silent prayer than a season of vain talking.

Sometimes it is well to bring the meeting to a close before the announced hour comes. Some leaders make the mistake of thinking that it is necessary to carry the meeting through to the announced hour, no matter how it drags.

F. Don't have bad air.

The air in the room has more to do with the excellence or dullness of the meeting than most people suspect.

G. Don't be stereotyped.

The fact that a prayer meeting conducted in a certain way was a good prayer meeting does not prove that every prayer meeting should be conducted in just that way. It is well to do unexpected things; it wakes people up; but be sure that you do not do foolish things in your desire to do unexpected things.

REVIVAL MEETINGS

BY REVIVAL MEETINGS WE MEAN consecutive meetings, day after day and night after night, for the quickening of the life and activity of the church and for the salvation of the lost. We speak of them as revival meetings because such meetings result from new life either in individuals or in the church as a whole and, if properly conducted, always result in the impartation of new life to the church and the salvation of the lost.

I. IMPORTANCE AND ADVANTAGES

The importance of revival services can scarcely be overestimated. There are those who say that we ought not to have special revival meetings, but should have a revival in the church all the time. It is true that there should be a revival in the church all the time. There was a continuous revival in the apostolic church; there are churches that have a continuous revival in these days; but it is almost always the case that the churches that have a continuous revival are those that believe in and make use of special revival services and what are known as "revival methods."

A. Repeated and consecutive impression can bring people to Christ.

An unsaved person hears a sermon on Sunday evening. An impression is made by the truth heard, but the impression has not been profound enough to lead to acceptance of Jesus Christ then and there. Before the next regular preaching service of the church comes, the impression has faded away, and an entirely new impression has to be made. If the Sunday evening sermon had been followed up by another on Monday evening, the impression of Sunday evening would have been deepened; if that had been followed by still another sermon on Tuesday evening, the impression would have been made deeper still, and very likely before the week was over the person would have been converted. Only those who have made a careful and prolonged study of this matter can realize how important in the work of bringing people to Christ is the element of repeated and consecutive impression. Folks who have attended church for years, and who have been only superficially impressed, are oftentimes readily brought to Christ in a series of consecutive services.

B. If properly conducted, there will be an unusual amount of prayer and unaccustomed earnestness in prayer.

Someone may say that Christians ought always to pray, and so they should, but we have to take the people as they are. As a matter of fact, the average Christian does far more praying in a time of special revival services than he does at any other time. The professed Christians who spend as much time as they ought in regular prayer day by day, when there is no special effort being made for the salvation of the lost, are very rare indeed.

C. At such times, Christians put forth special efforts for the salvation of the lost.

Every Christian should do everything in his or her power every day of life to lead people to Christ, but in point of fact very few Christians do this. How often those who are cold and indifferent, and do almost nothing at all for the salvation of the lost under ordinary circumstances, will display a great activity at the time of special services, and not seldom those who have never been known as workers before not only take hold of the work during special meetings, but continue it after the meetings are over.

D. Revival services awaken an unusual interest in the subject of religion in the community.

The outside world is aroused to the fact that the church exists and that there is such a thing as religion. They begin to think about God, Christ, the Bible, eternity, heaven, and hell. People who are never seen in the house of God at any other time in the year will flock there during revival meetings. Many of them will be converted, and others will become attendants at the church. They find out what the church has to offer and suddenly wake up to the fact that what the church has to offer is just what they need.

E. As a matter of experience and history, revivals have been greatly honored of God.

This is true in the history of the church as a whole and also in the history of local churches. The church of Christ has been saved, humanly speaking, from utter ruin by the revivals that God has graciously sent from time to time in its history. As regards local churches, the churches that have grown and prospered are those that have believed in and made use of revivals. Study the yearbooks of the various denominations, and you will find that the ministers who have believed in revivals and have fostered them in their churches are the ones who have been able to report from year to year accessions to their churches and gifts to the various branches of Christian activity. On the other hand, it will be found as a rule—an almost universal rule—that the ministers who have disrespected revivals have had their churches run down on their hands. If there is anything that the history of the church of Jesus Christ absolutely demonstrates, it is the tremendous importance, if not the imperative necessity, of revivals.

II. TIME TO HOLD REVIVAL MEETINGS

When shall revival meetings be held in a church or community?

A. When there are indications of special blessing

An alert pastor who keeps in touch with the people and the community will often be able to detect signs of special interest and blessing. There will be a new interest in preaching on the part of the congregation. There will be a new sense of liberty and power in preaching. There will be tears in the eyes of the congregation during preaching about sin and its consequences. People will come for spiritual counsel and to be shown the way of life. Perhaps members of this church who are more spiritually alert will say that they think there are signs of blessing in the church or community. All these things are indications that God is ready to favor that church or community with an especial outpouring of His Spirit, and arrangements should be made at once to take advantage of these favorable conditions—and to gather a harvest of souls—by holding special revival services.

B. When there is spiritual dearth in the community and church

When the Gospel seems to have lost its hold upon the people, when the congregations are constantly declining and conversions are few, when iniquity and unbelief are rampant in the community, such a time is also an important one. Special effort should be put forth to arouse the church and to save the perishing. God has promised His special blessing at such a time. He has said, "When the enemy comes in like a flood, the Spirit of the Lord will lift up a standard against him" (Isaiah 59:19). When everything goes hard in a church, and unbelief and irreligion and immorality seem to triumph, the minister whose trust is fixed upon God and in His Word need not become discouraged. Let the preacher cry to God with a new earnestness and faith and then go to work to bring about the conditions upon which God is always ready to bless His people.

C. In every church every year

This is entirely feasible. The writer of this book has been the pastor of four different churches, all quite different from one another: a village church with the usual village congregation and environment, a young suburban church in a large city, a church just organized for the masses in the heart of a large city, and an established metropolitan church with a large and varied membership. In each of these churches, he found it quite possible to have special revival meetings every year. Largely as a result of these special revival meetings, each of these churches had what could probably justly be termed a continual revival, there being accessions to the church at every communion. Many other pastors ministering to churches of still different varieties from these here described testify to the same experience.

As to the time in the year when these services can most wisely be held, this depends upon local conditions. It seems to be the experience of most pastors that the especially favorable time is the week of prayer and the weeks immediately following. People expect something to be done at that time, and to a certain extent are ready for it. There is, however, a growing tendency to begin these meetings during Easter week or earlier in Lent. This is an especially favorable time in large cities on account of the Roman Catholic and Episcopalian element. In large cities the social life is at an ebb at that time. Even the theaters take this fact into consideration. While we may not personally believe in observing times and seasons and days, we ought not to lose sight of the fact that other people do believe in it, and we should take advantage of this fact as giving us an especially good opportunity of getting hold of people and getting them out to hear the Word of God.

III. HOW TO ORGANIZE AND CONDUCT A REVIVAL MEETING

A. Send a letter to church members.

When it has been decided that the time has come to hold special services, a letter should be addressed to every member of the church, stating the plans and requesting their interest and prayer and cooperation in every way.

It is sometimes well, in connection with this letter, to give every member of the church some book to read that will stir them up to self-examination, to prayer, and to effort. A book largely used by some evangelists and many pastors for this purpose is the book *How to Pray*, by the author. It can be secured in paper cover for this purpose at a very low price. In the letter there should be a request that each member should answer it, pledging themselves not only to read the book that is sent, but also to prayer and cooperation in the work. The members of the church who have been absenting themselves from the church service or from the prayer meeting should be visited personally and dealt with gently, but earnestly, and led to realize their responsibility to Christ and His church, and also their responsibility regarding the unsaved in the community.

B. Meetings for united prayer should at once be begun.

Sometimes it is wisest to hold these at the central church, but oftentimes—especially when the membership of the church is very much scattered—it is better to have cottage meetings at first in the various neighborhoods of the parish. These separate cottage meetings can afterward be brought together for a united meeting at the church. If the revival services are to be of a union character, it is well for each church to begin prayer meetings by itself and for them afterward to come together for union prayer meetings. There short addresses should be given upon the importance of prayer and how to pray, but the major part of the meeting should be devoted directly to prayer. The people should be instructed as to what they should pray for; they should be drawn out in prayer for the membership of the church, then in prayer for the unsaved—and not merely for the unsaved in general, but for specific persons in whom they are interested. Their duty to uphold the hands of the pastor in prayer should be emphasized; they should be instructed as to the lines along which they should seek God's help for the pastor—personal life, selection of topics to preach upon, preparation of sermons, and especially that the preaching may be in demonstration of the Spirit and of power (1 Corinthians 2:4; Ephesians 6:19). They should be encouraged to pray for a special outpouring of the Holy Spirit in the community. Oftentimes, it is important to get them to take a higher outlook than the needs of their own local community, and to pray for a general outpouring of the Spirit throughout the world.

C. In the next place, a canvass of the entire community should be undertaken.

The whole village or city or section of the city should be carefully mapped out, different districts assigned to different workers, and every house and store in the community visited. Those visited should be informed of the meetings that are to be held, but more important than this, as far as possible, they should be dealt with and prayed with personally in regard to their salvation. If the services are to be of a union character, the visitors should go out two and two, each one representing a different church in the community.

D. After this preliminary work has been done, meetings should be announced at the church.

The number of meetings to be held each day will depend very much upon the location and the interest. In many places it will be possible to hold only an evening meeting at first. In other places the meetings can be begun with as many as three or four meetings a day, for what may be best in this line in one place is utterly impossible in another. The ideal is a meeting for prayer, a meeting for the study of the Bible on the part of believers, and an evening evangelistic service for the unsaved, with possibly a fourth meeting for children; but this ideal is not attainable in every community. Where it is not, there should at least be, in addition to the evening meeting, a gathering for prayer. It may be held for prayer and prayer alone, or it may be wiser to have a meeting in the afternoon, part of the time being given to prayer and part to the study of the Word of God.

One great reason why our modern evangelistic movements have lacked the old-time power is because the emphasis is not laid upon the prayer meeting that was in former days. In the great revival of 1857, more time and strength was put into prayer meetings than into anything else. In many places the meetings were entirely prayer meetings. We have swung to the other extreme, and in many cases evangelistic meetings are entirely meetings for preaching and singing. This is a great mistake. Wherever the church becomes lax in united prayer, the meetings will soon lose in power and come to a close as far as any real results are concerned.

The question often rises whether it is wiser to hold the meetings at a church or in a hall. This will depend somewhat upon circumstances. Each method has its advantages. Doubtless many people can be gotten out to a hall or to an opera house who will not enter a church; on the other hand, if people are gotten out to church and converted there, they will be more likely to remain in the church after the special meetings are over than if the meetings are held in a hall or an opera house. The wisest plan in many instances is to begin the meetings in a church and then go to a hall or opera house, and then back to the church before they close, in order that those who have been interested in the opera house may be accustomed to an interest in the church before the special interest is over.

As to whether the meetings are held in a church or hall, oftentimes, too, is dependent upon whether they are meetings of an individual church or a union of several churches. Here again there are advantages in each plan. There is likely to be more harmony and united effort and less controversy and suspicion if the meetings are held by an individual church. On the other hand, there can be no doubt that a community is moved by a union of all the churches in it, as it is not moved and cannot be moved by revival services held by an individual church. If revival services are held in the summer, oftentimes it is well to hold them in a tent.

E. The children should never be forgotten in times of special interest.

Special meetings for the children should be held. As a rule, they should be held in the afternoon just at the time the school is closing, so that children can go directly from school to the meeting. They should be held at least five afternoons in the week. More about these children's meetings will be said in the chapter upon children's meetings.

F. Of course the preaching is of very great importance in the conduct of revival services.

1. *Who should preach?*

The first question that arises is who should do the preaching. Wherever it is possible, it is well for the pastor of the church to do the preaching himself. It is said that some pastors do not have the evangelistic gift, and this is doubtless in a measure true, but most pastors can, to some extent, cultivate the evangelistic gift if they only will. There is a great advantage in the pastor himself preaching. There is not such a likelihood that the interest shall suddenly die out when the special services are over. When it is not possible for the local pastor to do the preaching, call in the help of some neighboring pastor who does possess the evangelistic gift.

Even when the pastor is an evangelist, there is an advantage in calling in a fellow pastor for a special series of meetings. It is good to hear a new voice and preaching the truth from another standpoint from that to which people have become accustomed. Many will go out of curiosity who might not attend special services conducted by the pastor. But we cannot depend altogether upon the local pastor or upon fellow pastors. It is by the ordination of God that there are evangelists in the church, and evangelists as a class have been greatly honored of God in the past history of the church. However clear it is that the pastor is possessed of the evangelistic gift, and however much God may have used the messages in leading the unsaved to Christ, it is good occasionally to call for help from someone God has especially appointed to the work of an evangelist. Of course, there are evangelists and evangelists. Some evangelists are mere adventurers; others are indiscreet and do much harm, but there are beyond question many whom God has called to this specific work, and whom He wants in it; and there are indications that God is going to multiply the number of really reliable ministers who are in evangelistic work.

2. What to preach?

What shall we preach in times of revival interest? (1) First of all, we should preach the Gospel, the Gospel that Christ died for our sins according to the Scriptures, was buried, and rose again. We should never get far from the Cross. We should preach the Atonement over and over and over again. (2) We should also preach the utterly lost and ruined condition of man. (3) We should preach the bitter consequences of sin here and hereafter. We should declare the whole counsel of God regarding the judgment and regarding hell. (4) We should present the truth about conversion, regeneration, and justification. (5) We should preach the divinity of Christ. There is great correcting and converting and saving power in that doctrine (Acts 2:36–37; 9:20, 22; John 20:31). (6) We should also preach to Christians about the Holy Spirit and His work, prayer, the power of the Word of God, and the necessity of Bible study. One will find much instruction in regard to what to preach at such a time from the sermons of such preachers as Moody, Spurgeon, and Finney. A study of the texts given in the first division of this volume in connection with the different classes with whom we have to deal in personal work will suggest many texts and topics for sermons.

G. In revival services the music is of great importance.

If possible, there should be a large choir of converted men and women. They should have the leadership of a godly chorister who not only knows how to sing, but who can get others to sing. If there are in the community, or if there can be secured, men or women who can sing Gospel solos effectively in the power of the Holy Spirit, their services should be obtained. Impress upon the singers that they are to sing not merely to interest the people, but to convert them, and that they need a definite anointing of the Holy Spirit for their work.

H. The testimony of saved people to the power and blessing of the Gospel is of great value in special revival services.

Especially is the testimony of those recently converted effective. When folks hear one who has recently come out from their ranks tell of what Jesus Christ has done, a longing is awakened in their hearts to find the same Savior.

I. A noon meeting can be held for businesspeople.

When the meetings are held in a city of considerable size, it is well to have a noon meeting to which those in business and others are invited.

Many can be gotten hold of in this way that can be reached in no other way. It is well, usually, in a series of special services to hold meetings for men alone in which sin is very plainly dealt with and Christ as the remedy for sin presented. Meetings for women are also desirable. As a rule, they should be conducted by women, though there are some men who seem to have a special gift in preaching to women. Generally, however, the men who are most inclined to take such meetings are least qualified to do it.

J. Classes to train the workers in how to deal with inquirers are of the highest importance.

Oftentimes, it is well to hold these training classes before the general meetings begin, so that from the very first meeting you can have workers whom you may depend upon to do the work.

K. Every general meeting should be followed by an after meeting.

Definite instructions as to the conduct of after meetings will be given in a separate chapter.

L. All the Christian people in the community should be set to work.

They should be so aroused upon the subject of religion that all they will talk about everywhere is Christ and His claims. They should be encouraged to go from house to house and store to store laboring with people and endeavoring to get them to accept Christ. Harm may be done in this way by indiscreet workers, but the harm that is done will be small indeed in comparison with the good that is accomplished.

M. It is very important to make use of good religious literature in times of special interest.

Tracts and books should be generously used.

CHILDREN'S MEETINGS

I. IMPORTANCE

No form of special meetings are of more importance than those that are intended for the purpose of reaching the children, bringing them to Christ, and building them up in Christ. They are important for many reasons.

A. The conversion of children is important.

The conversion of the children to Christ is a matter of the very first importance.

1. *The conversion of a child is important in the first place because children oftentimes die.*

Most people in Chicago die in childhood. For everyone who dies between twenty and forty, there are many who die between birth and twenty. So with very many of the children at any time upon the earth, they must be converted in childhood or pass into eternity unconverted. In spite of the large number of children's caskets that pass us in hearses, it is hard to bring people to realize how likely children are to die. We look at the white-haired man and say he is likely to die soon, but we look at the little child and think that child has many years before it. That is not at all sure. We have very rude awakenings from this dream. Mothers and fathers, do you realize that your children may die? Up quick, then, and lead them to Christ before that day comes. If you do not, it will be the darkest day you ever knew, but if you have led them to Christ it will not be a dark day. Lonely it will be, but not dark. Nay, it will be glorious with the thought that the voyage is over and the glory land reached quickly by one you love. Sunday school teachers, do you realize that any one of the boys or girls in the class you teach may die any day? Up, then, and win them to Christ as speedily as you may.

⌐◡ Although child mortality rates in North America have declined greatly since Torrey's day, the need remains great. There are still many children in poor urban and rural areas who are in mortal danger. Further, the need in other parts of the world is even more grave than Torrey describes here in America one hundred years ago. The devastation of AIDS in Africa and its ravaging impact on children is one dramatic example. But Torrey's point about taking advantage of the opportunities that you have is true even if children don't die. They might move away or be impacted negatively by many sorts of influences. It is crucial that we deal with children in an urgent way today that takes seriously the eternal consequences and the possibility that we may not have an opportunity tomorrow.

2. *The conversion of children is important, in the second place, because it is much easier to win a child to Christ than an adult.*

Dr. E. N. Kirk once said: "If I could live my life over again, I would labor much more among children." Children have no old prejudices to overcome as many grown people have. With the help of the Holy Spirit, they are easily led to feel the great love of Christ in giving Himself to die for them, and when the simple story of His suffering and death is read and explained from God's Word, they believe it and exercise saving faith, and there and then the Holy Spirit effects a change of heart. Mr. Spurgeon once said: "I could spend days in giving details of young children whom I have known and personally conversed with, who have given evidence of a change of heart," and he added,

I have more confidence in the spiritual life of such children whom I have taken into my church, than I have in the spiritual condition of adults thus received. I will go further and say that I have usually found a clearer knowledge of the Gospel and a warmer love toward Christ in the child convert than in the man convert. I may astonish you by saying that I have sometimes met with a deeper spiritual experience in a child of ten or twelve than in some persons of fifty or sixty. I have known a child who would weep himself to sleep by the month together under a crushing sense of sin. If you would know deep and bitter and awful fear of the wrath of God, let me tell you what I felt as a boy. If you want to know what faith in Christ is, you must not look to those who have been bemuddled by the heretical jargon of the times, but to the dear children who have taken Jesus at His word, and believed on Him, and therefore know and are sure that they are saved.

Every year that passes over our heads unconverted, our hearts are less open to holy impressions. Every year away from Christ, our hearts become harder in sin. That needs no proof. The practice of sin increases the power of sin in our lives. God and heaven and Christ and holiness lie very near childhood, but if the child remains away from Christ, every year he becomes farther and farther away. When I see a child walk into the inquiry room on a Sunday evening, I feel quite certain that if a worker of any sense gets hold of that child, he or she is going to be converted; but when I see a man or a woman walk in there, I do not feel at all as sure. The adult has become so entangled in sin; the mind has become so darkened by the error and skepticism that arise out of sin; there are so many complications added by each year, that the case of an adult is very difficult as compared with that of a child. The fact is that, with very many, if they are not converted in childhood, they will never be converted at all. Fathers and mothers, that is true of the children in our homes. Sunday school teachers, that is true of the children in your Sunday school classes. It is now or never.

3. *The conversion of the children is important, in the third place, because converted children are among the most useful workers for Christ.*

They can reach persons who are inaccessible to everyone else. They can reach their schoolmates and playmates, the Jewish children, the Catholic children, the children of worldly parents and unbelievers. They can bring them to Sunday school or to children's meetings and to Christ. You and I cannot get close enough to them to show them how beautiful Jesus is and what joy and blessing He brings. They can. Then they can reach their parents oftentimes when we cannot. The parents will not listen to us, but they will to their children.

There was a rough, drunken gambler in Minneapolis, Minnesota. He often went by the mission door, but when a worker invited him in, he repelled him with rude insults. But his child, about ten years old, was gotten into the Sunday school and won for Christ. Then she began to work and pray for her drunken papa, and a cottage meeting was at last held in his wretched home. The father took down his overcoat to go to the saloon. Little Annie asked him if he would not stay to the meeting. He roughly answered, "No." "Won't you stay for my sake, Papa?" The man hung up his coat. The meeting began, and the man was surly and wished he was out of it. They knelt in prayer while he sat on the end of the sofa. One after another prayed. Then all were silent. Then Annie's little voice was heard in prayer something like this: "God, save my papa." It broke the wicked man's heart, and then and there he accepted Christ. He afterward became a deacon in my church. When New Year's Day came and many had testified for Christ, Annie arose and said: "Papa is a Christian now, and Mamma is a Christian now, and Grandpa is a Christian now, and Grandma is a Christian now, and Uncle Joe is a Christian now, and Auntie is a Christian now. I guess we are all Christians down to our house now." But the little girl herself led the way. Wasn't the conversion of that child important? Many a hardened sinner and many a skeptic has been led to Christ by a child.

4. *The conversion of children is important because persons converted in childhood make the best Christians.*

If one is converted when old, there are many bad tricks of character and life that have to be unlearned, and it is generally a pretty slow process. But when one is converted in childhood character is yet to be formed, and it can be formed from the beginning on right lines. If you wish to train a tree into a thing of beauty and symmetry, you had better begin when it is young. If you want to form a character of Christlike symmetry and beauty, you would better begin in childhood. That Christlike man of the olden time, Polycarp, who ended his life as a martyr at ninety-five, was converted at nine. That fine young man of the New Testament, Timothy, was brought up on Scripture from a babe. I rejoice with all my heart when an old broken-down drunkard is brought to Christ. It means so much. But it means so much more when a child is brought to Christ.

5. *The conversion of children is important, once more, because there are so many years of possible service before them.*

If one is to live to eighty, say, if converted at seventy there is a soul saved plus ten years of service. When the boy Polycarp was converted, there was a soul saved plus eighty-six years of service. I think enough has been said to show that the conversion of the children is tremendously important, in fact, the most important business the church has on hand. Surely it was well that Jesus said, "Take heed that you do not despise one of these little ones."

B. Many children will be brought to Christ in special meetings held in their interest who will not be reached in any other way.

It is a well-proven fact that no other kind of meetings brings such definite results in the way of conversions as meetings held for the specific purpose of bringing the children to Christ.

II. WHEN TO HOLD CHILDREN'S MEETINGS

A. In seasons of special revival interest

No revival is what it ought to be if a great deal of attention is not given to the children and much prayerful effort put forth for their conversion. Whatever other meetings are held or omitted in times of special revival interest, meetings for children should not be omitted under any circumstances. Every pastor and evangelist should lay to heart the warning of our Master, "Take heed that you do not despise one of these little ones" (Matthew 18:10).

B. At summer conferences

At many summer conferences, a great deal of attention is given to the children, with the most encouraging results. At other summer conferences, the children are almost altogether neglected.

C. At summer resorts

Children are found in great numbers at summer resorts. Oftentimes they have but little to do. It is frequently a rare opportunity to win them to Christ if wisely conducted meetings are held for their benefit. In England the services that are held upon the beach in summer have yielded remarkably encouraging results. The children gather there in great numbers.

D. Regularly every week

About all that the average church does for the children is to have the Sabbath school services and perhaps the junior Endeavor meeting. This is not enough. There should be regular evangelistic services held for the children every week, especially in our city churches. In Newman Hall's church in London, a children's meeting was begun that was conducted for many years every week. It began in the special revival services for children held by E. P. Hammond in London years ago. At one of these regular weekly children's meetings, I was told that a large share of the best workers in the church at that time had been originally converted during the revival services for children, and I saw from personal observation deep interest among the children still, and many were being constantly led to Christ.

III. HOW TO CONDUCT CHILDREN'S MEETINGS

A. The first matter of importance is the arrangement of the children when they reach the appointed place of meeting.

They should not be allowed to huddle together at will but, as they come in the door, should be met by competent ushers and seated in classes of four or five with experienced Christian workers at the end of each class. There should first be a class of boys, then a class of girls. This will do very much toward preventing disorder during the meeting. The object of having a teacher at the end of the class is not merely to keep order, but that the teacher may deal personally with the children at the close of the service.

B. Great care should be bestowed upon the singing.

There should be a great deal of singing, for children love it, and the hymns should be bright and cheerful, and of a character that the children can understand. They should be taught the hymns verse by verse, and the meaning of the words of the hymn should be explained. Hymns setting forth God's love and the atoning death of Christ should be especially used. Children enjoy singing the same verse over and over again, more and more heartily, under the conduct of an enthusiastic leader. In this way the truth is deeply impressed upon the heart, and will probably never be forgotten. A priest once said to a lady manager of an orphan asylum in Brooklyn that they did not object to the religious lessons that they gave the children, but they did object to the hymns they taught them. "For," said he, "when once they have learned one of those hymns, it is very difficult for us to get them to forget it."

C. Prayer is very important in the children's meeting.

The prayer should be of such a character that the children can understand exactly what is meant, and there should often be prayers in which the children follow the leader sentence by sentence as he prays. This, of course, should not be done formally, but the children should be taught the meaning of the prayer and to offer it from the heart. It is necessary to teach children the purpose of prayer and to insist upon absolute attention and reverence while it is being offered.

D. There should be a Gospel sermon that the children can understand.

This sermon may contain some of the profoundest truths of the Gospel, but these truths should be expressed in words of which the children know the meaning.

1. *The sermon should be short; children were not made to sit still.*

A wise woman worker once said, "A boy has five hundred muscles to wriggle with, and not one to sit still with." There are a few rare men and women who can hold the attention of children for half an hour, or even an hour, I have seen it done; but for the average speaker to attempt to hold the attention of children more than fifteen or twenty minutes is positive cruelty.

2. *The sermon should be simple.*

This does not mean that it should be foolish, but the statements should be of such a character that the child takes in their meaning at once. There should be no long or involved sentences; there should be no complicated figures of speech. But one who would preach to children must be very careful about his illustrations. If some of our speakers to children should question their audiences afterwards as to what they had said, they would be astonished at the remarkable idea that the children had gained. One should be very careful to find out that the children really understand what he has said.

3. *The sermon should be full of illustrations.*

We do not mean that it should be nothing but a collection of stories; it should be a definite presentation of important truth with clearly stated points, but each one of these points should be illustrated so as to hold the attention of the child and fix it in his or her mind.

4. *The sermon should emphasize the following great and fundamental truths:*

a. *That all adults and all children are sinners, real sinners*

Some people think of children as if they were angels; they are not, but sinners in the presence of a holy God, and in their inmost heart they know this themselves. I do not know that I have ever seen deeper conviction than that which the Holy Spirit has awakened in the heart of a child.

b. That Jesus died in our place

The most successful preachers to children are those who focus on the doctrine of substitution. This truth should be illustrated over and over again in a great variety of ways. It is wonderful how children, whose minds haven't been corrupted by the errors of the day, grasp the great, saving doctrine of the Atonement.

c. The need of a new heart

Regeneration is a big word, and a child will not understand it, but a child can understand what is meant by a new heart. Of course this will need explanation. I once asked a boy if he was saved, and he replied that he was. I asked him if he knew that he was, and he said he did. I asked him how he knew it, and he said because he had had a change of heart. I asked him how he knew he had had a change of heart. He said, "The other night when I was praying I felt a pain here" (placing his hand over his stomach). The boy had heard about a change of heart, and really thought that it was the change of the location of the heart from one part of the body to another, and that the pain he felt while praying was occasioned by this change in the location of his heart. The boy really had received a new heart, as he showed by years of devoted and active Christian service, but he had not understood the language used by those who spoke to him.

> ⟶⌒ *One must always be sensitive to what children understand. It is very easy to use terms that can be misunderstood. For a catalog of some excellent resources to help you to communicate effectively in accordance with what children are able to understand, write Child Evangelism Fellowship, P.O. Box 348, Warrenton, MO 63383.*

d. That a new heart is God's gift in Jesus Christ

E. At the close of the service, the children should be given an opportunity to decide for Christ.

This opportunity may be given by having them stand, or hold up their hands, or in any other way the evangelist thinks wise; but every experienced worker knows that children go in crowds, and that if one child stands up other children are likely to follow, and one cannot safely take it for granted that every child who stands up knows what he is doing. It is well that the call for an expression be preceded by a season of silent prayer and a very careful explanation made to the children what you propose to do and what you want them to do. After a time of silent prayer, and also an explanation of what you want them to do in the time of silent prayer (never forget that children have to be taught line upon line, precept upon precept), go over your instructions again and again in different ways until you are satisfied that you are understood.

F. After the expression of a desire to become a Christian, there should be prayer for the children and prayer in which the children who have taken the stand are instructed to follow.

G. When you are through dealing with the children in a body, have each teacher deal with her own class individually, making as clear as possible the way of life and finding out definitely whether each child has accepted Christ or will accept Christ.

Each child who professes to accept Christ should be prayed with individually.

H. Use children's tracts.

Tracts can be secured with attractive covers that the children will like to get. Be sure that the tracts contain the Gospel. Oftentimes, it is well to read the tract to the children and preach upon it before you give it out, and then have them take the tract home to fix the sermon in their minds.

I. Many find the blackboard very useful in children's meetings.

Children are oftentimes more easily reached through the eye than through the ear, and words or sentences written upon the board are more deeply impressed upon their hearts than those that are merely uttered to them. A few people have the gift of drawing well, but one can use the blackboard to advantage who cannot draw at all. Children are gifted with imagination, and if you tell them what your pictures are, they will understand, and it will do the work.

Blackboards and chalk are now less popular than "whiteboards" with markers.

J. Objects that the children can touch or even handle are very useful as illustrating the truth.

A person of any ingenuity can draw many lessons from a few candles and a tumbler of water, a magnet, and other objects that are easily secured. There are good books upon object teaching for children.

K. The use of the Stereopticon will always draw a crowd of children.

Children never tire of Stereopticon pictures. If you can get children without the Stereopticon, there will oftentimes be better results, for sometimes the children will be too much taken up with the pictures; but if you cannot get the children without using it, get the Stereopticon. A bright little girl whose father uses a Stereopticon a great deal was taken to a meeting for children where it was used. After a time she exclaimed, "I wish Papa would show us more pictures and talk less." Nevertheless, Stereopticon services are oftentimes followed with abundant results in the conversion of children as well as adults.

The Stereopticon was a mechanism that provided vivid projection of images, something like a cross between two modern slide projectors and a Viewmaster.

L. Be sure and bear in mind the purposes for which children's meetings are held.

They are not held simply for the sake of amusing children. It is a poor use of time simply to amuse people. They are held, first, to convert the children, to lead them to a personal acceptance of Jesus Christ as their Savior, to surrender themselves to Him as their Lord and Master, and to confess Him as their Lord before the world. Second, they are held in order that the children may be instructed in true Christian living, and in the fundamental truths of the Gospel.

M. If the work among the children is to be really successful and produce permanent results, our dependence must be upon Bible truth, preached, or sung, or personally taught in the power of the Holy Spirit.

LEARNING ACTIVITIES

1. In reviewing the lesson on prayer, it would be good to evaluate your own prayer life and the place of prayer in your church. Where is it strong? Where does it need improvement? Identify two or three specific things that can be gleaned from this lesson in order to improve your prayer life (or the place of prayer in your church).

2. Pause right now and spend several minutes in prayer. If you are studying with others, devote a long season to prayer. Ask the Lord to be preparing those He has for you to reach. Ask Him to bless the efforts that you have already made in personal work. Ask Him to shape you and use you for most effective service.

3. Identify what big events could take place in your church that would draw your community's attention to the Lord. What terms, in addition to revival, would you use to label the events? What are the aspects of a revival that you would want to make sure were present in your events?

4. Rate your personal work from 1 to 10 in terms of its priority on outreach to children. Rate your church also. What could you do to help improve the rating by one point, especially if the rating is very low?

5. Ask the pastor and a few other leaders in your church about the place of ministry to children in your church. How do they rate the church? What do they think could be done to improve? How do they think that you could help it improve?

CHAPTER NINE

PORTABLE OUTREACHES

THIS CHAPTER ADDRESSES outreach ministries that are portable. The most portable is the use of tracts. Most people are familiar with tracts, but Torrey takes their emphasis to a high level. He doesn't just encourage you to distribute randomly a "collection" of tracts; he challenges you to minister carefully with a "selection" of tracts. He even suggests that you keep tracts in other languages if you know that you will encounter people who speak other languages.

Other portable tools for ministry are tents and gospel wagons, both of which build on the principles regarding open-air work. Open-air meetings are the most flexible sorts of meetings since they can be held nearly anywhere, subject to legal and wise choices of location. Although not common today, Torrey provides fascinating stories of how open-air meetings have been used with great results. Of course, open-air, tent, and gospel wagon ministries are not for the faint of heart. Instructions in these lessons make clear the obstacles that one is likely to face. It takes tremendous commitment, abilities, and dependence on God to take on these ministries.

The technical descriptions of tents and gospel wagons are significantly outdated, but the principles that are clear in these descriptions allow the contemporary Christian worker to make adjustments for use of modern inventions. Better material for tents and various types of automobiles have given us even more potential for effective portable ministry. Many churches in the South often still make use of tent meetings.

Moody Press was founded as the Bible Institute Colportage Association. We have included many references to it in order to maintain the emphasis of Torrey. However, there are now many sources of materials that can be used in this manner, including numerous books by Moody Press. There may not be as many opportunities to earn a living selling books these days, but the principle of making accessible quality reading materials is still relevant. It is possible to make an arrangement with a local bookstore or mail-order book distributor to sell their books in your ministry at a discounted price.

THE USE OF TRACTS

COMPARATIVELY FEW CHRISTIANS realize the importance of tract work. I had been a Christian a good many years, and a minister of the Gospel several years, before it ever entered my head that tracts were of much value in Christian work. I had somehow grown up with the notion that tracts were all rubbish, and therefore I did not take the trouble to read them, and far less did I take the trouble to circulate them, but I found out that I was entirely wrong. Tract work has some great advantages over other forms of Christian work.

I. IMPORTANCE AND ADVANTAGES

A. Any person can do it.

We cannot all preach; we cannot all conduct meetings; but we can all select useful tracts and then hand them out to others. Of course, some of us can do it better than others. Even a blind person or someone who cannot speak is able to do tract work. It is a line of work in which every man, woman, and child can engage.

B. A tract always sticks to the point.

I wish every worker did that, but how often we get talking to someone and are gotten off onto a side track.

C. A tract never loses its temper.

Perhaps you sometimes do. I have known Christian workers, even workers of experience, who would sometimes get all stirred up, but you cannot stir up a tract. It always remains calm.

D. Oftentimes, people who are too proud to be talked with will read a tract when no one is looking.

There are many who would repulse you if you tried to speak to them about their souls who will read a tract if you leave it on a table or in some other place where they might come upon it spontaneously.

E. A tract stays close.

You talk to people and then they go away, but tracts stay with them. Some years ago, a man came into a mission in New York. One of the workers tried to talk with him, but he would not listen. As he was leaving, a card tract was placed in his hands that said, "If I should die tonight I would go to _____. Please fill out and sign." He put it in his pocket, went to his steamer ship (for he was a sailor) and slipped it into the edge of his bunk. The steamer started for Liverpool. On his voyage he met with an accident and was laid aside in his bunk. That card stared him in the face, day and night. Finally he said, "If I should die tonight I would go to hell, but I will not go there; I will go to heaven. I will take Christ right here and now." He went to Liverpool, returned to New York, went to the mission, told his story, and had the card still in his pocket, filled out and signed with his name. The conversation he had had in the mission left him, but the card stayed by him.

F. Tracts lead many to accept Christ.

The author of one tract received before his death upwards of sixteen hundred letters from people who had been led to Christ by reading it.

II. PURPOSES FOR WHICH TO USE A TRACT

A. For the conversion of the unsaved

A tract will often succeed in winning a person to Christ when a sermon or a personal conversation has failed. There are a great many people who, if you try to talk with them, will put you off; but if you put a tract in their hands and ask

God to bless it, after they go away and are alone they will read the tract and God will carry it home to their hearts by the power of the Holy Ghost. One of our students wrote me, in great joy, of how he had at last succeeded in winning a whole family for Christ. He had been working for that family for a long time but could not touch them. One day he left a tract with them, and God used that tract for the conversion of four or five members of the family.

Another student held a cottage meeting at a home and by mistake left his Bible there. There was a tract in the Bible. When he had gone, the woman of the house saw the Bible, picked it up, opened it, saw the tract and read it. The Spirit of God carried it home to her heart, and when he went back after the Bible, she told him she wanted to find the Lord Jesus Christ. The tract had done what he could not do in personal work. I once received a letter from a man saying, "There is a man in this place whom I tried for a long time to reach but could not. One day I handed him a tract, and I think it was to the salvation of his whole family."

B. To lead Christians into a deeper and more earnest Christian life

It is a great mistake to limit the use of tracts to winning the unsaved to Christ. A little tract on the second coming of Christ, once sent me in a letter, made a change in my whole life. I do not think the tract was altogether correct doctrinally, but it had in it an important truth, and it did for me just the work that needed to be done.

There is a special class of people with whom this form of ministry is particularly helpful, those who live where they do not enjoy spiritual advantages. You may know someone who is leading a very unsatisfactory life, and you long to have that person know what the Christian life really means. His pastor may not be spiritual and may not know the deep things of God. It is the simplest thing in the world to slip into a letter a tract that will lead to an entirely new Christian life.

C. To correct error

This is a very necessary form of work in the day in which we live, since it is full of error. In our personal work, we have not always time to lead one out of error, but oftentimes we can give a tract that can do the work better than we can. If you tried to lead someone out of an error by personal work, you might get into a discussion, but the tract cannot. The one in error cannot talk back to the tract.

D. To set Christians to work

Our churches are full of members who are doing nothing. A well-chosen tract may set such to work. I know of a young man who was working in a factory in Massachusetts. He was a plain, uneducated sort of fellow, but a little tract on personal work was placed in his hands. He read it and reread it, and said, "I am not doing what I should for Christ." He went to work among his companions in the factory, inviting them to the church, and to hear his pastor preach. Not satisfied with this, he went to doing personal work. This was not sufficient, so he went to work holding meetings himself. Finally, he brought a convention to his city. Just that one plain factory man was the means of getting a great convention and blessing to that place, and all from reading that little tract. He was also instrumental in organizing a society that was greatly blessed of God. It would be possible to fill this country with literature on Christian work that would stir up the dead and sleeping professors of religion throughout the land and send them out to work for the Lord Jesus Christ.

III. WHO SHOULD USE TRACTS

A. Ministers of the Gospel

Many ministers do make constant use of them in their pastoral work, leaving well-chosen tracts where they make their pastoral calls, handing out tracts along the line of the sermons that they preach. It is said of Rev. Edward Judson of New York that he seldom makes a call without having in his pocket a selection of tracts adapted to almost every member of the family, and especially to the children. "At the close of the Sunday evening preaching service, he has often put some good brother in the chair, and while the meeting proceeds he goes down into the audience and gives to each person a choice leaflet, at the same time improving the opportunity to say a timely word. In this way he comes into personal touch with the whole audience, gives each stranger a cordial welcome, and leaves in his hand some message from God. At least once a year he selects some one tract that has in it the very core of the Gospel. On this he prints the notices of the services, and selecting his church as a center, he has this tract put in the hands of every person living within half a mile in each direction, regardless of creed or condition. He sometimes uses 10,000 tracts at one distribution, and finds it very fruitful in results."

B. Sunday school teachers

Every Sunday school teacher should be on the lookout for tracts to give to students. In this way, the teacher can do much to supplement the work done in class.

C. Travelers

Travelers have a rare opportunity for doing tract work. They are constantly coming in contact with different people and finding out their needs. A Christian traveler with a well-assorted selection of tracts can accomplish immeasurable good.

D. Businesspeople

Businesspeople can use tracts to good advantage with the very ones with whom they have business engagements. They can also do excellent work with their own employees. Many a businessperson slips well-chosen tracts into letters, and thus accomplishes an effective ministry for the Master.

E. Schoolteachers

It is very difficult for schoolteachers in some cities and towns to talk very much with their pupils in school. Oftentimes, the rules of the school board prevent it entirely, but a wise teacher can learn all about students and their home surroundings, and can give them tracts just adapted to their needs.

F. Housekeepers

Every Christian housekeeper should have a collection of well-assorted tracts. These can be handed out to other workers, the grocer, the market vendors, the butcher, and even to the tramps who come to the door. They can be left upon the table in the parlor and in bedrooms. Only eternity will disclose the good that is accomplished in these ways.

IV. HOW TO USE TRACTS

A. Use a tract to begin a conversation.

One of the difficulties in Christian work is to begin. You see a person with whom you wish to talk about the Lord Jesus Christ. The great difficulty is in starting. It is easy enough to talk after you have started, but how are you going to start a conversation naturally and easily? One of the simplest and easiest ways is by slipping a tract into the person's hand. After the tract has been read, a conversation naturally follows. I was once riding in a crowded car. I asked God for an opportunity to lead someone to Christ. I was watching for the opportunity for which I had asked, when two young ladies entered. I thought I knew one of them as the daughter of a minister. She went through the car looking for a seat and then came back. As she came back and sat down in the seat in front of me, she bowed, and of course I knew I was right as to who she was. I took out a little bundle of tracts, and selecting one that seemed best adapted to her case, I handed it to her, having first asked God to bless it. She at once began to read, and I began to pray. When she had read the tract, I asked her what she thought about it. She almost burst into tears right there in the car, and in a very few moments that minister's daughter was rejoicing in the Lord Jesus Christ as her personal Savior. As she afterward exited the car, she said, "I want to thank you for what you have done for me in leading me to Christ."

B. Use a tract to close a conversation.

As a rule, when you have finished talking with someone, you should not leave without giving something definite to take home to read. If the person has accepted Christ, put some tract in his or her hands that will show him or her how to succeed in the Christian life. If the person has not accepted Christ, some other tract that is especially suited should be left.

C. Use tracts where a conversation is impossible.

For example, one night at the close of a tent meeting in Chicago, as I went down one of the aisles, a man beckoned to me and intimated that his wife was interested. She was in tears, and I tried to talk with her, but she stammered out in a broken way, "We don't talk English." She had not understood a word of the sermon, I suppose, but God had carried something home to her heart. They were Norwegians, and I could not find a Norwegian in the whole tent to act as interpreter, but I could put a Norwegian tract in her hand, and that could do the work. Time and time again, I have met with men deeply interested about their soul's salvation, but with whom I could not deal because I did not talk the language that they understood.

One day as I came from dinner, I found a Swede waiting for me, and he said he had a man outside with whom he wished me to talk. I went outside and found an uncouth-looking specimen, a Norwegian. The Swede had found him drunk in an alley and dragged him down to the Institute to talk with me. He was still full of whisky and spit tobacco juice over me as I tried to talk with him. I found he could not talk English, and I talked English to the Swede, and the Swede talked Swedish to the Norwegian, and the Norwegian got a little bit of it. I made it as clear as I could to our Swede interpreter, and he in his turn made it as clear as he could to the Norwegian. Then I put a Norwegian tract in his hands, and that could talk to him so that he understood perfectly.

Oftentimes, a conversation is impossible because of the place where you meet people. For example, you may be on the streetcars and wish to speak to someone, but in many instances it would not be wise if it were possible, but you can give a fitting tract. You may be able to say just a few words, and then ask God to bless the tract.

D. Use tracts to send to people at a distance.

It does not cost a tract much to travel. You can send them to the ends of the earth for a few cents. Especially use them to send to people who live in out-of-the-way places where there is no preaching. There are thousands of people living in different sections of this country where they do not hear preaching from one year's end to another. It would be impossible to send an evangelical preacher to them, but you can send a tract and it will do the preaching for you.

V. SUGGESTIONS AS TO THE USE OF TRACTS

A. Always read the tracts yourself before giving them to others.

This is very necessary. Bad tracts abound today, tracts that contain absolutely pernicious doctrine. They are being circulated free by the million, and one needs to be on guard, lest harm be done rather than good in distributing them. Of course, we cannot read all the tracts in foreign languages, but we can have them interpreted to us, and it is wise to do so. Besides positively bad tracts, there are many tracts that are worthless.

B. Suit your tract to the person to whom you give it.

What is good for one person may not be good for another.

C. Carry a selection of tracts with you.

I do not say a collection, but a selection. Tracts are countless in number, and a large share of them are worthless. Select the best, and arrange them for the different classes of people with whom you come in contact.

D. Seek the guidance of God.

This is of the very highest importance. If there is any place where we need wisdom from above, it is in the selection of tracts and in their distribution after their selection.

E. Seek God's blessing upon the tract after you have given it out.

Do not merely give out the tract and there let the matter rest, but whenever you give out a tract ask God to bless it.

F. Oftentimes give a tract with words and sentences underscored.

People are curious, and they will take particular notice of the underscoring. It is oftentimes a good thing to have a tract put up in your office. Those who come in will read it. I know a man who had a few words put upon his paper-weight. A great many who came into his office saw it, and it made a deep impression upon them.

G. Never be ashamed of distributing tracts.

Many people hand out tracts to others as if they were ashamed of what they were doing. People are not likely to read tracts if you hand them to them as if you were ashamed to do it; but if you act as though you were conferring a favor upon them, and giving them something worth reading, they will read your tract. It is often well to say to a person, "Here is a little leaflet out of which I have gotten a good deal of good; I would like to have you read it."

OPEN AIR
MEETINGS

I. THEIR IMPORTANCE AND ADVANTAGES.

A. They are scriptural.

Jesus said, "Go out quickly into the streets and lanes of the city, and bring in here the poor and the maimed and the lame, and the blind" (Luke 14:21). Every great preacher of the Bible was an open-air preacher. Peter was an open-air preacher, Paul was an open-air preacher, and so were Elijah, Moses, and Ezra. More important than all, Jesus Christ Himself was an open-air preacher and preached for the most part out-of-doors. Every great sermon recorded in the Bible was preached in the open air: the sermon on the Day of Pentecost, the Sermon on the Mount, the sermon on Mars Hill, etc. In this country we have an idea that open-air preaching is for those who cannot get any other place to speak, but across the water they look at it quite differently. Some of the most eminent preachers of Great Britain preach in the open air.

B. Open-air meetings are portable; you can carry them around.

It would be very difficult to carry a church or mission building with you, but there is no difficulty about carrying an open-air meeting with you. You can get an open-air meeting where you could by no possibility get a church, a mission hall, or even a room. You can have open-air meetings in all parts of the city and all parts of the country.

C. Open-air meetings are more attractive in the summer than hot, sweltering halls or churches.

When on my vacations, I used to attend a country church. It was one of the hottest, most stifling and sleepy places I ever entered. It was all but impossible to keep awake while the minister attempted to preach. The church was located in a beautiful grove where it was always cool and shady, but it seemed never to enter the minds of the people to go out of the church into the grove. Of course, only a few people attended the church services. One day a visiting minister suggested that they have an open-air meeting on the front lawn of a Christian man's summer residence near at hand. The farmers came to that meeting from miles around in wagons, on foot, and every other way. There was a splendid crowd in attendance. The country churches would do well in the summer to get out of their church building into some attractive grove near at hand.

D. Open-air meetings will accommodate vast crowds.

There are few church buildings, especially in the country, that will accommodate more than one thousand people; but people by the thousands can be accommodated by an open-air meeting. It has been my privilege to speak for several summers in a small country town with fewer than a thousand inhabitants. Of course, the largest church building in the town would not accommodate more than five hundred people. The meetings, however, were held in the open air, and people drove to them from forty miles around, and at a single meeting we had an attendance of fifteen thousand people. Whitefield was driven to the fields by the action of church authorities. It was well that he was. Some of his audiences at Moorfields were said to number sixty thousand people.

E. Open-air meetings are economical.

You neither have to pay rent nor hire a janitor. They do not cost anything at all. God Himself furnishes the building and takes care of it. I remember that at a Christian Worker's Convention a man was continually complaining that no one would hire for him a mission hall in which to hold meetings. At last I suggested to him that he had all outdoors, and could go there and preach until someone hired him a hall. He took the suggestion and was greatly used of God. You do not need to have a cent in your pocket to hold an open-air meeting. The whole outdoors is free.

F. You can reach people in an open-air meeting that you can reach in no other way.

I can tell of instance after instance where those who have not been at church or a mission hall for years have been reached by open-air meetings. The persons I have known to be reached and converted through open-air meetings have included thieves, drunkards, gamblers, saloon-keepers, abandoned women, murderers, lawyers, doctors, theatrical people, society people—in fact, pretty much every class.

G. You can reach backsliders and people who have drifted away from the church.

One day when we were holding a meeting on a street corner in a city, a man in the crowd became interested, and one of our workers dealt with him. He said, "I am a backslider, and so is my wife, but I have made up my mind to come back to Christ." He was saved and so was his brother-in-law.

H. Open-air meetings impress people by their earnestness.

How often I have heard people say, "There is something in it. See those people talking out there on the street. They do not have any collection, and they come here just because they believe what they are preaching." Remarks like this are made over and over again. Those who are utterly careless about the Gospel and Christianity have been impressed by the earnestness of men and women who go out on to the street and win souls for Christ.

I. Open-air meetings bring recruits to churches and missions.

One of the best ways to fill up an empty church is to send your workers out on the street to hold meetings before the church service is held, or better still, go yourself. When the meeting is over, you can invite people to the church (or mission). This is the divinely appointed means for reaching men and women who cannot be reached in any other way (Luke 14:21). All Christians should hear the words of Christ constantly ringing in their ears, "Go out quickly into the streets and lanes of the city, and bring in here the poor."

J. Open-air meetings enable you to reach men.

One of the great problems of most ministers of the Gospel today is how to get hold of the men. The average church audience is composed very largely of women and children. One of the easiest ways to get hold of the men is to go out on the streets; that is where the men are. Open-air meetings are, as a rule, composed of an overwhelming majority of men.

K. Open-air meetings are good for the health.

An English preacher was told that he was going to die due to an illness. He thought he should make the most of the few months he had allotted to live, so he went out on the streets and began preaching. The open-air preaching cured his disease, and he lived for many years and continued to conduct open-air meetings.

II. WHERE TO HOLD OPEN-AIR MEETINGS

To put it in a single word, hold them where the people are that you wish to reach. But a few suggestions may prove helpful.

A. Hold meetings where the crowds pass.

Find the principal thoroughfare where the crowds throng. You cannot hold your meeting just at that point, as the police will not permit it, but you can hold it just a little to one side of that point, and the crowds as they pass will go to one side and listen to you.

B. Hold them near crowded tenements.

In that way, you can preach to the people in the tenements as well as on the street. They will throw open their windows and listen. Sometimes the audience that you do not see will be as large as the one you do see. You may be preaching to hundreds of people inside the building that you do not see at all. I knew of a poor, sick woman being brought to Christ through the preaching she heard on the street. It was a hot summer night and her window was open, and the preaching came in through the window and touched her heart and won her to Christ. It is good to have a good strong voice in open-air preaching, for then you can preach to all the tenements within three or four blocks. Mr. Sankey once sang a hymn that was carried over a mile away and converted a man that far off. I have a friend who occasionally uses in his open-air meetings a megaphone that carries his voice to an immense distance.

C. Hold meetings near circuses, baseball games, and other places where the people crowd.

One of the most interesting meetings I ever held was just outside of a baseball ground on Sunday. The police were trying to break up the game inside by arresting the leaders. We held the meeting outside, just back of the grandstand. As there was no game to see inside, the people listened to the singing and preaching of the Gospel outside. On another Sunday, we drove down to Sell's circus and had the most motley audience I ever addressed. There were people present from almost every nation under heaven. The circus had advertised a "Congress of Nations," so I had provided a congress of nations for my open-air meeting. On that day I had a Dutchman, a Frenchman, a Scotchman, an Englishman, an Irishman, and an American preach. We took care at the open-air meeting to invite the people to evening meeting at the mission. That night a man came who told us that he was one of the employees of the circus, had been touched that afternoon by the preaching of the Gospel, and had come to learn how to be a follower of the Lord Jesus Christ. He accepted the Savior that night.

> *This list represents some of the larger groups of non-Americans in Chicago at the time. Today, such an event in Chicago would need to include African-Americans, Polish, Vietnamese, Pakistanis, and perhaps dozens of others.*

D. Hold meetings in or near parks or other public resorts.

Almost every city has its resorts where people go on Sunday. As the people will not go to church, the church ought to go out to the people. Sometimes permission can be secured from the authorities to hold the meetings right in the parks. Wherever this is impossible, they can be held near at hand. One who is now a deacon of our church spent his Sundays at Lincoln Park before he was converted; an open-air meeting was held close at hand, and here he heard the Gospel and was converted.

E. Hold meetings in groves.

It would be well if every country church could be persuaded to try this. Get out of the church into a grove somewhere, and you will be surprised at the number of people who will come who would not go near the church at all.

F. Hold open-air meetings near your missions.

If you have a mission, be sure and hold an open-air meeting near it. It is the easiest thing in the world to keep a mission full even during the summer months, if you hold an open-air meeting in connection with it, but it is almost impossible to do so if you do not.

G. Hold open-air meetings in front of churches.

A good many of our empty churches could be filled if we would only hold open-air meetings in front of them. Years ago, when in London, I went to hear Newman Hall preach. It looked to me like a very orderly and aristocratic church, but when I left the church after the second service, I was surprised to find an open-air meeting in full blast right in front of the church, and people gathered there in crowds from the thoroughfare.

H. Be careful about the little details in connection with the location.

On a hot day, hold the meeting on the shady side of the street. On a cool day, on the sunny side. Make it as comfortable for the audience as possible. Never compel the audience to stand with the sun shining in their eyes. Preach with the wind, and not against it. Take your own position a little above the part of the audience nearest you, upon a curbstone, chair, platform, rise in the ground, or anything that will raise your head above others so that your voice will carry.

III. THINGS TO GET

A. Get it thoroughly understood between yourself and God that He wants you to do this work, and that by His grace you are going to do it whatever it costs.

This is one of the most important things in starting out to do open-air work. You are bound to make a failure unless you settle this at the start. Open-air work has its discouragements, its difficulties, and its almost insurmountable obstacles, and unless you start out knowing that God has called you to the work, and come what may you will go through with it, you are sure to give it up.

B. Get permission from the powers that be to hold open-air meetings.

Do not get into conflict with the police if you can possibly avoid it. As a rule, it is quite easy to get this permission if you go about it in a courteous and intelligent way. Find out what the laws of the city are in this regard, and then observe them. Go to the captain of the precinct and report that you wish to hold an open-air meeting, and demonstrate that you are not a disturber of the peace or a crank. Many would-be open-air preachers get into trouble from a simple lack of good sense and common decency.

C. Get a good place to hold the meeting.

Do not start out at random. Study your ground. You should operate like a general. We are told that the Germans studied France as a battleground for years before the Franco-Prussian war broke out, and when the war broke out there were officers in the German army that knew more about France than the officers in the French army did. Lay your plan of campaign, study your battle-field, pick out the best places to hold the meetings, look over the territory care-fully, and study it in all its bearings. There are a good many things to be con-sidered. Do not select what would be a good place for someone to throw a big panful of dishwater upon you. These little details may appear trivial, but they need to be taken into consideration. It is unpleasant, and somewhat disconcert-ing, when you are right in the midst of an interesting exhortation, to have a panful of dishwater thrown down the back of your neck.

D. Get as large a number of reliable Christian men and women to go with you as you possibly can.

Crowds draw crowds. There is great power in numbers. One man can go out on the street alone and hold a meeting; I have done it myself; but if I can get fif-teen or twenty reliable men or women to go with me, I will get the people every time. Please note that I have said reliable Christian men and women. Do not take anybody along with you to an open-air meeting that you do not know. One who is in the habit of being foolish should be left at home so as not to disturb your whole meeting. Do not take someone with you who has an unsavory reputation. Probably someone in the crowd will know it and shout out the fact. Take only peo-ple who are of established reputation, and well balanced. Never pick up a stranger out of the crowd to speak. Someone will come along who appears to be just your sort, but if you ask him or her to speak you will wish you had not done so.

E. Get the best music you can.

Get a baby organ and a cornet if you can. Be sure and have good singing if it is possible. If you cannot have good singing, have poor singing, for even poor singing goes a good ways in the open air. One of the best open-air meetings I ever attended was where two of us were forced to go out alone. Neither of us was a singer. We started with only one hearer, but a drunken man came along and began to dance to our singing, and a crowd gathered to watch him dance. When the crowd had gathered, I simply put my hand on the drunken man and said, "Stand still for a few moments." My companion took the drunken man as an illustration for a sermon, and when he got through I took him for a text. People began to whisper in the crowd, "I would not be in that man's shoes for anything." The man did us good service that night. He first drew the crowd, and then furnished us with an illustration.

If you can, get a good solo singer, or even a poor solo singer will do splendid work in the open air, if he sings in the power of the Spirit. I remember a man who attempted to sing in the open air, who was really no singer at all, but God in His wonderful mercy gave him that night to sing in the power of the Spirit. People began to break down on the street, tears rolled down their cheeks, and one woman was converted right there during the singing of that hymn. Although the hymn was sung in such a miserable way from a musical standpoint, the Spirit of God used it for that woman's conversion.

F. Get the attention of your hearers as soon as possible.

When you are preaching in a church, people will oftentimes stay even if they are not interested, but unless you get the attention of your audience at once in the open air, one of two things will happen: Either your crowd will leave you, or else they will begin to heckle you. In the first half-dozen sentences, you must get the attention of your hearers. I was once holding a meeting in one of the hardest places of a city. There were saloons on three of the four corners, three breweries nearby, and four or five Roman Catholic churches were close at hand. There was scarcely a Protestant in that part of the city. The first words I spoke were these, "You will notice the cross on the spire of yonder church." By this means I secured their attention at once, and then I talked to them about the meaning of that cross. On holding a meeting one Labor Day, I started out on the subject of labor. I spoke only a few moments on that subject, to lead them around to the subject of the Lord Jesus Christ. Holding a meeting one night in the midst of a hot election, near where an election parade was forming, I started out with the question, "Whom shall we elect?" The people expected a political address, but before long I got them interested in the question of whether or not we should elect the Lord Jesus Christ to be the Ruler over our lives.

G. Get some good tracts.

Always have tracts when you hold an open-air meeting. They assist in making permanent the impressions and fixing the truth. Have the workers pass around through the crowd, handing out the tracts at the proper time.

H. Get workers around in the crowd to do personal work.

Returning from an open-air meeting years ago in the city of Detroit, I said to a minister who was stopping at the same hotel that we had had several conversions in the meeting. He replied by asking me if a certain man from Cleveland was not in the crowd. I replied that he was. He told me that he thought if I looked into it I would find that the conversions were largely due to that man, that while the services were going on, he had been around in the crowd doing personal work. I found that it was so.

IV. DON'T

A. Don't unnecessarily antagonize your audience.

I heard of a man addressing a Roman Catholic audience in the open air and pitching into the Roman Catholic Church and the pope. That man did not have good sense. Another man attempted a prohibition discourse immediately in front of a saloon. He got a brick instead of conversions.

B. Don't get scared.

Let Psalm 27:1 be your motto: "The Lord is my light and my salvation; whom shall I fear? The Lord is the strength of my life; of whom shall I be afraid?" There is not a particle need of being scared. You may be surrounded by a crowd of howling hoodlums, but you may be absolutely certain that you will not be hurt unless the Lord wants you to be hurt; and if the Lord wants you to be hurt, that is the best thing for you. You may be killed if the Lord sees fit to allow you to be killed, but it is a wonderful privilege to be killed for the Lord Jesus Christ. One night I was holding a meeting in one of the worst parts of Chicago. Something happened to enrage a part of the crowd that gathered around me. Friends near at hand were in fear lest I be killed, but I kept on speaking and was not even struck.

C. Don't lose your temper.

Whatever happens, never lose your temper. You ought never to get angry under any circumstances, but it is especially foolish to do so when you are holding an open-air meeting. You will doubtless have many temptations to lose your temper, but never do it. It is very hard to hit someone who is serene, and if you preserve your serenity the chances are that you will escape unscathed.

D. Don't let your meeting be broken up.

No matter what happens, hold your ground if you can, and you generally can. One night I was holding a meeting in a square in one of the most desperate parts of a large city. The steps of an adjacent saloon were crowded. A man came along on a load of hay, went into the saloon, and fired himself up with strong drink. Then he attempted to drive right down upon the crowd, in the middle of the square in which there were many women and children. Some man stopped his horses, and the infuriated man came down from the load of hay, and the howling mob swept down from the steps of the saloon. Somehow or other, the drunken driver got a rough handling in the mob, but not one of our number was struck. Two policemen in citizen's clothes happened to be passing by and stopped the riot. I said a few words more, and then formed our little party into a procession, behind which the crowd fell in, and marched down to the mission singing.

E. Don't fight.

Never fight under any circumstances. Even if they almost pound the life out of you, refuse to fight back.

F. Don't be dull.

Dullness will kill an open-air meeting at once and drive the whole audience away. In order to avoid being dull, do not preach long sermons. Use a great many striking illustrations. Keep wide awake yourself, and you will keep the audience awake. Be energetic in your manner. Talk so people can hear you. Don't preach, but simply talk to people.

G. Don't be soft.

One of these nice, sentimental sort of people in an open-air meeting the crowd cannot and will not stand. The temptation to throw a brick or a rotten apple is perfectly irresistible, and one can hardly blame the crowd.

H. Don't read a sermon.

Whatever may be said in defense of reading essays in the pulpit, it will never do in the open air. It is possible to have no notes whatever. If you cannot talk long without notes, so much the better; you can talk as long as you ought to. If you read, you will talk longer than you ought to.

I. Don't use crass language.

Use language that people are acquainted with, but do not use crass language. Some people think it is necessary to use slang, but there is language that is popular and easily understood by the people that is adequate to communicate.

J. Don't talk too long.

You may have a number of talks in an open-air meeting, but do not have any of them over ten or fifteen minutes long. As a rule, do not have them as long as that. Of course, there are exceptions to this when a great crowd is gathered to hear some person in the open air. Under such circumstances, I have heard a sermon an hour long that held the interest of the people, but this is not true in the ordinary open-air meeting.

V. THINGS ABSOLUTELY NECESSARY TO SUCCESS

A. Consecrated men and women

None but consecrated men and women will ever succeed in open-air meetings. If you cannot get such, you might as well give up holding open-air meetings.

B. Dependence upon God

There is nothing that will teach one his dependence upon God more quickly and more thoroughly than holding open-air meetings. You never know what is going to happen. You cannot lay plans that you can always follow in an open-air meeting. You never know what moment someone will come along and ask some troublesome question. You do not know what unforeseen event is going to occur. All you can do is to depend upon God, but that is perfectly sufficient.

C. Loyalty to the Word of God

It is the one who is absolutely loyal to God's Word, and who is familiar with it and constantly uses it, who succeeds in the open air. God often takes a text that is quoted and uses it for the salvation of some hearer. Arguments and illustrations are forgotten, but the text sticks and converts.

D. Filling of the Holy Spirit

If anyone absolutely needs the filling with the Holy Spirit, it is the open-air worker. This is the great secret of success in open-air work.

TENT
WORK

I. ITS IMPORTANCE AND ADVANTAGES

A. You can reach people by the tent you cannot reach by any other method.

People who you cannot get inside of a church or mission hall, people who will not even listen to preaching from a Gospel wagon, people whom you could not step up to and talk with personally, will come into a tent. The tent itself awakens curiosity. It looks like a circus. Time and again I have preached in a tent where six-sevenths of the audience were Roman Catholics; and not only did we get them into the tent, but many of them were won to Christ. It is stated in the official report of a large and successful tent work that 95 percent of the audience was composed of thieves, murderers, drunkards, and abandoned women. The other 5 percent were respectable people. A great many of the abandoned classes were converted. People who tried to pull the tent down, threw stones at the workers, cut ropes, and stood outside and tried to prevent people going in, before the meetings had been going on very long were on their knees calling on God for pardon. One of these had recently been released from prison where he had served fourteen years as a safe-cracker. He became a very bright convert.

B. Tents are portable.

Wherever you put a church up, there it must stay; you cannot easily move it. But if you put a tent up in one neighborhood, if it proves to be a poor neighborhood you can move it to another, or when that neighborhood is worked out, you can move it to a new one at a small cost.

C. Tent ministry is inexpensive.

A new tent can be purchased inexpensively, or you can get them second-hand, but this does not pay. You have to pay extra for the seats. For many reasons benches are better.

D. Tent work turns the season of the year that is regarded the poorest for evangelistic effort into the very best.

Ask almost any pastor what he regards as the best season for evangelistic work, and he will tell you the second week in January or Lent. If you ask him what is the worst season, he will tell you July and August, but with a tent July and August prove to be the best season in the year for evangelistic work. This has been demonstrated in Chicago, Philadelphia, New York, Boston, in many smaller cities, and in country towns. There can be little doubt that the number of conversions in tents in the summer far exceeds the number of conversions in evangelistic services in churches in the winter.

II. HOW TO CONDUCT TENT MEETINGS

A. Have the right sort of a person in charge of the tent.

The most important thing in any tent work is the person who serves as superintendent of the tent. If you have the right person, the rest will take care of itself, and if you have the wrong person, nothing that you can do will make a success of the work. What sort of a person is needed? A person who is perfectly fearless, who can stand up when ruffians are stoning the tent and not be the least bit ruffled if a stone comes through the tent and strikes him on the back of the head; a person who can stand boys shooting at him with tacks and sharp double-pointed tacks striking him in the face; a person who can stand perfectly unmoved with a lot of roughs shaking the gasoline lamps until it seems as if the tent would be set on fire; a person who trusts God and believes that God is going to take care of things.

In the next place, he should be a person who has handled others before; someone who can go into a mixed crowd of Protestants and Catholics; a person who has control of his own temper as well as control of the crowd; a person who is never ruffled, just stands there perfectly serene with sunshine in his face but with a grip like iron upon the audience; a person who can preach a plain direct Gospel sermon; a person who can hold the attention of people who are not in the habit of paying attention to ministers when they preach. To put it in a word, you want a person filled with the Holy Ghost who preaches the Gospel in the power of the Spirit.

> *Although many of the details that need to be taken care of in contemporary ministry settings are quite different than in Torrey's day, one thing remains the same: It is crucial that ministries be managed well. Many ministries fail to be effective because they are not organized and implemented appropriately. Sometimes this takes the form of not being able to respond to the antagonistic efforts of opponents, but often it is being made ineffective by things that could have been avoided with proper planning and operation. We may not think of these management roles as "spiritual," but they are vital to the effectiveness of ministry.*

B. Have the right sort of a tent.

The larger the tent is, the better, other things being equal. It is a great mistake to get too small a tent; they are unserviceable. If enough people do not come at first to fill your tent, you can so arrange the seats in the middle of the tent that it is not noticed that there is a large vacant space on the outside. If the tent is small, people will think it is a small thing, and your attendance will be small. A big tent makes a large impression upon the neighborhood.

C. Get the right place to locate your tent.

A good place is one where the crowds gather, upon some great thoroughfare where they are sweeping past by hundreds and by thousands. Tents should often be taken into rough neighborhoods. Someone may ask, "Is it safe there?" The safest place on earth is where the Lord takes you. The safest place for Moses was out in the river among the crocodiles, when God was taking care of him in the little ark. You can put a tent anywhere with safety if God leads you to put it there. We located a tent once where there were two murders during the first week within a block of the tent. One of the men was in the tent a half an hour before he was stabbed. He was urged to take the Lord Jesus Christ that night, but he said, "No, I cannot do it tonight; I will come Sunday night." Within half an hour he was found dying in a lot, where he had been stabbed.

Always select a dry spot. Be careful not to get into a place where you are going to be flooded out. If you are not on your guard at this point, you will oftentimes see what seems to be a beautiful place for a tent, but the first thunderstorm that comes up, the tent will be useless.

D. Choose the right sort of a person to be an usher.

The person who acts as usher is next in importance to the person who superintends the tent. The person must be fearless, exceedingly wise, and extremely patient. If your usher loses his temper, you are going to get into trouble. If you have a Christian who is wise and firm and gentle and loving and fearless, you are all right.

E. Be determined that you are going to have your own way in your tent.

Set about that in the very first meeting. If you let the crowd get the upper hand of you once, they will have it for all time; but if you show them the very first time that you are going to have your way, you will have it. Be very pleasant, but be as immovable as a rock. If it becomes necessary, take a person by the collar and help him out of the tent, but be sure you do it with a genial, winning smile. This often proves a means of grace to this kind of people. Do not turn someone out if you can help it, but do so rather than have your meeting broken up or seriously disturbed. Those who are drunk may be allowed some liberties because they know no better, but have it distinctly understood that they cannot go beyond a certain point.

F. Give a good deal of thought to the singing.

Have the very best singing that you can get. Have as big a choir as you can possibly gather together, but allow no one in the choir who is not saved. It is well to have an orchestra if you can get it.

G. Have the very best preaching that can be secured.

But what is good preaching for a church is not always good preaching for a tent. A tent preacher should be able to hold the attention of plain people. Many a person who can preach to great audiences in a church is an utter failure in a tent.

H. Always have an after meeting and do personal work.

The purpose of tent meetings is not to keep folks out of the saloons; they do keep folks out of the saloons, but the purpose of tent meetings is to bring folks to Christ. A man once said to me, "This is magnificent. Here are almost a thousand people here who are not Christians. It is magnificent if not a soul of them was converted, for it keeps them out of the saloons." But if all we do for them is to keep them out of the saloons for an hour or two, not much is accomplished. What tent work is carried on for is to lead them to a personal acceptance of the Lord Jesus Christ. The best way to accomplish this is by definite, personal, hand-to-hand work in the after meeting.

I. Have children's meetings in connection with your tent work.

The neighborhoods where tents are ordinarily put up are thronging with children. It would be easy to fill the tent with children, but it is not best to allow them in the evening service unless they come with their parents. If they are allowed in the evening service, they will crowd out the grown people; but the children must not be neglected; therefore, have special services for the children in the tent in the afternoon. Tell them they cannot be admitted to the evening service unless they bring their parents with them. In this way, a great many parents will be induced to come to the evening meetings for the sake of the children. The results that are accomplished among children in tent meetings are astonishing. These children come largely from utterly un-Christian homes, but many children are won to Christ.

A little boy came to one of our tents one afternoon. He heard the story of the Cross, accepted Christ, and went straight home. That night he brought with him his father and brother, and they were both converted, and then he brought two other brothers and two sisters, and these four were converted. His mother, who was a backslider, was brought back to the Lord. There were also two older daughters who led lives of sin. The whole family had been converted except these two abandoned girls. One of the workers started out with the determination to bring those two girls down to the meeting, and if possible get them to accept Christ. Some of the other workers stayed at home and prayed. This worker pled with the girls to come down to the meeting, and at last persuaded them to come. They got there very late, and just as they entered, Major Whittle was talking about wayward girls, and before the meeting was over these girls were rejoicing in Christ. Three boys, four girls, father and mother, brought to Christ through the conversion of a little boy.

J. Encourage the mothers to come and bring their babes.

If they can't bring their babies, they can't come at all. One very successful tent worker promised a rattle to every baby brought a certain night. The scheme took, and mothers and babies and baby carriages came pouring in that night. They had a wonderful meeting, and that man gained the love of the whole community.

III. WHERE TO CONDUCT TENT WORK

We have already spoken about putting up tents in crowded parts of our great cities, but that is not the only place.

A. In the portion of a city where you wish to organize a church

You may not be quite sure whether it would be wise to start a church in that locality. Set up a tent and make a test of it. In one locality in Chicago where a tent was set up, a Methodist church and Baptist church were organized, a Congregational mission revived, and one other mission started.

B. In country towns

One of the solutions of the summer problem in country churches is for the church to get a tent and hold its services in that during the summer months. Many will go to it who will not go to the church. Oftentimes, it is well for all the churches of a country town to combine in a summer tent work.

C. In religiously destitute sections of the country

There are many places in our country where there are many people but no church for miles. Tents can be set up in these remote parts of townships, and a splendid work done. It would be well for country pastors to take tents out on to the borders of their parishes and do Gospel work there.

D. In summer resorts

We think that if people go out to spend the summer anywhere, we cannot reach them, but there is no place where you can reach them better, provided you go at it wisely. Set up a tent near where the great vacation throngs congregate. People at these resorts do not know how to spend Sunday; they do not like to go to the country churches, but they will go to a tent.

GOSPEL-WAGON WORK

PRETTY MUCH EVERYTHING that can be said in favor of open-air meetings can be said in favor of Gospel-wagon work; in fact, it is a special form of open-air work. But many of these advantages are found in a larger degree in the work of the Gospel wagon, and there are other advantages that are peculiar to it.

I. THE GREAT ADVANTAGE OF GOSPEL-WAGON MEETINGS IS THEIR PORTABILITY.

A Gospel wagon can drive rapidly from one part of a city to another, carrying a large number of workers. A Gospel wagon can also go from town to town throughout the country, and readily reach places where there are no churches or other religious opportunities. One Gospel wagon in a single summer held meetings all through Connecticut and Massachusetts, and afterward went out to Chicago and then down into the Southern states, being blessed of God wherever it went, holding meetings all along the road.

> *Today some churches have sidewalk ministries, urban outreaches, and county fair ministries that still make very effective use of mobile "platforms." One ministry goes into the ghettos of New York City with basketball hoops mounted on pickup trucks. Although times have changed, there are some great parallels from this section to today.*

II. THE SECOND ADVANTAGE OF THE GOSPEL WAGON IS ITS NOVELTY.

While there are many Gospel wagons in operation today, in most communities the Gospel wagon is still a decided novelty. People love something new and flock to see it, and a large opportunity is thereby given for preaching the Gospel.

III. THE GREAT ADVANTAGE OF GOSPEL-WAGON WORK IS THAT IT REACHES AND CONVERTS THE PEOPLE.

Mr. Leonard Weaver, speaking of Harry Moorhouse's Bible-carriage work in England says: "I could tell of would-be suicides who have been arrested on their march to death and converted to God. They have flung the poison from their pockets. I could tell of men, ruined as the results of their lives of sin, accepting Christ and finding rest for their battered spirits in His embrace; of Christians being brought together on this basis of union, and losing the bitterness of sectarianism and learning to love one another; of workers being banded together and carrying on a weekly service in the open air after the van has been removed; of mission halls opened where they have large memberships, reaching thousands with the Gospel. Many a Gospel stream, the ripple of which is heard in the courts of heaven, can be traced back to this grand, God-honored Bible-carriage work." Gospel wagons are not an experiment; they are a work that God has approved. It is said that two consecrated Christian workers who will travel with a Bible carriage for six months will circulate more Bibles than any fifty workers from door to door. Mr. Leonard Weaver says again, "Let me say to the praise of God, with the help of another worker I have sold and given away over one million of the Scriptures. In two hours we have sold one thousand copies of the New Testament, not in quantities to one purchaser, but one by one. Then besides these we sent forth millions of Gospel books."

COLPORTAGE WORK

I. COLPORTAGE WORK DEFINED

What is Colportage work? By Colportage work we mean the distribution of religious literature from house to house. As a rule, the literature thus distributed is sold, sometimes for its full value, sometimes at less than cost.

II. ITS IMPORTANCE AND ADVANTAGES

A. People who fail in other lines of Christian work can succeed in Colportage work.

There are many who wish to work for the Lord, and feel they have a definite call to give their whole time to that work, who are unable to preach to edification, who are incompetent to run a mission, who would not even succeed as house-to-house visitors. What can they do? They can do Colportage work and oftentimes meet with great success in it. I have in mind one man who felt a call to Christian work, but it soon became evident that he had no gifts whatever that would warrant his preparation for the ministry. He was exceedingly slow and tiresome in speech, he lacked fire, and apparently lacked energy. He was induced to take up the Colportage work, and he became one of the most successful colporters I ever knew, not only making a very generous living by the work, but also reaching many homes and touching people who could be reached in no other way. Another man who could not even speak in prayer meetings, who was exceedingly limited in all ways, sold during a single month 1,200 volumes and cleared well above his expenses month after month. Going from town to town, he was the means of doing untold good. Retired ministers who have reached the point where their services are no longer in demand for churches do not need to give up the Lord's work. They can take up Colportage work, and perhaps be more useful than they were in their preaching days.

Ministers and other Christian workers who are broken down physically, and unable to bear the strain of regular work, can take up Colportage work with great advantage to their health, and accomplish very much for the Master.

B. Colportage work reaches neglected districts.

All over the land, there are stretches of country so sparsely settled that it would be impossible to maintain religious services, yet in these thinly settled districts taken together, there are thousands upon thousands of souls that need to hear the Gospel. Oftentimes, they can be reached by Colportage work better than in any other way. One solution of the religious problem in the country is to be found in Colportage work.

C. Colportage work is self-supporting.

The colporter needs to have no missionary society. He or she can go out and sell books for self-support, and perhaps make a comfortable living. Take, for example, the books of the Bible Institute Colportage Association. They contain some of the very best evangelical literature of the day, books adapted to the unsaved to lead them to Christ, books on the deeper Christian life, books on Christian work. They are written by some of the best-known and most gifted authors, men like F. B. Meyer, Campbell Morgan, Andrew Murray, D. L. Moody, Major D. W. Whittle, Charles Spurgeon, and others.

D. Colportage work converts sinners and builds up Christians.

All over our land today, there are many people who have been led to Christ, and many Christians who have been led into a deeper knowledge of Christ, through the work of colporters.

E. Its results are permanent and ever-widening.

A preacher goes away, but a book stays. One person reads a book and is blessed by it and hands it to another, and still to another. A single book may be read by scores of persons.

F. It opens doors to other work.

Many a person begins Christian work as a humble colporter, but going from house to house and village to village with the little books that carry the knowledge of Jesus Christ, he soon begins to preach the Word, and may in time receive a call to be a pastor or an assistant pastor.

G. Colportage work is a splendid preparation for other Christian work.

The colporter gets right into the home, gets acquainted with all kinds of people, and has to learn through necessity the modes of convincing. There is perhaps no better preparation for many phases of ministerial work than the work of a colporter.

III. HOW TO DO COLPORTAGE WORK

A. Get a few books to begin with, and then begin.

A man once came to me out of money and out of employment. I bought for him four Colportage books and sent him out. He came back in less than half an hour having sold the books. He took his share of the money and bought himself other books, and thus the work widened. The way to begin is to begin.

B. Visit every house and store and saloon.

When one undertakes to do Colportage work in any given district, as a rule it is well to visit every house and store and saloon in the district. Of course, if one continues to work the same district, it will be learned what houses can be visited again and again, and what places to avoid. Experience shows that many, even in saloons, will buy the books, and sometimes the saloon-keepers themselves, and no one can measure the good thus done.

C. Churches can employ a church visitor without expense to themselves.

Churches can equip the church visitor with Colportage books that he can sell, and thus meet his expenses. Of course, the visitor must have the public endorsement of the pastor of the church, and in this way get an entrance for the work. This plan has been adopted with great success in some quarters.

D. Attend religious conventions.

A great work can be done by colporters attending religious conventions, and there disposing of books along the lines of the subjects treated in the conventions.

LEARNING ACTIVITIES

1. As you look to your next week, try to identify all of the different types of people that you might only be able to reach through a tract. Then, go to a local Christian bookstore and select high-quality tracts that will minister to them.

2. Review the advantages of using tracts. Which advantages do you think are the most significant?

3. How might open-air meetings work in your community? Is anyone doing it already? What key factors must be considered for it to be successful? Where are the neediest areas of your community? How could open-air meetings be used to reach these areas?

4. Where do big groups of people gather in your region? How might tent meetings (or some modern variation) be used to reach these people? What practical considerations would you need to keep in mind in order to hold tent meetings?

5. How might you be able to use modern transportation technology to improve on the Gospel wagon concept? What are some areas near you that might only be reached through a very mobile means?

6. Does your church or ministry group have a ministry of distributing quality Christian literature? How might some of the ideas of colportage be used to improve its ministry (to provide income and to increase distribution)?

CHAPTER TEN

OTHER OUTREACHES

BY THIS POINT IN THE BOOK, you have certainly come to the realization that Torrey wants us to stretch in order to be more effective in our Christian work. Many of the aspects of ministry in the last chapter involved taking risks, particularly regarding physical safety. In this chapter, Torrey challenges us to take risks regarding our reputations. Certain Christian groups have strenuously avoided even the appearance of evil by not going near theatres. However, Torrey encourages us to wisely and cautiously try to use secular entertainment venues as opportunities to present the Gospel. Some contemporary ministries have already discovered how they can reach people in these places who would never come to a traditional church building. Of course, Torrey places great value on the local church and sees these outreaches as means to connect people with local churches. Gospel missions are buildings that are prepared as a permanent place for people to go who might not otherwise go to church or hear the Gospel. However, these must never become simply places of entertainment, but remain tools to bring people to Christ.

Other social institutions, like jails and hospitals, provide excellent contexts in which to do personal work. Torrey provides detailed instructions on how to maximize your effectiveness in these ministry settings. His sensitivity to the needs of people and the opportunities for ministry are seen vividly in his guidelines for how to provide music. It must be appealing, but it must also serve a deeper purpose.

Nearly everyone will have an opportunity at some point to participate in a funeral. Although it is a somber occasion, it is still one in which personal work should play a significant role. In this section, Torrey equips each of us for our roles in funerals of saved and unsaved persons.

SERVICES IN
THEATRES,
CIRCUSES, ETC.

I. IMPORTANCE AND ADVANTAGES

A. People feel comfortable attending.

Many people are likely to be reached by services in theatres, circuses, and other places of entertainment who are not likely to be reached elsewhere. Actors, actresses, and the other employees of theatres seldom attend services at churches; it is difficult also to find them in their homes, but they can be reached on their own ground. At the very first service in Forepaugh's circus tent in Chicago during the World's Fair, an actor was brought under deep conviction of sin and converted to Christ. In services held in the city of Minneapolis, I had frequent opportunity of speaking personally with the actors and other employees of the places. But not only can the employees be reached, but also the frequenters. We held services one New Year's afternoon in the Theatre Comique in the city of Minneapolis. A few days afterward, I received an anonymous letter from an Iowa city. The writer said that he had been present at the theatre service that day. It was the first time he had been in a religious service for years, although in the Old Country he had been a local preacher. In the two or three weeks preceding that service, he had squandered over $300 in that theatre, but the word spoken that afternoon had brought him back to Christ. The man afterward returned to Minneapolis and made himself known, and subsequently became a deacon and one of the most faithful workers in our church.

B. Another advantage of services in a theatre is their novelty and attractiveness.

The interest especially of young people is awakened by seeing a service advertised in a theatre. They go out of curiosity, and an opportunity is thus offered of bringing them to Christ. Everything about the place attracts them; they like the surroundings; they are off their guard; and the Gospel gets an entrance into their hearts.

C. Many are converted.

It has been the writer's privilege to conduct services every Sunday afternoon for several winters in the theatres of one of our American cities, and during the World's Fair to conduct theatrical services for many weeks, seven nights in the week. In both places most encouraging results followed. In the services in Chicago, many were converted every night. At a recent theatre service in a southern city, about one hundred and fifty professed conversion.

II. HOW TO CONDUCT

A. The first important matter in the conduct of theatre services is the choice of the theatre.

What sort of a theatre to choose depends upon the purpose for which the meetings are held. If the aim is to get hold of those who have sunken into the deepest depth of sin, of course a theatre of the lower order is preferable. On the other hand, there are objections to such a theatre. It is not a good place to take people, but you are not likely to take anybody there except those who frequent it already or those who go for a definitely Christian purpose. Nevertheless, great care should be exercised in the choice of workers for such a place. Girls and boys should not be taken to such a place unless they already frequent it. A young man approached a prominent businessman in the city of Minneapolis who was handing out flyers on the street, inviting people to the Theatre Comique for a Gospel service. The young man said, "Do you know what kind of a place the Theatre Comique is?" The businessman replied that he had not lived in Minneapolis twenty years not to know. The young man asked again, "Do you think that such a place is a proper place to hold a religious service?" The reply was made, "When you go fishing, where do you go?" The young man smiled and answered, "Oh, I see, I go where the fish are." A good many fish were caught in that pool, though it was a cesspool.

If the aim is to reach a better class of people, of course one must engage a theatre of the higher order. During the World's Fair the Haymarket Theatre and Columbia Theatre in Chicago were packed to overflowing each Sunday morning to hear the Gospel preached by leading preachers of this country and Europe, and there were a great many conversions.

Sometimes the size of the theatre will be a determining factor. Twenty thousand people could be crowded into the Forepaugh tent and were crowded into it each morning that services were held there; this in spite of the fact that the heat was almost insufferable. The circus men were so astonished at the vast audiences that came out to religious services that they approached Mr. Moody to see if he would not furnish a speaker to go around with their show and hold services every Sunday; they offering to pay all the expenses.

It is best to select, if possible, a theatre that is in use rather than one that is abandoned. If the theatre has been given up, the probability is that people did not go to it, and they will not be likely to go to a religious service in that place. I knew of a case of what appeared to be a very desirable theatre being purchased to hold religious services in. It seemed to be in a good locality and well adapted to the work. The theatre, however, had been abandoned by the theatrical people, and it was never possible to get the people to attend religious services there in any great numbers.

B. The second point of importance is securing the theatre for the services.

Oftentimes this is not a very difficult matter. Theatrical people are frequently very glad to have their building used for religious services. I once went to the proprietor of a very vile den to see if I could secure his place for Gospel meetings. To my surprise, he received me very cordially and said certainly we could have the place, and he only charged a nominal rent. Going the next year to another theatre in the same city, only a theatre of a much higher order—a very attractive and respectable place—I inquired of the manager if I could secure his theatre for Sunday afternoon services. He replied, "Certainly." When I asked him what he would charge for it, he asked me if there was any money in it. I told him none at all, that we were going to spend money and not take it in. "In that case," he said, "you can have the theatre for nothing." He stood to this agreement, furnished light and heat, ushers and everything, and would take absolutely nothing for it. Even the stage manager was in attendance every

Sunday to see that everything was in perfect order. As a rule, it is far better to rent a theatre than to buy it. If you buy it, it ceases to be a theatre and becomes your church, and the very people you wish to get hold of are no longer attracted.

C. Exercise great care about the music.

Provide just as large a choir as possible. Secure the very best leader possible; the best leader is a man with a good large voice, a great deal of enthusiasm and ability to get people to sing, who is filled with the Holy Ghost, and knows how to sing to save. In addition to a good leader and a large choir, it is well to have choruses, duets, quartets, and solos. A band is sometimes helpful, but not at all a necessity. A good cornetist is of great help, but the singing attracts as much as instrumental music, and does far greater execution.

D. Secure the best possible speakers.

No one is a good speaker for a theatrical service who does not preach the straight Gospel and preach it in a way to attract and hold the public. If there is one person in the community who has a peculiar gift in this direction, it is best usually to have this person do the major part of the speaking week after week. It will do to include another speaker occasionally, and good may be accomplished by it, but one speaker who knows the audience and the work, and follows one sermon up by another, will accomplish the most definite and most satisfactory results.

E. Be sure that the services are thoroughly evangelical, and emphatically evangelistic.

Very little good comes from holding meetings in theatres and similar places unless these meetings are emphatically Gospel meetings. Preaching along ethical and social and philanthropic lines accomplishes very little good. If, however, the meetings are thoroughly evangelical and evangelistic, the ethical and social results will necessarily follow. Drunkards will be converted and give up their drinking, gamblers will give up their gambling, impure people will forsake their impurity, politicians will be brought to Christ and thus their politics will be reformed. The night one politician came to the meeting where he was converted (during the World's Fair), he had been out with a number of his political friends. They had been planning for his election to an important office here in Chicago. At the service he heard nothing about political reform; he heard the simple Gospel, a Gospel that would save the slave of drink. He accepted Christ that

272

night. The result has been that his whole life, personal, domestic, commercial, and political, has been renovated. A sermon on political reform would not have touched him at all.

F. Advertise the meetings largely and widely.

Large billboards such as the theatrical people use for their own advertisements are perhaps the best of any, but the newspapers should also be used to the utmost. Newspapers are generally willing to do a great deal of free advertising for services of this character. Men with invitations to the meetings should be placed upon all the street corners for blocks around.

G. Have a thoroughly drilled corps of ushers.

Sometimes the theatres provide their own ushers, and for many reasons it is well to use them. They know the building, understand just how to seat people, and, furthermore, they need to hear the Gospel themselves and are likely to be converted.

H. Have wise and well-trained personal workers scattered through the audience.

This is of the very highest importance, even more important in a theatre than it is in a church. No speaker can take note of what is happening in every part of a theatre. Many men and women will be touched by the sermon, but only touched if gotten hold of right then and there by a watchful and wise worker, and the effect of the sermon followed up, will they be converted; whereas if they are allowed to go out, the impression will soon die away and the person may be lost forever. These workers should be carefully trained, as to exactly where to sit and what to do during the service and at the close of the service.

I. Have after meetings.

This is of the highest importance. For details regarding after meetings, see the lesson on "After meetings."

J. Invite the audience to the churches.

There is a prevalent opinion among the masses of the unchurched that they are not welcome at the churches. We should do everything in our power to disabuse them of this false notion. The theatre service affords a splendid opportunity for doing it. It is well to have the ministers themselves extend the invitation. In this way a permanence is given to the work. The church is the only thing that goes on continually. Missions, theatre services, tent services come and go, but the church was established by Christ and perpetually continues. A work that does not lead the people ultimately into the churches and get them connected seldom results in any permanent good. It is well to have printed invitations from the churches to distribute among the audience. These invitations should be gotten up in an attractive form so that the people will be glad to take them home and keep them.

ORGANIZING AND CONDUCTING A GOSPEL MISSION

I. IMPORTANCE OF GOSPEL MISSIONS

A. Many people are unreached.

In every large city, and in many of our smaller cities, there are great masses of the people whom the churches are not reaching. The reasons why they are not being reached by the church are various. First of all, because of the location of the churches. The churches, as a rule, in our larger cities are inaccessible to the great majority of our poorer population. The churches follow the well-to-do people uptown, as a rule, and where the thickest population is, where the people are to whom the Lord Jesus especially ministered during His life, there the churches are not. The churches are not reaching them because they are not near enough to where these people are.

In the second place, the services of the regularly organized church are of such a character that they do not reach the poorer people. Oftentimes when churches pretend to preach the Gospel they do not preach it; and, when they do preach the Gospel, it is preached in such a manner that it does not take hold of the common people. A laborer, the poor, a beggar, or a drunkard who wishes to be reformed goes into many of our churches, and the minister stands up and preaches the Gospel of the Lord Jesus Christ, and yet preaches the Gospel in such a manner that it does not leave any impression upon the listener's mind. The preacher is before everything else a scholar, and does not know how to get down to the hearts and lives of ordinary folks.

In the third place, the whole atmosphere of the church is not such that these people feel at home. Sometimes the style of dress, the social etiquette, the music, the whole general conduct of the church is such as to repel them. Down in the mission, on the other hand, there is an entire absence of conventionality, but there is a friendliness, a kindliness, a homelikeness that their hearts warm to. There is something that attracts them to the place, and they go again and again until the Spirit of God opens their hearts and they are saved.

It is the work of the mission to present the Gospel to these large masses of men and women and children existing in all our larger cities, and in many of our smaller cities, who are not reached by the ordinary ministrations of the church. It is to present the Gospel to the masses, not simply to reach them. It is of no great importance to know merely how to reach the masses; anyone can reach the masses, but the question is how to present the Gospel to them. The work of the mission is not to conduct innocent entertainments, nor to provide a nice, warm, pleasant place for the people to go into from the streets; it is not to clothe the poor and the naked; but the work of the mission is to bring the Gospel of the Lord Jesus Christ to bear upon the hearts and lives of lost men and lost women. What they find, or ought to find, in the mission is the Gospel of the Lord Jesus Christ seven nights in the week. If they desire amusement, they can get it elsewhere. The true business of the mission, as well as the true business of the church of the Lord Jesus Christ, is to preach the Word of God, and to bring it to bear upon lost souls. The Word of God is the one lever that will lift them, not only out of the ditch, but into the kingdom of God.

B. The Gospel mission is important as a soul winner.

The question of how to evangelize the masses is often discussed as if it were a problem that nobody had solved, but it has been solved. There is no experiment about it. There are many who know exactly how to reach the masses with the Gospel and prove that they know how by doing it. The Gospel missions are winning souls, and their chief importance lies in this fact. I have in mind a mission to which you can go any night in the fifty-two weeks in the year, and you will see anywhere from twelve to fifty kneeling at the altar and seeking the Lord Jesus Christ. Go to many other missions and you will see practically the same thing. The Gospel missions of America are winning thousands upon thousands of poor, lost men and women to Jesus Christ every year; winning them and saving them, transforming them, making them children of God, heirs of God and joint heirs with Jesus Christ, by the power of the Gospel of our Lord Jesus Christ. Here is where the prime importance of the mission lies, not because it is trying to do the work, but because it is doing it.

C. Gospel missions are important as an inspiration to the churches.

Some of the most satisfactory local revivals in the history of the country have come from some member of a church attending a mission, getting a new conception of the power of the Lord Jesus Christ, and going home and kindling his church. The fire has gone through the whole church, and the church has been awakened to a mighty work for God. Oftentimes, when people who have not even attended a mission have read reports of the work, they have wakened up to the fact that Paul meant just what he said when he wrote that the Gospel was the power of God unto salvation to everyone who believed, and they have gone to work with new faith and new energy, and the Gospel has proved a saving power in their own community.

D. Gospel missions are important as a feeder to the churches.

Many of the best-working members, and sometimes the best-paying members, in our churches today are converts of missions. Many rich people have gone from the regular churches down to the missions and have been there converted and have gone back to their churches to be a power and blessing. Some people get an idea that all who are converted in missions have no gifts or promise. It is a great mistake. Many a person who has been converted in a mission is indeed from the deepest depths of poverty and ruin, but it is sin that has brought the present condition. When the mission has gotten hold and won him or her to Christ, oftentimes, the person regains an old position in society and business. A man who had been mayor of a large Southern city, but who had gone down through drink until he was a penniless tramp, was converted in a New York mission. He afterward became the manager of one of the largest publishing houses in America. The night of his conversion, discouraged, disheartened, despairing, he had started from his lodging house to go and commit suicide in the East River. He had gone to a saloon to get one more drink, was thrown out because he was penniless, was brought into a mission by one who saw him thrown out of the saloon, and was converted that night. Many who are today in the regular Gospel ministry were converted in a mission. One of the brightest and most promising congregational ministers that I know in our land, the beloved pastor of a well-to-do church, was converted in a New York mission.

E. Missions are important as furnishing a place where members of our
   churches can work.

A Christian cannot grow without work. One of the great troubles in many of our churches today is that there is nothing to do. The members go Sunday after Sunday and are fed and fed and fed until they are dying of spiritual dyspepsia, apoplexy, or both. A minister once said to me, "My greatest difficulty is that I haven't anything for my members to do." It was literally true. It was a college church, and a parish in which there were more workers than work. A mission gives Christians something to do, something exceedingly inspiring to do, something in which there is a tremendous uplift to their own spiritual energy.

What a blessing would come to many of our wealthy churches if the members of these churches, who go Sunday after Sunday and hear the Gospel of the Lord Jesus, would go out from these churches down into the lowest parts of the city and come right into living touch with lost men and women and try to use the Gospel of the Lord Jesus Christ to lift them up where they ought to be. If they should do this, we would have new life in our prayer meeting, we would not have two or three long and labored prayers; we would have prayer after prayer, short, right to the point, appeals to God for His blessing upon this man or that woman. We would have a new conception of the power of the Gospel of the Lord Jesus Christ; we would have a new vision of the Lord Jesus Christ Himself. I never knew Jesus as I know Him today until I knew what it was to go down among the poor and outcast and kneel right beside a dirty drunkard and put my arm about his neck, and whisper to him that Jesus died for him, and that Jesus came to save him and could save him, and then hear him with breaking heart lift his voice to God in prayer, and then see him rise a new man in Christ Jesus. I understood the Gospel then; I understood Jesus then; I saw Jesus then as I never saw Him before.

If you wish to be a better Christian than you ever were in all your life; if you wish to understand the Lord Jesus as you never understood Him before in all your life; if you wish to have the spirit of prayer as you never had it before in all your life, go to work in a mission. If you are a pastor and wish to have a better membership than you ever had in your life, send your members out to work in a mission. If you have not a mission where they can do it, start one, have one anyhow. I pity from the bottom of my heart the man or woman who does not know the inspiration, the joy and uplift, that comes from going down into some mission where perhaps there are five, ten, or one hundred lost men and women, and just pleading with them in the simplest language you can command, to take the Lord Jesus Christ who saved you.

II. HOW TO START A MISSION

The way to start a mission is to start it. A great many people talk about starting, but they never start. In one city, they had a great gathering and were going to build an expensive building. They had a wonderful meeting, and one man promised much of the money. Someone who was present was asked what he thought about it, and he replied, "I can tell you better after they have started." They never started. The whole thing went to pieces. Our country is full of people who are going to start missions and other Christian enterprises, but they never do it. The way to begin is by beginning.

A. In the first place, be sure God wishes you to start a mission.

It is not enough to be sure that you wish to start one. It is, as a rule, far better to go and help a mission already existing than to go and begin a new one of your own. Many people hear of the wonderful work people are doing in some mission and then go and start one without consulting the Lord. There have been hundreds of missions opened in this country that the Lord never wished opened, and if those who started them had gone to Him about it, they would never have been started.

B. If you are sure that it is the Lord's desire that you start a mission, start with the determination to go through with it.

People attend conventions or read articles about missions and see only the bright side; they do not see that the work is also full of discouragements. If there is any work that is full of discouragements, it is mission work; so when you start, begin with the determination that you will go through every obstacle, and then you will get through.

C. Be sure you get the right location.

That is very important. Be sure to consult God about the place. There is a great deal in the place, and the place that you think best may not be the best place. Here are a few hints as to location:

1. *Go where there is the hardest work, not the most attractive work, to do.*

2. *Go where there is the most need for work.*

3. *Go where there are a great many passersby.*

4. *As a rule, the first floor is best for many reasons, but there are some advantages in a second-floor mission.*

5. *A vacant store, saloon, or theatre will answer the purpose for a mission excellently.*

6. *Don't start on too large a scale.*

Everybody seems to wish a bigger mission than anybody else and, if they start on a large scale, as a rule in a few months they have enough of it. Sometimes the best place to start a mission is on a street corner. Go and hold an open-air meeting, and if the Lord approves of your work, He will give you a more permanent place.

7. *The location of the mission must be largely determined by the purpose of the mission.*

If the purpose of the mission is to reach drunkards, the place for the mission is near the saloons; if the purpose of the mission is to reach fallen women, oftentimes it is desirable to have the mission right among the places that these women haunt, though, if possible, there should also be a home remote from the dens of iniquity to which the converts can be sent. If the purpose of the mission is to reach the respectable poor, of course the location of the mission has to be determined by that fact.

D. Furnish plainly.

Fancy missions, as a rule, are failures. They are nice in theory, but plain ones do the work.

E. Advertise.

When you have made up your mind where you are going to start and have gotten everything ready, advertise your meetings everywhere: in the houses, in the stores, in the saloons, and on the street. Send men and women out to bring people in; "compel them to come in." Get as many consecrated Christian workers as you can together. Be sure you have the power of the Holy Spirit, and then go in and win souls.

III. HOW TO SUPPORT THE MISSION

A. Don't support it on credit.

Many people get in debt and call it walking by faith. God says, "Owe no one anything." Running into debt is not faith, but disobedience. It is better to shut a mission up than to run it into debt. Debt dishonors God. If you run into debt you will be discredited, the church will be discredited, God will be discredited, and sinners will stumble to perdition over the dishonor brought to the name of Christ.

B. Be careful about fund-raising.

Do not support your mission by fairs, socials, imitation dime museums, or anything of that sort. The man who goes into the disgraceful methods of raising church finances that are so common in our day lacks faith in God.

C. Do not support your mission by indiscriminate solicitation.

Never go to ungodly people for money. God says that the sacrifice of the wicked is an abomination unto the Lord. He certainly does not wish us to use an abomination to support His work.

D. If you are able to do it, it is oftentimes well to support a mission out of your own pocket.

In almost every large city, there are many Christians who could support a mission. One of the most efficient missions in the world was for years supported by a businessman out of his own pocket. He worked six days in the week the entire day, spent all the evenings at the mission, then went fourteen miles to his home, and before he could go to bed would have a long list of people to pray for. He was past fifty years old when he began this work; he kept it up for many years, and the work continues to this day. Another man of wealth in another city put $10,000 or more each year into a mission that he organized. He found that that work paid so much better than his business that he finally turned his back upon his business and put himself into the work. He is still in the work, a young man at nearly threescore years and ten. It does not require a very rich man to support a mission. Four young men in one city, each of them working on a meager salary, supported a very successful mission with scarcely any help from others. Of course, it required self-denial, but they felt that the self-denial abundantly paid.

E. One of the best ways to support a mission is to have an individual church back of it.

The church will be a blessing to the mission, and the mission to the church. Every rich church ought to have one or more missions that it is supporting.

F. The best way to support a mission in many cases is to support it by the freewill offerings of those who attend it.

This is best even where the attendants are all poor people. Very few realize how much poor people can give and will give if they are interested in a work, and if the work really is of God. Far more missions as well as churches could be self-supporting if the people only believed it and undertook it. The people always appreciate the mission better, and think more of it, when they have money in it.

G. Missions can be supported by faith.

If you are sure the Lord wishes you to carry on mission work, ask Him for means, and He will supply them. You will not need to make personal solicitations from anybody but the Lord. I say this not from speculation, but from experience. Many others have had the same experience.

IV. HOW TO CONDUCT A GOSPEL MISSION

A. Let God conduct it.

Missions often fail because there is too much of machinery and management. Cast-iron rules and cast-iron methods of conducting missions, red tape, and other nonsense shut God out. Give your mission over unreservedly to the control of God. Be sure you do it—seek His guidance and wait for it. The promise of the thirty-second Psalm applies as well to mission work as to other work: "I will instruct you and teach you in the way you should go; I will guide you with My eye." The trouble is, oftentimes we are not near enough to see the glance of the Father's eye.

B. Conduct your mission along strictly Gospel lines.

Refuse to be switched off onto side issues. Amusements and entertainments may be a good enough thing in their place, but the time is short and the Lord is at hand. We cannot afford to be reaching out in such indirect and indefinite ways. Thousands of souls are perishing, and the only thing that has God's power in it to save is the Gospel (Romans 1:16). A fine text for the mission worker is, "I am not ashamed of the gospel of Christ, for it is the power of God to salvation for everyone who believes." The missions that have been successful are the missions that have held strictly to the Gospel, the missions that have given the Gospel clearly, simply, and constantly. Experiments along other lines are nothing new. They have been tried for over a quarter of a century. I remember a church that in my early life seemed to me a model church. It had most cunningly devised machinery for reaching the people—lectures, entertainments, clubs, classes, etc., etc. It did reach the people, but it did not convert them. It grew marvelously, but it was made up of such heterogeneous and unconverted material that it went to pieces and ended in a free-for-all fight; yet every little while some new work is springing up, along these old and discredited lines, yet imagining that it is striking out in new and promising paths. The Gospel alone can do the work we aim to do. Run your mission along Gospel lines seven nights in the week.

C. Tend strictly to business.

Missions will not run themselves. People attend a few meetings of a successful mission, or read about them, and conclude that missions are a fine thing. Then they open one somewhere and expect it to go of itself, and it does go— to pieces. This has occurred again and again. There is no form of Christian work that demands more careful and prayerful watching and attention to business than mission work. A single ill-conducted service in a church may not do much harm, but a single ill-conducted service in a mission is likely to have far-reaching consequences of evil. One unfortunate meeting in a mission may mar the work for years.

D. Put only proven workers in the leadership of the mission.

Use only people of irreproachable character and who have a good understanding of God's Word, who have good common sense and uncommon push. It is too much the custom, if a notorious sinner is converted, to open a mission at once and put that person in charge. However, the leader has not been tested, and nothing is known of his qualifications. The condition of many missions is simply horrible because of this sort of thing. Of course, such a person ought to be set to work, and there is much that can be done, and done well without any risk. He could be used to hand out fliers and to get people into the mission, or testify humbly and effectively as to what God has done, or very likely do most efficient personal work. For his own sake and for Christ's sake, do not put someone into any place of leadership until he or she is tried and proven with regard to stability of Christian character, gifts, and Bible knowledge.

E. Make much of the Bible.

People in a mission should be given a great deal of the Word of God. Stable and well-rounded Christian character is built upon a study of the Word of God. The Christian character that is built merely upon the foundation of experience is unreliable: It breaks down easily; but the Christian character that is built upon the Word of God never goes to pieces. The converts and attendants ought to be encouraged to study the Word for themselves. There should be classes also for thorough systematic instruction in Bible truth. There should be training classes where they are taught how to use the Bible in leading others to Christ. They should be encouraged to make much use of the Bible in giving their experience. In some successful missions, the men always begin their testimony by a quotation from Scripture, giving chapter and verse.

F. Make much use of testimony.

There can be no doubt of the great power of living testimony, especially in mission work. Men and women who regard themselves as not only lost, but hopelessly lost, come into the mission and there hear some other man or woman who has been as deep down in sin as themselves tell the story of the saving power of Christ. Hope is kindled in their hearts, and they turn to Christ and are saved. There are thousands of earnest Christians in our land today who were saved through the testimonies of redeemed men and women. Of course, care has to be exercised as to the character of the testimonies thus given. We should be careful to see that it is genuine and not hypocritical; we should see to it that they live out in their daily lives what they testify to in the evening meeting. If they give their testimony about their past sinful life in a boastful way, they should be instructed in private not to do this. Sometimes it is necessary to say a word about it publicly. But the fact that there are evils connected with the relation of our experience is not a sufficient reason for altogether giving up this mighty weapon of testimony.

G. Make much use of music.

Get the best music you can. Be sure it is converted music. Tolerate nothing but a converted chorister, a converted organist, and a converted choir. Have an organist that you can depend upon. An organist of modest ability who is always there is much better than a much better organist who is sometimes late or absent. Get the best soloist you can, but be sure they sing hymns that contain the real Gospel and sing them in the power of the Holy Spirit. Have duets, quartets, and choruses, but best of all, have lively congregational singing. Be careful in your selection of hymns. Choose hymns that are full of life and full of the Gospel. Sing them over and over again until you have sung them into the hearts of the hearers. Many will go out of the mission unconverted, but the hymn that has been heard will go on singing itself in his or her heart until it has sung him or her into the kingdom of God. It is wonderful how the Gospel in song sticks in the minds of hearers.

H. Make a great deal of personal work in the mission.

It is not enough to get those who desire to be saved up to the altar, though that is a good thing to do; have workers deal with them individually. Be sure that the workers themselves know how to do personal work. One great cause of the instability of much of our mission work is that there has been no thorough hand-to-hand dealing with the converts.

I. Look after your converts.

Keep a list of them, and hunt them up in their homes if they have any. If they have no homes, hunt them up in their lodging houses or wherever they may be. Follow them up persistently; instruct them individually as to how to succeed in the Christian life. Be watchful to see that they follow the instructions given. Get them into some live church of Jesus Christ. We ought to be careful as to the church that mission converts join. Many churches would prove to be an icehouse to them and would freeze them to death. It is oftentimes best to have the mission itself organized into a church, where there is regular church life, and where the sacraments of baptism and the Lord's Supper are administered.

J. Give as much of the work as you can to the converts of the mission.

Send them out into the streets and saloons to invite people in; be careful, however, about sending reformed drunkards into saloons. Put the converts out on the street corners and in front of the mission with fliers. Organize them into a choir and get them to sing. Train them to use their Bibles in dealing with inquirers. Work them into the Sunday school as officers and teachers as fast as it is wise. Organize them into lookout committees, sick committees, hospital committees, jail committees, etc. Set them to conducting cottage meetings. Use them in open-air work.

K. Have plenty of good ushers.

Let them meet people at the door and give them a warm handshake and show them a seat.

L. Let no one go out without a personal invitation to come to Christ.

The best work in many a mission is that which is done with those who start to go out before the meeting is over. Someone stays near the door and follows out everyone who leaves and preaches Christ to him or her. Many have been won to Christ this way, just outside the mission.

M. Have no cast-iron form of service.

It is well to begin one way one time and an entirely different way another. Let everything be unconventional. Avoid getting into ruts.

N. Never be afraid of drunkards, thieves, thugs, or cranks.

You have God back of you and, if you look to Him, He will give you the victory every time. Many things may happen that would frighten an ordinary preacher out of his wits, but out of these very unforeseen incidents blessing oftentimes comes.

I was once conducting a meeting when a drunken man rose in the back part of the audience and wanted to speak. As he came forward I said, "Do you want us to pray for you?" The man faced the audience and broke out, "I am a damned fool!" then he apologized for swearing. He said, "I did not mean to swear." I said, "My friend, you told the truth; you are a fool and you are damned, but Christ can save you. Do you wish us to pray for you?" And down the man went upon his knees. In a little while, a tall, muscular, drunken lumberman rose to his feet and said he wished to ask a question. I replied, "All right, what is it?" He said, "I wish to ask about the blessed Trinity." I said, "Never mind that now; Christ died for you. Do you wish us to pray for you?" The man replied, "I am not such a fool but what I am willing to be prayed for," and down he dropped upon his knees.

The power of God came upon the meeting, and there was great blessing that night.

O. Depend upon the Holy Spirit.

You may have the right machinery; you may have the building and the crowds; you may have even the Word of God itself, but unless you have the power of the Holy Spirit to accompany the divine seed as you sow it, your work will come to nothing. All this machinery, unless the power of the Holy Spirit is in it, is worse than useless; but if you have the fire from above, you will win souls.

MEETINGS IN JAILS, HOSPITALS, POORHOUSES, ETC.

JAILS, HOSPITALS, POORHOUSES, and other public institutions offer a very important and much-neglected field of operations for the devoted soul winner.

I. IMPORTANCE AND ADVANTAGES

A. Many of the inmates of these institutions must be reached while there, or not at all.

Many of them, in fact, spend pretty much all of their lives there, and many others still will die there.

B. The inmates are oftentimes in a favorable mood for the reception of the Gospel.

Things have gone against them. Life looks hopeless. The Gospel, which is full of hope, just appeals to their need. Take, for example, those in jail. They have found out by bitter experience that "the way of the unfaithful is hard"; they are humbled and sobered. They are very likely to be in a thoughtful mood; they have much time for thought, little opportunity in fact for anything else; furthermore, the whisky is out of them, and with many of them the only time the whisky is out of them is when they are in jail or prison. There could not be a more favorable opportunity for preaching the Gospel. I have known many who thanked God that they were ever sent to jail, for there they heard the Gospel, some of them for the first time, and others of them in a different mood from that in which they had ever heard it before.

C. The converts can be followed up.

A prisoner is reached with the Gospel one Sunday in jail and is likely to be there the next Sunday as well, and perhaps for many Sundays to come, and there is an opportunity for him to get thoroughly established before being out in the world again. The same is true of a resident of a hospital who is reached one day, and is likely to be there for many days to come.

D. The inmates have to attend.

In some instances, attendance is compulsory. When one is confined to a sick bed in the ward of a hospital where a religious service is being held, they are obliged to hear the Gospel preached and sung. Further than this, where the inmates of such institutions are not compelled to attend, there is so little to do that they are willing to go to anything for a novelty.

E. The results of such services are very large.

It has oftentimes been our privilege in the Cook County Jail to preach to fifty or more persons there under charge of murder, besides great numbers of others. Very many of the most desperate and hardened characters have been converted in jail services. There is scarcely any other work that yields so important and so good results as jail work. Some of the leading ministers and other Christian workers of this country were converted while incarcerated. One of the leading ministers of one of our evangelical denominations, a man whose name is known not only in this country but in Europe, a man who has a remarkable power of preaching the Word of God, was first reached while in jail. At that time, he was a brilliant but drunken lawyer. He was converted in jail and has been for many years an honored preacher of the Gospel.

In one of our cities, a reckless young man was incarcerated under charge of arson. He had burned the property of his own father. His father was himself a godless man. While in jail this young man was brought to Christ and has been for years a most devoted Christian at the head of a very successful mission work. Jerry McAuley, perhaps the leader in rescue mission work in this country, was converted while in Sing Sing prison. Christian workers should see to it that every jail, poorhouse, and similar institution in the land has a regular evangelistic service. The formal services held under the city or state in such institutions frequently are purely formal and of no real value. As a rule, the best work is that which is done by volunteers. Services should also be held in every hospital in the land where it is possible to get an entrance.

II. HOW TO CONDUCT

A. First of all, you must get permission.

The way to get permission is to ask for it. The request should not be made in the way of a demand; it should be made with great tact and courtesy. If it is possible to get influence back of your request, get it.

B. Keep the good will of the attendants.

Here is a place where many zealous but unwise workers make a mistake; they unnecessarily antagonize jailers or keepers or nurses or other attendants. This is the height of folly. It does not cost much to keep the good will of people, and in a case like this it is of inestimable value.

C. Be sure to violate none of the rules of the institution.

Be careful at the outset to find what the rules of the institution are, and then observe them to the very letter. It makes no difference whether you think the rules of the institution are wise or not; keep them anyhow. It is not your business to make the rules, but to observe them.

D. Attend strictly to your own business.

Don't try to run the whole jail or hospital. Some, when they go to preach in an institution, seem to be seized with the idea that they own the whole institution. I have known workers to go to work among the inmates of a hospital and then try to get them to give up the use of medicine and accept divine healing, or sometimes try to get them to go to some other hospital they thought was better. In such a case, the authorities are of course warranted in sending them out of the hospital.

E. Go regularly.

Regular services, week after week, month after month, year after year, accomplish far more than spasmodic efforts. One great trouble in all this kind of work is that there are so many people who get enthusiastic for some weeks, and then their enthusiasm cools. When institutions have a number of experiences with this kind of work, they become unwilling to permit a new band of workers to take up again a work that has so often failed in the past.

F. Have good music, and plenty of it.

These people get very little music, and they enjoy it. Frequently, they enjoy the music more than they do the preaching, and it is easier to reach many of them by a solo sung in the power of the Spirit than it is by a sermon. Adapt your music to the circumstances; for example, in a hospital the music should not be loud or exciting; it should be bright and comforting. A doleful tune in a hospital may hasten the death of some of the patients, but a bright, cheerful, Gospel tune is likely to save the lives of some of the patients. The music that is adapted to a hospital is frequently not adapted to a jail, and vice versa.

G. Preach the Word.

Stick close to the Bible. Be simple, plain, vivacious, right to the point.

H. Be wise in your prayer.

An indiscreet prayer in a hospital may do much harm; so may an indiscreet prayer in a jail or workhouse.

I. In a jail, be careful to avoid all air of superiority.

Many an inexperienced preacher begins to talk to the inmates in jail as if he was an angel and they were demons. Such a preacher will get no hearing. Let the prisoners feel that you realize that you are their brother. Do not assume a patronizing air; avoid all unnecessary sentimentality and gush.

J. Make use of testimony.

Jerry McAuley was converted through the testimony of Orville Gardner. He had known Orville Gardner in the old days as a desperate character in New York, going by the nickname of "Awful Gardner." When he went to Sing Sing prison and saw Orville Gardner in the pulpit, he could hardly believe his own eyes; but when Orville Gardner rose and gave his testimony, it went home to Jerry McAuley's heart and thoroughly roused him to a study of the Bible itself, with the result that he was converted in his cell. There are many in this country today who have been inmates of jails and prisons—notorious criminals—but who are today living consistent Christian lives. The testimony of such a person has great weight with other convicts.

K. Deal individually with the inmates.

The public preaching does much good, but the personal work does more; it brings matters to a personal decision. The great majority of converts in jail work come through individual work. It may be difficult at first to get permission to deal individually with the inmates, but if you are wise, and win the confidence of the authorities, you will get the opportunity in time.

L. Make a large use of tracts and other Gospel literature.

Prisoners have so much time on their hands that they are ready to read anything. Select your literature very wisely. Goody-goody religious literature is not what is needed, but that which shows real ability and strength and goes right to the heart of things. There is no better literature for use in jails and hospitals than that published by the Bible Institute Colportage Association.

M. Pray much in secret.

Prayer is one of the great secrets of success in all forms of religious enterprise, but this is peculiarly true regarding work in jails, hospitals, and similar institutions. If a record could be kept and published regarding God's answers to prayers for work under such circumstances, it would make a most interesting and inspiring book.

CONDUCT
OF
FUNERALS

I. IMPORTANCE OF FUNERAL SERVICES AS A MEANS OF REACHING PEOPLE WITH THE GOSPEL

Funerals offer an excellent opportunity for getting hold of people and winning them to Christ. Many will attend a funeral service, out of regard for the deceased or his family, who will not go to any other religious service. Atheists, Roman Catholics, and utterly irreligious people are often seen at funeral services. It is a time when peoples' hearts are made tender by sorrow, and when men are solemnized by the presence of death and the nearness of eternity. He is a poor minister of Jesus Christ who does not seize upon such an opportunity for preaching the Gospel and bringing men to Christ.

It was once the writer's privilege to conduct the funeral services of a man who up to a short time before his death had been an out-and-out infidel. His wife was a Roman Catholic. A little while before his death I had pointed him to Christ, and he had found forgiveness of sins and had died rejoicing in the Savior. As I stood by his casket, many of his old friends were gathered around him. The opportunity was seized to preach the Gospel. The hearers were reminded of the long-standing unbelief of their friend and then of how his unbelief had failed in the trying hour and how he had found hope in Christ. As the sermon closed, I made an appeal to any who would then and there accept Christ as Savior. One man stepped forward and, reaching his hand across the coffin, said, "I have been an infidel just as my friend who lies here, but I will now take Christ as my Savior," and he gave me his hand upon it then and there. The wife of the man was also converted and united with our church and became a very faithful member.

II. HOW TO CONDUCT A FUNERAL SERVICE

Very few directions are needed as to the proper conduct of a funeral service. It should be conducted very much as any other Gospel service, with a special reference, of course, to the circumstances.

A. It is important to have wisely selected music, rendered in the power of the Holy Spirit.

One needs to be careful in regard to hymns sung at a funeral service. Some hymns that are supposed to be especially choice for such an occasion are sentimental trash. Hymns that are suitable for the funeral of a Christian are oftentimes not suitable for the funeral of an unconverted person. A good soloist who can sing effectively in the power of the Holy Spirit is a great help. A song properly rendered at such a time is likely to prove the means of someone's salvation. There is no place where a godless singer is more utterly out of place than at a funeral, and there is no place where a consecrated singer is more likely to be used of God.

B. Great dependence should be placed upon the reading of the Word of God.

Passages should be selected full of comfort for the sorrowing, but also passages that drive home to the minds of the unsaved the lesson of the occasion, namely, the nearness of death and the certainty of judgment. The Scriptures should not be read carelessly, but with the purpose of impressing their truth upon the hearts of the hearers. The presence and power of the Holy Spirit is greatly needed to this end.

C. The prayer is of great importance.

It should not be, as funeral prayers so often are, a mere attempt to say nice things, a smooth-flowing current of really meaningless words: It should be a real prayer and a prayer of faith. There should be petition to God for His comfort to those who are in affliction; there should also be prayer that the lesson of the hour should not be forgotten and direct prayer for the conversion of the unsaved who are present.

D. Great wisdom and skill are necessary in the sermon or address.

All unwarranted eulogy of the deceased should be renounced utterly. If there have really been things worthy of imitation in the life of the one who has departed, it is well oftentimes to mention these, but to do it not for the sake of glorifying the dead but for the sake of instructing the living and leading them to the imitation, in these respects, of the one who has gone. If the one who lies in the casket has been beyond question a true child of God, it is well to call attention to the fact and emphasize how it pays at such an hour to have been a Christian. It is well sometimes to drive home the thought that if some of those who were present were in the casket instead of the one who is there, there would have been no hope. There should always be a direct appeal to the unconverted to accept Christ then and there.

If the deceased was unsaved, there need be no personal reference at all. Of course, there should be no pronunciation of doom either, but there should be a plain declaration of the one way of salvation through Jesus Christ. This truth should not be applied to the deceased, but to those who are still living. They can draw their own inferences as to the application, but experience proves that in such an instance, if the work has been wisely done, the hearers will apply the truth to themselves instead of to the departed.

If there have been any special circumstances in connection with the death, these should be laid hold of as a point of interest that can be made to lead up to the truth. For example, if the deceased was clearly a true child of God and some of the friends are Roman Catholics, it is well to emphasize the truth, backing it up well by Scripture, that the deceased has not gone to purgatory, but has departed to be with Christ. It was once my privilege to conduct the funeral of an earnest Christian woman, almost all of whose relatives were Roman Catholics. The church was filled with Roman Catholics. I made no reference whatever directly to the Roman Catholic Church, and did not use the word "purgatory," but I dwelt at considerable length upon the truth that those who have been saved by a living faith in Jesus Christ pass into no purgatory of torment, but pass at once to be with Christ. The Roman Catholic audience listened with great attention, and I have reason to think that the sermon was blessed of God. Of course, if direct reference had been made to the fact that the woman had come out of the Roman Catholic Church and become a Protestant, there would have been trouble at once and no good accomplished.

E. Always follow up your funerals by visitation.

When you have been invited to conduct the funeral services of any person in a home, you have a right of entree into that home. Use it to the utmost. Take advantage of the circumstances. Deal with the people while their hearts are still tender with their great grief, and if possible lead them to the Savior. Many an irreligious home has become a Christian home because a wise minister has followed up the advantage that has been given by being invited to conduct a funeral service there.

1. As you evaluate your church and ministries, how limited are you to the church building itself? What opportunities are available for you in your community to have spiritual events in secular places?

2. What do you feel about using places like theatres? What risks does it involve? What potential benefits are possible?

3. Are blatant sinners welcome in the services at your church? Is your church being effective at reaching the truly needy? How does your church accomplish it? How could it accomplish it even better?

4. Review the reasons that ministry in jails and hospitals can be so effective. Interview a few people in your church or community regarding their ministry in these settings. How does their experience match the guidelines given by Torrey?

CHAPTER ELEVEN

SPECIAL COMPONENTS OF EFFECTIVE OUTREACH

IN THIS CHAPTER, TORREY PRESENTS two aspects of ministry that need to be connected to most of the others. Perhaps the most important part of any meeting is the "after meeting." This is a time for follow-up on those who have been moved by the main part of the service. It is usually held near the main meeting hall and allows a prime opportunity for personal work. So many contemporary ministries make an impact on people's lives, but don't bring that impact to its full potential. Torrey stresses the importance of making sure that those who have been reached during the service are brought to Christ for salvation or fulfillment of their other spiritual needs. Although it may take various forms, the concept of strong immediate follow-up is crucial.

The practicality of Torrey's instruction is evident in the final section of this chapter. It may not be as overtly spiritual as some of the other guidelines, but the instructions on advertising are very important. The best event in the world will have no impact if no one shows up. Advertising helps deliver the people who need to be there. Although some of the specific details are from another era, it is surprising how many of Torrey's ideas about advertising are still true today.

This chapter provides bookends for the rest of the instructions about meetings. On the one end, it helps to get people to the meetings. On the other end, it helps you to serve them as fully as possible once they come and respond. There is a great need for both in contemporary ministry. Many ministries are being run with high quality, but to very few people. They desperately need to do better promotion so that the people who need to be there come. Others provide a tremendous initial impact, but don't follow through. It is not enough to just warm people's hearts. Rather, they need to be brought to the point of personal salvation and dealing with their matters of need. Too often, we let needy people just come to our events and slip back into a life of sin. Torrey challenges us to make sure that we are trying diligently to meet the deep and most significant needs.

THE
AFTER
MEETING

I. IMPORTANCE AND ADVANTAGES

In successful soul-winning work, the after meeting is of the highest importance. Every tent meeting, mission meeting, and revival service should be followed by an after meeting. The wise and active pastor will also follow up every Sunday evening service with an after meeting. Many a mighty preacher fails to get the results from preaching, because of not knowing how to draw the net. He is successful at hooking fish, but does not know how to land them. A friend told me a short time ago that he heard a man one evening preach to a large congregation of men one of the best sermons he ever heard, and my friend continued, "I believe there would have been fifty decisions just then, but just at the critical moment the evangelist did not know what to do, and let the meeting slip through his fingers." He asked them to stand up and sing some hymn, and the men began to go out in crowds. He tried to get them together again, and there were some inquirers, but nothing like the results there should have been. Much good preaching comes to nothing because it is not driven home to the individual, and the individual brought then and there to an acceptance and confession of Jesus as Savior and Lord.

A. It gets rid of those who will hinder the work.

The first advantage of the after meeting is that it gets rid of that portion of the audience which is not in sympathy and is a hindrance to close work. It enables us to get near to the inquirer and meet his immediate need. Many things that it is impossible to do in the general meeting are very easily done in the smaller meeting that follows it. Some workers are very anxious to have everyone stay to the after meeting, but frequently it is very fortunate that all do not stay. The smaller gathering is not only easier to handle, on account of its size, but it is also more sympathetic and more in keeping with the purpose of soul saving that is now in view.

B. People are brought to a point of decision.

The second advantage of the after meeting is that people are brought to an immediate decision for Christ. This advantage rises partly out of the first. In almost every wisely conducted evangelistic service, there will be some who have not really decided for Christ, but who are on the verge of a decision. Of course some of those, if allowed to go home, will decide for Christ in the home; but there will be many others who, unless the impressions are followed up then and there, will lose their interest before another meeting is held. There is great need in all soul-winning work that we strike while the iron is hot. A wise worker, and one of much experience, recently wrote substantially as follows about a meeting that she had attended in the East: "The sermon was grand, the Holy Spirit was manifestly present in power, and I could not help feeling if some experienced person was only present to conduct an after meeting then and there we should have had great results, but the benediction was pronounced and the students allowed to go to their rooms. We have been trying to follow up the work since, and many have come out positively, but we could have had much larger results with much less labor on our part if an after meeting had been held at once." It would be difficult to put too much emphasis upon the after meeting.

II. HOW TO CONDUCT AN AFTER MEETING

A. Announce the meeting.

The number who attend the after meeting and the character of those who attend will depend very much upon the announcement. The announcement should be very clear and definite so there can be no mistaking what is meant. The announcement should also be earnest. If the announcement is indifferent, people will think that the after meeting is of little consequence and, therefore, will not stay to it. If the announcement is earnest, the people will think that the minister or evangelist thinks the meeting is of some importance and will be likely to think so also. The announcement should be given in a winning and attractive way; it should also be urgent, but in our urgency we should avoid the impression that we think that any Christian who does not stay to the after meeting is necessarily committing some great sin. Many Christians have good reasons why they cannot stay to the after meeting, and if we are indiscreet in our urgency in giving the invitation to it, they will either stay to the after meeting when they ought not, or they will go away with the morbid sense that they have done something wrong—or worse yet, we shall bring them under the condemnation of the irreligious people who go away, and thus injure the cause of Christ.

Sometimes an indiscreet urgency in the invitation to the after meeting keeps people away from the first meeting. The way we put the invitation, even in seemingly insignificant matters, is oftentimes of great consequence. For example, if we say, "Now, if there is anyone here tonight who is interested, we should be glad to have them stay to the after meeting," this will cause some person who may be interested to think that probably he or she is the only one in the whole audience who is, and, as few people like to be considered singular, he or she will not be likely to stay. If, on the other hand, we say, "We hope that everyone here tonight with whom the Spirit is working will stay to the after meeting," this will cause those who are somewhat interested to think, *Well, I am not alone; there are others interested beside myself,* and so they will be likely to stay to the after meeting.

We do well to put our invitation in such a way that those who are not wanted in the after meeting will not feel at liberty to stay. For example, there are those who crowd after meetings out of mere curiosity and are a great hindrance. If possible, the invitation should be so worded as to shut this class out. There are others who go to oppose the work. The invitation should be so put as to shut this class out. It will not be possible to do it altogether in whatever way the invitation is put, and if the invitation does not succeed in doing it, other means will sometimes have to be taken. There are a third class who are very angry if you deal with them personally, but if the invitation has been wisely put, when anyone gets angry when you approach them personally you can call their attention to what was said in the invitation, and show them courteously that, by coming to the after meeting, they expressed a willingness to be dealt with.

B. Hold it in the right place.

The second matter of importance in the conduct of an after meeting is as to where it shall be held. As a rule, it is better to hold it in another room from that in which the general meeting is held. If the after meeting is held in the same room as the general service, when the invitation is given for the general audience to withdraw, many who might have stayed to the after meeting are carried out with the tide, whereas if the meeting is held in another room, they see the tide setting in there and are carried in with it. Of course, oftentimes there is no other room that is available, and the after meeting has to be held in the same room as the general service; and there are times when it is better to hold it in the same room even when another room is available.

If the meeting is to be held in another room, it is very desirable that it should be a room that the people have to pass as they go out. Workers should be posted at every door of this room, to invite and urge the people to go in as they pass. It is exceedingly important that these workers be wise men and women. I have heard workers shouting out invitations to this second meeting as if it were a sideshow to a circus. Oftentimes, the best way to give the invitation is to quietly slip up beside the one that you wish to get into the after meeting, hold out your hand, and engage him in a few moments of conversation and almost imperceptibly draw him into the meeting. Gentleness and courtesy and winsomeness in this matter are of great importance.

When the interest is very deep, you can have the second meeting in another building. Have the singing begin at once, just as soon as the people begin to pass the door.

C. Make much of prayer in the after meeting.

The meeting should be begun with prayer. Wait until everyone is in and all is quiet. Insist upon absolute silence, then have all the Christians engage in silent prayer. It is well to suggest to them objects of prayer, as for example, that they pray for those who have gone to their homes undecided, then that they pray for the presence and power of the Holy Spirit in the meeting, then for the unsaved who are in the room. Two or three or more audible prayers by men and women whom you can trust should follow. Do not take any chances at this point and let any troublemaker spoil the meeting. Unless you know your people very well, it is usually best to name those who shall lead in prayer. Of course, one can trust the Holy Spirit to take charge of the meeting—and should—but this does not mean that we should not exercise a wise control over the meeting. There will also be places for prayer later in the meeting, but there should certainly be prayer at the opening. If it should turn out in any meeting that there are no unsaved people there, it is oftentimes well to give the entire meeting up to prayer. A few months ago it turned out in an after meeting that there were only two or three unsaved people in the whole audience. These were taken to another room to be dealt with, and then I urged it upon the people that there must be something wrong with us or with the work because there were so few coming to Christ. The Holy Spirit carried the message home, and then we got down on our knees before God in prayer. The next night, largely as an outcome of that season of prayer, we had a meeting of great power.

D. Explain the gospel in as plain and simple a manner as possible.

This is especially important if there are few workers present to deal with individuals. After explaining the way of life and the steps one must take to be saved then and there, an invitation can be given to those who are willing to take these steps at once. They should be asked to rise, hold up their hands, come forward, or in some other definite way express their desire to begin the Christian life.

E. Find out just as early as possible in the meeting where the people present stand.

Then you will know what to do next. It is frequently desirable to take some sort of an expression in the general meeting, though this should usually be done in such a way as not to put those who are not Christians in an awkward position. Indeed, as a rule, the moment the last word of the sermon is uttered there should be an opportunity for decision. This opportunity may be given in a variety of ways. You may ask the audience to bow a few moments in silent prayer, insisting courteously but firmly that no one go out for a few moments. If the interest is deep enough, you can then ask all those who wish to be saved or all who have made up their minds "now and here" to accept Christ as their personal Savior, to surrender to Him as their Lord and Master, and to begin to confess Him as such before the world to rise, or to "come forward and give me your hand," or come and kneel at the altar. If the interest hardly warrants that, you can ask all in the audience who are burdened for unsaved friends or all who are anxious for the salvation of some friend in the audience to rise, and when they have risen, invite all who wish to be saved "right now" to rise. It is not well usually in the general meeting to ask all Christians to rise, as this makes it awkward for the unsaved, and they may not come back again.

Another good way is to say, "We are going to sing a hymn, and I do not wish anyone to go out until it is finished. The Holy Spirit is evidently working in this meeting (don't say this unless it is true), and anyone moving about may distract someone who is on the verge of a decision for Christ. Now, while we are singing the second verse, let all who will accept Christ (don't say *if* anyone will accept Christ) arise." Stop when the second verse is sung and call for decisions, and then sing the third and fourth in a similar way. If there is an altar in the church where you are preaching, it is often better to have them come to the altar. If there is no altar, you can have the front seats emptied and use them for an altar. A solo may often be used in place of the congregational hymn, but be sure of your soloist and the solo that has been selected. It is safer, as a rule, to select the solo yourself.

Still another way is to say as you close your sermon, "We are going to have a second meeting, and all those who have been converted here tonight and who desire to enter the joy of the Christian life, are invited to remain. We also want everyone who is interested in his soul's salvation, and all Christians, to stay to that second meeting—you cannot afford to go away." Once in the second meeting, there are a variety of ways of finding out where the people stand. If the interest is very deep, call at once for those who wish to accept Christ to rise and come forward. On other occasions, ask all who have accepted Christ and know that they are saved and are walking in fellowship with Him to rise. Now you and your workers can readily see who the persons are with whom you ought to deal. They are, for the most part, those who are still seated. Next ask those who wish to become Christians to arise. It may be well to sing one or several verses as this is done. One and then another and then many at once will often rise.

Whenever it is possible, it is well to have now still a third room into which those who have risen and desire to become Christians shall go. Have a wise person in charge of this room until you get there yourself. Put one worker, and one only, with each inquirer. These workers should be trained for the work. Every church and mission should have a training class for this purpose. When you have gotten all you can into the inside room, turn the outside meeting into a meeting for testimony and prayer, which either you or some wise worker manages. It is a great advantage to have a choir leader who can do that. The unconverted ones who have not gone into the inside room can be gotten hold of personally in this testimony meeting or afterward. Do not have any holes anywhere in your net if you can avoid it.

Sometimes it is well in the second meeting to ask all who were converted after they were fifty to rise, and then those who were converted after they were forty, thirty, twenty, ten, before they were ten; then ask all who will accept Jesus "tonight" to rise, and then all who really desire to know the way of life. In other meetings, all who have been Christians fifty years may be asked to stand, then those who have been Christians forty years, thirty, twenty, and so on down. A good method to use occasionally in the second meeting is to ask all who were converted after they were fifty to come forward and gather about the platform, and then those who were converted after they were forty, and so on. This will gradually thin out those who are seated, and the unconverted will begin to feel that they are left in the minority, and it may lead them to desire to be saved also. Especially will this be true if a man sees his wife leaving him, or a son his mother.

Some may say there is too much method or maneuvering in all this, but it wins souls, and this is worth maneuvering for. Jesus Himself told us to be as wise as serpents (Matthew 10:16), and again we are told that the children of this world are wiser in their generation than the children of light. Evidently Jesus would have us exercise all honest ingenuity in accomplishing His work, especially the work of soul-winning. The methods suggested will suggest others. The great purpose of all these methods is to get many to commit themselves, and to bring them to a decision to accept Christ.

F. The most important part of the after meeting is the hand-to-hand dealing with individuals.

There has already been a suggestion as to how this should be done, but the hand-to-hand work should not be limited to those who go into the third room. Trained personal workers should be scattered all over the meeting, each worker having his own assigned place, and feeling his responsibility for that section of the room. He should be on the lookout for persons with whom he can deal either during the testimony meeting or after the formal meeting is over. These workers, however, should be instructed to obey at once any suggestion of the leader of the meeting. I have been in meetings where the leader requested absolute silence, but indiscreet workers would go on talking to those with whom they were dealing. I have heard other workers talking with an inquirer when there has been a call for prayer. Such irreverence does much harm.

G. There should always be workers near the door of the meeting to follow anyone who goes out before the meeting is over.

They should approach such a one personally and deal with him about his soul. Much of the best work that is done is done with people who have become so deeply interested that they try to run away from the meeting but are followed out by some wise worker. It may be necessary for the worker to follow the fugitive down the street. I knew of one case where a very successful worker tried to engage a young man in conversation, and he started off on a run. The worker followed, and having better wind than the runaway, caught him after two or three blocks. The young man was so amazed, and so awakened by the worker's earnestness, and afterward so instructed by his wisdom, that he accepted Christ then and there on the street. This would probably not be a wise method under ordinary circumstances.

H. A good use may be made of the testimony of saved people in the after meeting.

As a rule, however, there should not be a call for testimonies until those who are ripe for hand-to-hand work are taken into another room. Great caution needs to be exercised in the use of testimony. In almost every community, there are men and women who are always willing to give their testimony at the first opportunity, but who kill any meeting where they are allowed to speak. It may be that they have no sense; or it may be that there is something crooked in their lives, and their testimony simply brings reproach on the cause that they pretend to represent. You must manage somehow to keep these people silent. You need to be on your guard, too, that the testimonies are not stereotyped or unreal. They should be short, to the point, real, and, above all, in the power of the Holy Ghost. There is a special power in the testimonies of those who have been recently saved. It is always a great help to the young converts themselves to be trained to give their testimony.

I. When anyone has clearly accepted Christ, insist upon an open confession of Christ.

If it can be done without disturbing other workers, have him or her stand right up then and there and confess Jesus as Lord, and his or her acceptance of Him. If the inquirer has been taken into an inside room, ask him out into the room where the general after meeting is going on, and have him give his confession there. Many a young Christian does not come out into the clear light for many days, if ever, because he is not shown the necessity of a public confession of Christ with his mouth. There is nothing more important for a young Christian's life than a constant confession of the Lord.

J. Do not hold the after meeting too long.

Oftentimes, it is well to tell the people in the first meeting that the after meeting will only be fifteen or twenty minutes long, or whatever you have decided upon. Many will be encouraged to stay by this who would not think it possible to stay if it were to be a long meeting. When you have made a promise of this kind, be sure you keep it.

1. IMPORTANCE

It is of the utmost importance that wherever meetings are held they be properly advertised. Judicious advertising is important for three reasons:

A. Advertising is important because it gets people out to hear the Gospel.

There is no hope of saving people unless they hear the Gospel, and they will not come and hear it unless they are informed that it is being preached. A mere general notice will not arouse their attention, but wise advertising will. The advertisement that gets a man out to hear the Gospel is just as important in its place as the sermon through which he hears the Gospel. The contempt in which some people hold all advertising is utterly irrational. Experience demonstrates that wise advertising has very much to do with the number of people who are reached and converted by the Gospel. I could tell from personal experience of many remarkable conversions that have resulted from judicious advertising.

B. Advertising is important because it sets people to thinking.

It is of the very highest importance to get people to thinking upon the subject of religion. The very simple reason why many people are not converted is because they give the subject of the claims of Christ upon them no attention whatever. It never enters their thoughts from one day's end to another. But a wise advertisement will arrest their attention and set them to thinking. It may bring up memories of childhood. It reminds them that there is a God. It tells them that Jesus saves. Some sentence in the advertisement may follow them for days, and result in their conversion to Christ. Instances could be multiplied of those who have never gone near the meeting advertised but have been set to thinking and thus have been brought to Christ.

C. Advertising is important because of its direct converting power.

Enough Gospel can be put in a single advertisement to convert anybody who notices it and will believe it. On every invitation card that goes out from the church of which the author is pastor is placed some pointed passage of Scripture, and many are those who have been won to Christ by the power of the truth thus set forth.

II. HOW TO ADVERTISE

A. In your advertisements aim to reach the nonchurchgoers.

The church today is ministering largely to those who are already in attendance. A church that is truly Christian has the missionary spirit, and its first aim is to get hold of those who do not go to hear the Gospel. The churchgoers will hear the Gospel anyhow, and our chief responsibility in our advertising work is to get the ear of those who are never found in the house of God. Theatres and saloons make every effort to get the attention of those who are not already patrons. These institutions do it in order to get people's money and destroy their souls. How much more should the church do it in order to save them? Stores, papers, and magazines offer special inducements to those who are not already their patrons; the church of Christ should do the same for a far higher purpose.

B. Aim to set people to thinking.

A commonplace advertisement does very little good, but an advertisement so phrased as to awaken the attention of those who see it and set them to thinking accomplishes great good. Of course, one ought not to stoop to anything that is in a true sense undignified or grossly sensational to awaken attention; but an advertisement may, at the same time, have proper dignity and yet set forth the truth in such a striking way that even the godless cannot help but notice it. For example, a sermon was announced upon "A Converted Infidel's Preaching." This part of the advertisement was in large black letters on a white background. At least one infidel came to find out what this infidel preached about. The converted infidel was Saul of Tarsus. What he preached about is found in Acts 9:20. That verse was the text of the sermon. The infidel mentioned was deeply impressed and went to the inquiry room, and two weeks after looked me up and told me that both he and his wife had accepted Christ. Several years before that a sermon had been preached on "A Bitter and Brilliant Infidel Converted." One of the leading daily papers was deeply interested as to who this converted infidel was and sent for an outline of the sermon. Of course it was Saul of Tarsus, and the sermon was printed Monday with great letters running clear across the top of the page, "A Bitter and Brilliant Infidel Converted." Another sermon was announced on the subject, "Five Things That No Man Can Do Without." Tickets were scattered all over the city with the announcement of the subject upon them. Even the schools took it up, and the teachers discussed with their scholars what were the five things that no man could do without. The sermon was really a Bible reading upon such texts as "Without [holiness] no one will see the Lord," "Without faith it is impossible to please Him."

C. In your advertisements, make much use of the Scripture that will convert.

There are many who will read your advertisements who will not go to the church. Put enough Scripture on the advertisement to convert them.

D. Advertisements of religious services should be well printed.

They should be printed so they can be readily seen and so that they will make an impression upon the mind. It is well oftentimes to have them printed in such a way that people will like to keep them as souvenirs, and thus they will go on doing their work for a long time.

E. Use bulletin boards.

1. *Every church should have one or more large bulletins standing out in front of the church constantly.*

On these, announcements should be made of the services of the church, regular or special, from time to time. Something should always be upon the bulletin. The notice should be constantly changed so that people will be looking for something new. If there is no special service to be announced, a striking text of Scripture can be put upon the bulletin. It is usually desirable to have these bulletins on feet so that you can move them from place to place.

2. *There should also be large bulletins in conspicuous places throughout the city.*

Put these in places where many cars or carriages pass. The announcements upon these bulletins should be in such large letters that they can be read by people in the carriages or cars as they go by. One bulletin in a good place is worth ten in poor places. Make a study of locations for your bulletins.

3. *Secure, wherever possible, the use of the bulletin boards of theatres.*

There are oftentimes seasons of the year when the theatres are closed, and many theatrical proprietors will be willing to allow you the use of their bulletins, if not free, for a small compensation. Just the class of people you wish to reach will notice advertisements on these bulletins.

F. Use the public billboards of the city.

This is a very successful way of advertising. Have your notices larger and more striking than those of others. Do not have too many words upon them, but big letters that can be read a block or more away. A very small body of Christians once used all the bulletin boards of Chicago with enormous notices, stated in a very striking way, about the coming of Christ. There was no notice at first as to where their meetings were to be held. Thousands of people in the city wondered what it all meant and who put these notices up. The whole city was talking about the meaning of it. Reporters were sent here and there to find out who was back of it. When the meetings were held, they were attended by large audiences. Unfortunately, they had but very little to give the people when they got there, but as an advertisement it was a notable success. Of course, these things cost money, but they usually bring in more than they cost. But cost however much they may, if they win souls for Christ, it pays.

G. Use a large van with advertisements on all sides.

A van can be driven up and down the thickly traveled streets for a very useful and comparatively inexpensive form of advertisement. In connection with evangelistic meetings recently held in Chicago, a van eighteen feet long and ten feet high was covered with black cloth on which was printed in white letters the announcement of the meetings and speaker. This was driven up and down the main thoroughfares and read by thousands. Many may say that this is undignified, but it serves to fill the church and bring people to Christ. It is better to sacrifice your dignity and fill your pews and save souls than to keep your dignity and have an empty church and allow people to go down to hell.

H. Transparencies are very useful and inexpensive as a means of advertising meetings.

A transparency consisting of a wooden frame, say eighteen to twenty-four inches in length and twelve inches high, with white cloth around the four sides on which are printed in black letters announcements of the meetings can be made by almost anybody for a little cost. To the wooden bottom of the transparency, tallow candles are secured. When the candles are lighted, and the transparencies carried up and down the street, they will attract more people than the most artistic printed matter. The novelty of the thing is one of the strongest points in its favor. As many as possible of these transparencies should be sent out every evening. Sometimes it is well to organize the whole crowd of transparency bearers into a procession and send them through the more thickly populated part of the city. They may be laughed at, or even stoned, but what matters that if people are brought out to hear the Gospel and saved? I know personally of three conversions in two days from the transparencies that were carried up and down the streets of Chicago.

I. Use large printed cards.

Cards twelve by eighteen inches printed so that they can be read from the street are very useful, not only for special meetings, but to announce the regular services of the church or mission, and all kinds of special services. These should be handed around among the members of the church, or mission workers and their friends, to hang up in their windows. A man who placed one of these cards in his window sat behind the curtain of another window and watched results. It seemed as though almost everyone who went by, men, women, and children of all classes, stopped to read the sign through. Good is often accomplished by placing a pointed text in the window where people will read it. Many have been blessed by these texts. People are very ready to cooperate in this kind of work. A single church found several hundred persons in its membership who were willing to put these cards in their windows. When a large number of cards are noticed on different streets, they at once awaken comment on the part of the passersby. They wonder what is going on, and go to the church to find out. Still larger cards, or better still, bulletins that are inexpensive, can be furnished to such members of the church as have stores. These bulletins can be placed out in front of the stores. They can even be used to advantage in private houses, where the houses stand in conspicuous places.

J. Banners across the street attract attention.

These, however, are very expensive, and should not be used unless it is in a place where very many people pass.

K. Elevated cars and surface cars can be used to advantage for advertising purposes.

We all know how many people read the advertisements that are seen in the elevated and other cars. This form of advertising, however, is very expensive, and if the city has been well placarded, is unnecessary. If the great billboards are used all over the city, it is doubtful if anyone will see the advertisement in the cars who does not see it on the billboards.

L. Small invitation cards should be used.

These should be handed out on the street corners, should be carried into houses, saloons, hotels, stores. It is well for the pastor on prayer-meeting night to have a supply of these tickets present, and before the meeting closes have them handed out to each individual, urging them to take them and give them out. The same method can be employed in other meetings. Very frequently, when Mr. Moody was not getting the attendance at his services that he desired, he would have a large supply of tickets at one service, and have them distributed among the people to give out, and at the very next service there would be a large increase in attendance.

M. Issue tickets for the meeting.

It is well sometimes to issue tickets for a meeting, and allow no one to enter before a certain time without a ticket. This puts a premium on admission to the services, and people believe that it is something worth going to. Of course, these tickets should be free, but people should be obliged to take some trouble to get them, to send a stamped envelope or call at a certain place to get them. If you do ticket a meeting, be sure and keep faith with the people. Never say no one will be admitted up to a certain hour without a ticket and then let people in whether they have a ticket or not. The people who have taken the trouble to get a ticket will justly feel that they have been outraged.

N. No other form of advertising is as good as personal invitation.

Whatever else is done to advertise the meetings, be sure and get individuals to talk about the meetings to individuals and to urgently invite them to come. There should be a systematic canvass of the entire neighborhood where meetings are held. The names and addresses of all non-churchgoers should be secured. Notices should be sent again and again to these non-churchgoers. They should be followed up by letters and post cards. These things cost money, but these are the methods that are used by successful business houses in building up their business, and the church of Christ can afford to be no less active and earnest than a business house.

O. Never forget the papers in your advertising.

1. *First of all, make as much use as possible of the news columns of the paper.*

Most newspapers are willing to assist to the utmost of their ability in pushing the work of any church that shows it is alive and aggressive. If notices and descriptions of meetings, and outlines of sermons, and other interesting matter is sent to them, they will publish it. They will often send reporters to the meeting if there is anything worth reporting. It is not fair to leave it to the papers to find out what is going on when it is more our interest than theirs that is in hand. If you are not satisfied with the reporting of the newspapers by their own people, usually you can report the meeting yourself, and they will accept your report if it is readable. Of course, if the newspapers get the idea that someone is trying to advertise for personal gain, they will despise and ignore—as they ought to—but if it is a legitimate way of making public the work being done, the papers appreciate it. Many ministers and churches complain of not getting satisfactory reports from the newspapers, but they are more to blame than the newspapers. They think that the newspapers ought to know that they are alive and important, but newspaper staff are very busy and cannot be expected to know everything. Churches abuse the newspapers and then wonder why the newspapers do not support them.

2. *Make use of the advertising columns of the newspaper.*

This should not be done too generously, as it is not necessary, but an attractive advertisement should now and then be put in the amusement column. I say in the amusement column, for that is the column read by people looking for someplace to go, by travelers and commercial men, by the very class that the church wishes to reach, and oftentimes fails to reach. A very large church that we know, whose audience used to fill only one floor, advertised a special evening service with a special subject in the amusement column of the paper. The following Sunday evening the church was filled upstairs and down. There were perhaps eight hundred or one thousand extra people present. The church kept up this special advertising for only a week or two, but the church has kept full from that day to this, though more than five years have passed.

P. In your advertising, never forget God.

All your advertising will come to absolutely nothing unless God blesses it. His guidance should be sought as to how to advertise and His blessing asked upon the advertisements that are sent out. A minister of the Gospel who found it difficult to get men to go out with the transparencies finally decided to carry them himself. As he went down one of the leading streets of the neighborhood, he did not enjoy the work, but he prayed that God would bless the transparency to the conversion of someone. The next night a man came to another member of the church and told him how he had been brought out to church by seeing the transparency at a certain point, and how he had been converted. This other member called the minister who had carried the transparency and introduced him. The minister questioned him and found out that it was undoubtedly by his transparency this young man had been attracted, as he stood upon the steps of a hotel. Thus he found that his prayer was answered. A few evenings after another young man told his story, and he had evidently been converted by means of the same transparency as it was carried back up another street. God is willing to bless everything we do, our advertising as well as our preaching, if we do it to His honor and under His guidance, and we should look to Him to thus definitely bless it.

LEARNING ACTIVITIES

1. Does your church and other outreach ministries do an effective job of serving those who are reached by the presentation of the Gospel? Do you use an "after meeting" approach?

2. What else could be done in your setting to reach fully the needs of those who are responding? What are the common needs that they have? How can you set up the ministry to be ready to serve them if they express further interest?

3. Evaluate the advertising of your church or other outreach ministry. Is it actually bringing people in?

4. What creative techniques could be used to be more effective in drawing people to your events? How are you going to be able to tell for sure that they have been effective?

CHAPTER TWELVE

PREACHING
AND
TEACHING

PREACHING IS NOT JUST FOR PASTORS on Sundays. Although we don't always call it preaching, most Christians have opportunities to present God's Word to audiences, whether they be small groups at work or at home, or larger groups gathered to hear us. It is important that everyone be able to speak clearly from God's Word. This chapter includes the basic instructions for how to prepare a message. It enables every Christian to prepare messages and deliver them effectively. Once one develops the ability to speak in public, there are countless opportunities that appear in which to use that ability.

Many liturgical churches and some other organizations still use Bible readings. A Bible reading is simply a time designated for the presentation of a reading from Scripture and perhaps some brief comments. In recent decades, Bible reading has been prohibited from some public settings; however, it seems to be more welcome now. A postmodern worldview has opened these settings for just about anything, including the Bible. Thus, it is increasingly important that Christian workers be prepared to take advantage of situations where they can present God's Word.

This section is also a challenge regarding the place of the Bible in our churches and ministries. We talk about the Bible a lot, but how much time do we give for the simple reading of God's Word? Torrey has repeatedly emphasized the importance of the Bible. Bible readings are one way in which the Bible is given priority, even in our church services and other gatherings.

The concluding section of this chapter and the book is given to the subject of teaching the Bible. Torrey has provided many excellent examples of how to use illustrations effectively in this book. The combination of the clear presentation of God's Word with a vivid story of application is a powerful communication device.

This book is only one aspect of preparation for ministry. It has focused on the practical aspects of personal work. Another key aspect of preparation for ministry is the systematic teaching (and learning) of God's Word. This book ends with an emphasis on paying attention to the whole of the Bible. Studying the Bible is one of the most important aspects of a healthy Christian life and ministry. It is a fitting conclusion to Torrey's emphasis on the power of God through His Word.

HOW TO
PREPARE
A SERMON

THERE IS NO INTENTION in this chapter of presenting an elaborate treatise on preaching. It simply aims to give practical suggestions for the preparation of sermons that will win souls for Christ and edify believers.

I. GET YOUR TEXT OR SUBJECT.

A great many neglect to do that, and when they get through preaching they do not know what they have been talking about; neither does the audience. Never get up to speak without having something definite in your mind to speak about. There may be exceptions to that rule. There are times when one is called on suddenly to speak, and one has a right then to look to God for subject matter and manner of address. There are other times when one has made full preparation, but it becomes evident when he is about to speak that he must take up some other line of truth. In such a case also, one must depend upon God. But under ordinary circumstances, one should either have something definite in his mind that he is to speak about or else keep silent. It is true God has said in His Word, "Open your mouth wide, and I will fill it" (Psalm 81:10), but this promise, as the context clearly shows, has nothing whatever to do with our opening our mouths in speaking. Most people who take this promise as applying to their preaching, and who make their boast that they never prepare beforehand what they are going to say, when they open their mouths have them filled with anything but the wisdom of God. Christ did say to

His disciples, "Do not worry about how or what you should speak. For it will be given to you in that hour what you should speak; for it is not you who speak, but the Spirit of your Father who speaks in you" (Matthew 10:19–20); but this promise did not have to do with preaching, but with witnessing for Christ in circumstances of emergency and peril. In all cases of similar emergency, we have a right to rest in the same promise, and we have a right also to take the spirit of it as applying to our preaching. But if one has an opportunity to prepare for the services before him and neglects that opportunity, God will not set a premium upon his laziness and neglect by giving him a sermon in his time of need.

How shall we select our text or subject?

A. Ask God for it.

The best texts and topics are those that you get on your knees. No one should ever prepare a sermon without first going alone with God, and there definitely seeking His wisdom in the choice of a text or topic.

B. Keep a textbook.

I do not mean the kind that you buy, but the kind that you make for yourself. Have a small book that you can carry in your vest pocket, and as subjects or texts occur to you in your regular study of the Word, or in hearing others preach, or in conversation with people, jot them down in your book. Oftentimes, texts will come to you when you are riding on the streetcars or going about your regular work. If so, put them down at once. It is said that Ralph Waldo Emerson would sometimes be heard at night stumbling around his room in the dark. When his wife would ask him what he was doing, he would reply that he had a thought and he wanted to write it down. Oftentimes when you are reading a book, a text will come to you that is not mentioned in the book at all. Indeed, one of the best ways to get to thinking is to take up some book that stimulates thought. It will set your own mental machinery in operation. Not that you are going to speak on anything in that particular book, but it sets you to thinking, and your thought goes out along the line on which you are going to speak. Very often while listening to a sermon, texts or subjects or sermon points will come to your mind. I do not mean that you will take the points of the preacher, though you may sometimes do that if you will thoroughly digest them and make them your own, but something that is said will awaken a train of thought in your own mind. I rarely hear someone preach but the sermon suggests many sermons to me.

Put but one text or subject on a page of your textbook. Then when points or outlines come to you, jot them down under the proper text or subject. In this way, you will be accumulating material for future use. After a while texts and topics and outlines will multiply so rapidly that you will never be able to catch up with them and will never be at a loss for something to preach about.

C. Expound a book in order.

Take a book of the Bible and expound it. You should be very careful about this, however, or you will be insufferably dry. One of the best preachers in an eastern State undertook to expound one of the long books of the Bible. He made it so dry that some of his congregation said they were going to stay away from church until he got through that book; they were thoroughly tired of it. Study the masters in this line of work, men like Alexander Maclaren, William H. Taylor, and Horatius Bonar. F. B. Meyer's expositions on Abraham, Jacob, Elijah, Moses, etc., are very good.

D. Read the Bible in course, and read until you come to a text that you wish
   to use.

This was George Mueller's plan, and he is a safe man to follow. He was wonderfully used of God. When the time drew near to preach a sermon, he would take up the Bible and open it to the place where he was reading at that time, first going down upon his knees and asking God to give him a text, and then he would read on and on and on until he came to the desired text.

II. FIND YOUR POINTS.

I do not say make your points—find them; find them in your text, or if you are preaching on a topic, find them in the various texts in the Bible that bear upon that topic. It is desirable often to preach on a topic instead of on a single text. Never write a sermon and then hunt up a text for it. That is one of the most wretched and outrageous things that someone who believes that the Bible is the Word of God can do. It is simply using the Word of God as a label or endorsement for your idea. We are ambassadors for Christ, with a message. Our message is in the Word of God, and we have no right to prepare our own message and then go to the Word of God merely to get a label for it.

How shall we find our points?

A. Carefully analyze the text.

Write down one by one the points contained in the text. Suppose, for example, your text is Acts 13:38–39: "Therefore let it be known to you, brethren, that through this Man is preached to you the forgiveness of sins; and by Him everyone who believes is justified from all things from which you could not be justified by the law of Moses." By an analysis of the text, you will find the following points taught in it:

1. Forgiveness is preached unto us.
2. This may be known (not merely surmised, or guessed, or hoped, or believed).
3. It is known by the resurrection of Christ. Forgiveness is not a mere hope, but a certainty resting upon a solid and uncontrovertible fact. The one who here speaks had seen the risen Christ.
4. This forgiveness is through Jesus Christ. In developing this point, the question will arise and should be answered, How is forgiveness through Jesus Christ?
5. Everyone who believes is forgiven.

B. Ask questions about the text.

For example, suppose you take Matthew 11:28 as a text: "Come to Me, all you who labor and are heavy laden, and I will give you rest." You might ask questions on that text as follows:

1. Who are invited?
2. What is the invitation?
3. What will be the result of accepting the invitation?
4. What will be the result of rejecting the invitation?

One of the easiest and simplest ways of preaching is to take a text and ask questions about it that you know will be in the minds of your hearers, and then answer these questions. If you are preaching upon a subject, you can ask and answer questions regarding the subject. Suppose, for example, that you are to preach upon the subject of the new birth. You could ask the following questions and give Bible answers to them and, thus, prepare an excellent sermon:

1. What is it to be born again?
2. Is the new birth necessary?
3. Why is it necessary?
4. What are the results of being born again?
5. How can one be born again?

If you answer the questions that suggest themselves to your own mind, you will probably answer the questions that suggest themselves to the minds of others. Imagine your congregation to be a lot of question marks. Take up their questions and answer them, and you will interest them.

C. If you are going to preach upon a topic, go through the Bible on that topic and write down the various texts that bear upon it.

As you look these texts over, they will naturally fall under different subdivisions. These subdivisions will be your principal points. For example, suppose you are going to preach on "Prayer." Some of the passages on prayer will come under the head of "The Power of Prayer"; that can be your first main point. Others will come under the head of "How to Pray"; that will be your second main point, with doubtless many subordinate points. Other passages will come under the head of "Hindrances to Prayer," and this will make your third main point.

III. SELECT YOUR POINTS.

After finding your points, the next thing is to select them. You will seldom be able to take up all the points that you find in a text, or upon a topic, unless you preach much longer than the average congregation will stand. Few ministers can wisely preach longer than thirty or forty minutes. To a person just beginning to preach, twenty minutes is often long enough and sometimes too long. At a cottage meeting, fifteen minutes is certainly long enough and usually too long. The more you study a subject the more points you will get, and it is a great temptation to give the people all these points. They have all been helpful to you, and you wish to give them all out to them, but you must bear in mind that the great majority of your congregation will not be so interested in truth as you are. You must strenuously resist the temptation to tell people everything you know. You will have other opportunities to give the rest of the points if you give well the few that you now select; but if you attempt to tell all that you know in a single sermon, you will never have another chance. In selecting your points, the question is not which points are the best in the abstract, but which are best to give to your particular congregation at this particular time. In preaching on a given text, it will be wise to use certain points at one time and certain other points at another time. The question is, which are the points that will do the most good and be the most helpful to your congregation on this special occasion.

IV. ARRANGE YOUR POINTS.

There is a great deal in the arrangement of your points. There are many preachers who have good points in their sermons, but they do not make them in a good order. They begin where they ought to end, and end where they ought to begin. What may be the right order at one time may not be the right way at another time. There are, however, a few suggestions that may prove helpful:

A. Make your points in logical order.

Put those first that come first in thought. There are many exceptions to this rule. If our purpose in preaching is not to preach a good sermon, but to win souls, a point will oftentimes be more startling and produce more effect out of its logical order than in it.

B. Do not make your strongest points first and then taper down to the weakest.

If some points are weaker than others, it is best to lead along up to a climax. If a point is really weak, it is best to leave it out altogether.

C. Put that point last that leads to the important decision that you have in view in your sermon.

It may not in itself be the strongest point, but it is the one that leads to action; therefore, put it last in order that it may not be forgotten before the congregation is called upon to take the action that you have in mind.

D. Give your points a natural way.

The first leads naturally to the second and the second to the third and the third to the fourth, etc. This is of great importance in speaking without notes. It is quite possible to so construct a sermon that when one has once gotten well under way, everything that follows comes so naturally out of what precedes it that one may deliver the whole sermon without any conscious effort of memory. When you have selected your points and written them down, look at them attentively and see which point would naturally come first, and then ask yourself which one of the remaining points this would naturally suggest. When you have chosen the two, in the same way select the third, and so on.

V. PLAN YOUR INTRODUCTION.

One of the most important parts of the sermon is the introduction. The two most important parts are the introduction and conclusion. The middle is of course important; do not understand me that you should have a strong introduction and conclusion and disregard all that lies between, but it is of the very first importance that you begin well and end well. In the introduction you get the attention of the people; in the conclusion you get the decisive results, so you should be especially careful about these.

You must catch the attention of people first of all. This you should do by your first few sentences, by the very first sentence you utter if possible. How shall we do this? Sometimes by a graphic description of the circumstances of the text. Mr. Moody was peculiarly gifted along this line. He would take a Bible story and make it live right before you. Sometimes it is well to introduce a sermon by speaking of some interesting thing that you have just heard or seen—some incident that you have read in the paper, some notable picture that you have seen in a gallery, some recent discovery of science. In one sermon that I often preach, and that has been used of God to the conversion of many, I usually begin by referring to a remarkable picture I once saw in Europe. I start out by saying, "I once saw a picture that made an impression upon my mind that I have never forgotten." Of course, everybody wants to know about that picture. I do not care anything about the picture; I only use it to secure the attention of people and thus lead directly up to the subject. If you have several good stories in your sermon, it is wise to tell one of the very best at the start. Sometimes a terse and striking statement of the truth that you are going to preach will startle people and awaken their attention at the very outset. Sometimes it is well to jump right into the heart of your text or subject, making some crisp and striking statements, thus causing everybody to prick up their ears and think, *Well, I wonder what is coming next.*

VI. ILLUSTRATE YOUR POINTS.

Illustrate every point in the sermon. It will clinch the matter and fasten it in a person's mind. Think up good illustrations, but do not overillustrate. One striking and impressive illustration will fasten the point.

VII. ARRANGE YOUR CONCLUSION.

How shall we conclude a sermon? The way to conclude a sermon is to sum up and apply what you have been saying. One can usually learn more as to how to close a sermon by listening to a lawyer in court than he can by listening to the average preacher in a pulpit. Preachers aim too much at delivering a perfect discourse, while a lawyer aims at carrying his case. The sermon should close with application and personal appeal. It is a good thing to close a Gospel sermon with some striking incident, an incident that touches men's hearts and makes them ready for action. I have often heard sermons preached and right in the middle they would tell some striking story that melted and moved people, then they would go on to the close without any incident whatever. If they had only told the story at the close, the sermon would have been much more effective. It would have been better still if they had had that moving story in the middle and another just as good or better at the close.

A true sermon does not exist for itself. This, as has already been hinted, is the great fault with many of our modern sermonizers. The sermon exists for itself as a work of art, but it is not worth anything in the line of doing good. As a work of rhetorical art it is perfect, but as a real sermon it is a total failure. What did it accomplish? A true sermon exists for the purpose of leading someone to Christ or building someone up in Christ. I have heard people criticize some preachers and say that they broke nearly all the rules of rhetoric and of homiletics and that the sermon was a failure, when the sermon had accomplished its purpose and brought many to the acceptance of Christ. Again, I have heard people say, "What a magnificent sermon we have just heard!" and I have asked, "What good did it do you?" and they would say, "I do not know as it did me any good." I have further asked what good it did anyone else, what there was in it that would particularly benefit anyone. It was a beautiful sermon, but it was a beautiful fraud.

A few years ago a well-known professor of homiletics went to hear Mr. Moody preach. He afterward told his class that Mr. Moody violated every law of homiletics. Perhaps he did, but he won souls to Christ by the thousands and tens of thousands, more souls, probably, in one year than that professor of homiletics ever won to Christ in his whole lifetime. A scientific angler will get a fishing rod of remarkable lightness and elasticity, a reel of the latest pattern, a silk line of the finest texture, flies of the choicest assortment, and he will go to the brook and throw out his line with the most wonderful precision. The fly falls where he planned that it should, but he does not catch anything. A little boy comes along with a freshly cut willow stick for a rod, a piece of tow string for a line, a bent pin for a hook, and angleworms for bait. He throws out his line without any theoretic knowledge of the art and pulls in a speckled trout. The boy is the better fisher. The man has a perfect outfit and is wonderfully expert in throwing his line, but he does not catch anything. A good deal of our pretended fishing for men is of the same character. Let us never forget that we are fishers for men. Let us not try to save our sermons, but to save men's souls.

VIII. THINK YOUR SERMON OUT CLOSELY.

I would not advise you to write your sermons out because what you have written might afterward enslave you, but I would advise you to do a great deal of writing, not for the sake of preaching what you have written, but for the sake of improving your style. Most emphatically would I advise you never to read a sermon. The more preachers I listen to, the more firmly convinced do I become that a sermon ought never to be read. Of course, there are advantages in writing the sermon out and reading it, but they are counterbalanced many times over by the disadvantages. I once heard a man deliver an address who said before beginning that as he wished to say a great deal in a very short time, he had written his address. It was a magnificent address, but he had no freedom of delivery, and the audience did not get it at all. As far as practical results were concerned, it would have been a great deal better if he had said less and spoken without his manuscript. Furthermore, it is not true that a preacher can say more with a manuscript than without it. Anyone who really has a call to preach can be trained to speak just as freely as to write. It can be just as logical, packed full of matter and argument. Style can be just as faultless. It will be necessary, however, to think out closely beforehand just what is going to be said. After thinking your sermon all out carefully, when you come to preach, your mind will naturally follow the lines along which you have been thinking. You set the mental machinery going, and it will go of itself. The mind is just as much a creature of habit as any part of our body. After one has thought consecutively and thoroughly along a certain line, one's mind naturally runs in the grooves that have been cut out when the thought is taken up again.

PREPARATION AND DELIVERY OF BIBLE READINGS

I. DIFFERENT KINDS OF BIBLE READINGS

There are many different kinds of Bible readings, and it is well to bear in mind the distinctions between them.

A. The whole Bible topical Bible reading

By this we mean the Bible reading that takes up some topic and goes through the whole Bible to find its texts for the study of the topic. For example, if the Bible reading is on the subject "The Power of Prayer," passages for the illustration and exposition of the subject are taken from any book in the Bible where they are found.

B. The book topical Bible reading

By this we mean the taking up of a topic as it is treated in a single book in the Bible; for example, the Holy Spirit in John's gospel, or the Believer's Certainties in the first epistle of John. These subjects are handled simply as they are treated in these individual books.

C. The chapter topical Bible reading

In this, the subject is handled simply as it is found in a single chapter in the Bible; for example, the Freedom of the Believer in Romans 8; or the Priceless

Possessions of the Believer in Philippians 4; or the Glory of the Believer in 1 John 5; or Christ as seen in 1 John 2.

D. The general survey of a book Bible reading

In this form of Bible reading, there is a rapid survey of the salient facts or great truths of some book in the Bible.

E. The general survey of a chapter Bible reading

This varies from the preceding one, in that a single chapter is considered instead of an entire book.

II. THE CHOICE OF SUBJECTS

The first matter of importance in the construction of Bible readings is the choice of subjects. The following suggestions will help in this choice of subjects:

A. There are some great subjects that every pastor and teacher and evangelist should take up.

These include the following: The Power of the Blood of Christ, The Power of the Word of God, The Power of the Holy Spirit, The Power of Prayer, How to Pray Effectually, Justification, The New Birth, Sanctification, The Filling and Empowering of the Holy Spirit, Assurance, Faith, Repentance, Love, Thanksgiving, Worship, Future Destiny of Believers, Future Destiny of Impenitent Sinners, The Second Coming of Christ, Fulfilled Prophecies.

B. Go through Bible, textbooks, and concordances noting subjects for Bible readings.

C. Get suggestions from books of Bible readings.

D. Keep a blank book, and note down such subjects as occur to you from time to time.

E. Get your subject for the meeting immediately in hand, by prayer.

III. THE GETTING TOGETHER OF MATERIAL FOR BIBLE READINGS

A. Use a concordance.

Look up in the concordance the passages having the word or synonymous words in it. Suppose, for example, that the subject is "The Power of Prayer"; look up passages in the concordance under the words *pray, prayer, intercession, supplication, ask, cry, call,* and synonymous words. Some of these passages you will reject at once; many will not relate to prayer at all; others will relate to prayer, but not to the power of prayer; other passages you will note to be used or rejected later. It will save time if, instead of writing the passages down on first going through the concordance, you mark them by some sign on the margin of the concordance.

B. Look up the subject and related subjects in your topical textbook.

Suppose, for example, the subject in hand is "The Power of the Blood"; look up passages under the following subjects: reconciliation, atonement, redemption, death of Christ.

C. Look up the subject and related subjects in other resource books.

D. Look for passages on the subject.

In your general Bible study, always be on the watch for passages bearing on the subjects upon which you intend to teach. There are many passages that bear upon a subject that you will find neither in a concordance nor textbook; but if you study your Bible with an alert mind, these passages will be noticed by you and can be jotted down as you come to them.

E. Put on your thinking cap and see if you cannot call to mind passages on the subject in hand.

Sometimes it is well to construct a Bible reading absolutely without reference to concordance or textbook. Of course, this will be impossible for one who has not a good general knowledge of the Bible, but a Christian worker should always be growing into a walking concordance and Bible textbook.

IV. THE SELECTION AND ARRANGEMENT OF MATERIAL

A. Delete excessive material.

Having gotten your material together, see what you can dispense with, and strike it out at once. The following four points will be helpful in the exclusion of material:

1. *Substantially the same material in different forms*

2. *Comparatively unimportant material*

3. *Material not adapted to the needs of the congregation for which you are preparing*

4. *Material about which you are uncertain*

B. Form your principal divisions, and arrange your remaining material under them.

When you have excluded all the material that you can dispense with, look carefully at the material remaining. As you look at it, it will begin to classify itself. Some of it will fall under one division and some under another. When you have obtained your main divisions, look at the material in each division, and this oftentimes will begin to arrange itself in subdivisions.

C. Get your divisions in the best possible order.

Arrange the subdivisions under them also in the best order. The following suggestions will help in this:

1. *Bring together points that naturally go together.*

2. *As far as possible, have each point lead naturally up to the next point.*

3. *When possible, have a climax of thought with the strongest point last.*

4. *Put the points that lead naturally to decision and action last.*

V. THE DELIVERY OF THE BIBLE READING

A. Sometimes give the passages out to others to read.

1. *Write them out on slips of paper and hand them out.*

In such a case, be sure that those who take the passages will really find them and read them in a clear tone. Have them stand up to do it unless the audience is very small.

2. *Call the passages off, and have those who take them call them out after you.*

If two take the same passage, say which of the two shall have it.

B. Oftentimes read the passages yourself.

In order to do this, you will have to acquire facility in the use of your Bible, but this comes readily with practice. Some find it helpful to write in red ink in their Bible at the close of the first passage where the next one is to be found, and at the close of the second where the third is to be found, etc. If this is done, an index should be made on the flyleaf of the Bible of subjects, and of the first text under a subject. When the same text comes in a number of Bible readings, use various colored inks, or number the marginal text that follows it so that you will know which applies to the particular subject in hand.

ILLUSTRATIONS AND THEIR USE

NOTHING GOES FURTHER toward making an interesting, effective speaker than the power of illustration. All preachers who have been successful in reaching men and women have been especially gifted in their power of illustration. Much of the power of Spurgeon, Moody, and Guthrie lay in their power of apt and impressive illustration.

I. THEIR VALUE

A. To make truth clear

No matter how clearly an abstract truth is stated, many minds fail to grasp it unless it is put in concrete form. Ministers are probably better able to grasp abstract truth than any other class of people, and yet I have noticed that even they—in order to understand truth—need to have it illustrated in concrete form. It was once said of a certain minister by one of his parishioners, "He is a remarkable man; he is so profound that I cannot understand him." This was said in honest admiration and not as a criticism, but obscurity is not a mark of profundity. It is possible to take the profoundest truth and make it so plain and simple that a child can understand it. Obscurity is rather a mark of intellectual weakness than of intellectual power, for it requires brains to make a profound truth clear and simple. But nothing will go further to make clear a truth that is of difficult statement and profound than the skillful use of illustrations.

B. To impress the truth

It is necessary in a public speaker that he not only make the truth clear, but that he impress it upon his hearers. A truth may be so stated as to be clearly understood and yet make but little impression upon the mind. There is perhaps nothing that will do more to impress the truth upon the mind than the wise use of illustrations. Take, for example, Romans 1:16: "For I am not ashamed of the gospel of Christ, for it is the power of God to salvation for everyone who believes, for the Jew first and also for the Greek." This verse may be clearly understood and yet make little impression upon the mind of the hearer until you tell the story of some poor, degraded wretch who has been wonderfully saved by the Gospel. Then the truth is not only understood, but impressed, upon the mind.

C. To fasten the truth

How often you have heard a sermon, and the only thing that fastened itself in your memory was the illustration? You cannot forget an illustration, and with the illustration, you remember the truth that it was used to illustrate.

D. To attract and hold attention

There is little use in talking to people unless you have their attention. Nothing is more effective in accomplishing this object than the apt use of illustrations.

E. To rest the mind

If you talk continually for twenty minutes without an illustration, people begin to get very tired. Most people are not used to thinking consecutively for twenty minutes, and when you require them to do so without giving an illustration to rest and refresh the mind, they become very weary; but if here and there you drop in a good illustration, it serves to rest the mind. A two hours' sermon by a preacher successful in illustration will tire you less than a ten minutes' sermon by others. I once heard a man talk two hours to children. He held their attention spellbound from beginning to end, and they did not seem to be tired at the end, but would have liked to have had him go on. The whole secret of it seemed to be that he had marvelous power of illustration. When you find that your audience is growing tired or listless, drop in an illustration. This was Mr. Moody's constant practice. When he found his audience was heavy or getting restless, he would bring in one of his best stories out of his inexhaustible fund of anecdotes.

II. CLASSES OF ILLUSTRATIONS

A. Biblical illustrations

That is, incidents from the Bible and pictures of Bible scenes. Christ made much use of this kind of illustration. There is reason to believe that it is the very best method of illustrating a sermon. One of Mr. Moody's greatest gifts was his power to make a Bible incident live before you; Zaccheus, the woman who was a sinner, the woman with an issue of blood, and many other Bible persons became living, breathing beings in whom your deepest interest was aroused. In order to acquire this gift, study Bible incidents carefully, then write them out. Study them over and over again and rewrite them; tell these incidents to others, especially to children; endeavor to make them as living and interesting as you possibly can. The power to do this will grow rapidly. About the only genius there is in it is the genius of hard work. That is true of almost any form of genius. There is scarcely anything that a man cannot accomplish if he only puts his mind to it. Hard work will accomplish almost anything. If you are going to gain this power of biblical illustration, you must try and try and try again. Never be discouraged. You can certainly cultivate this faculty if you only work hard enough.

B. Incidents from your own experience

There is power in an incident that happened in your own experience that there is not in an incident which you have taken from somebody else. There is also great danger in the use of this class of illustrations; the danger is that you will make yourself too prominent. One has to be on constant guard against that. Unless one is very careful, one will soon find oneself parading oneself, one's excellences and wisdom and achievements. It is a very subtle snare. In using these incidents from your own experience, you must put yourself in the background just as far as possible. Cases are not rare where the imagination, in the use of incidents, has grown to such an extent that workers have been found borrowing incidents from the experiences and lives of others and transferring them to their own experience. Within the past month, I have received information of one who is going up and down the country telling of things which are known to have happened in the life of Mr. Moody as though they had happened in his own life. There is danger, too, that as you repeat a story again and again it will grow in its proportions, and at last there will be little likeness between the incident as you tell it and the event as it really occurred. And yet you will yourself get to believe, unless you are scrupulously truthful, that it actually happened that way. It may not be that "all are liars," but most storytellers get to be liars unless they are on their guard. When it is once found out that a speaker is given to exaggeration (lying), and it will always be found out sooner or later—his usefulness is at an end.

C. Anecdotes

Almost everyone is interested in a story. The great power of one of the best-known after-dinner speakers in our country lies in his power to tell a good story. Lawyers and politicians and platform speakers generally make a large use of the anecdote in their speeches. Preachers of the Gospel do well to make use of the same form of illustration. Anecdotes may not be as dignified as illustrations from science and poetry, but they are more effective; and effectiveness is what the true preacher is aiming at. There is, however, great danger that the matter of storytelling be much overdone. One hears sermons that are simply a string of anecdotes, and after a while this becomes disgusting to an intelligent hearer.

D. Illustrations from history

Illustrations from history have the advantage of dignity as well as forcefulness. The question is often asked me by young people preparing for the ministry and evangelistic work, "What do you think I ought to study outside the Bible?" and I always advise them, whatever else they study, to study history. It is a most useful branch of knowledge in itself, but it is of special value to the public speaker. Very few people know much about history, and if you can bring forward from history well-chosen incidents, both the truth and the illustration will be interesting, instructive, and effective. It serves furthermore to awaken the confidence of the people in the speaker. An argument from authentic history is one of the most unanswerable of arguments.

E. Illustrations from science

The natural sciences afford many beautiful and helpful illustrations. Striking and impressive illustrations of Bible truth can be found in astronomy, botany, chemistry, geology, physics, and other natural sciences. But this is a form of illustration in the use of which one needs to exercise great care. Be very careful that your illustration illustrates. I have heard scientific illustrations used when the illustration needed more explanation than the truth it was intended to illustrate. Be very careful that your science is correct. What is considered scientific knowledge today is likely to be found to be scientific error tomorrow. I have heard much scientific falsehood used in illustrating sermons. Do not use exploded science to illustrate Gospel truth. One great fault with the use of scientific illustrations is that the average preacher is likely to accept a scientific doctrine just about the time the scientific world gives it up.

F. Illustrations from the poets

An apt quotation from the poets often serves to illuminate and fix the truth. These are very easy to get, for there are excellent collections of classified quotations from the poets.

G. Illustrations by visible objects

It is sometimes well to use objects, not only in talking to children, but to grown-up people as well. For example, Rev. E. P. Hammond makes a very successful use of the magnet and different kinds of nails; small nails, large nails, straight nails, and crooked nails, in illustrating the doctrine, "And I, if I am lifted up from the earth, will draw all men unto me."

III. HOW TO GET ILLUSTRATIONS

A. Be on the lookout for them.

Cultivate the habit of watching for thoughts, watching for texts, watching for points, and watching for illustrations; in other words, go through the world with your eyes and ears open. One of the greatest faults in the training of children in the past has been that we have not trained the child's faculty of observation. Cultivate your own power of observation. Henry Ward Beecher was a striking example along this line. He was one of the most gifted men in the power of illustration. Wherever he went, he was always on the lookout for something with which to illustrate the truth. He would talk with all classes of men and try to get from them illustrations for his sermons. James A. Garfield was another example of the same thing. One day he was walking down a street in Cleveland, Ohio. He heard a strange noise coming out of the basement of a building he was passing. He said to the friend who was with him, "I believe that man is filing a saw. I never saw a saw filed; I am going down to see how he does it." Spurgeon was a most illustrious example. He not only went through the world with his own eyes open, but it is said that he kept three or four men in the British Museum all the time looking for illustrations for him. The one who would be a mighty preacher to men must associate much with men.

B. Keep a book of illustrations.

Take this book with you wherever you go. Whatever you see on your travels that seems to afford likely matter for an illustration, jot it down. Whenever you hear a good illustration in a sermon or address, jot it down. The book of illustrations that you make for yourself is far better than the book of illustrations that you purchase; too many others have that book, and sometimes when you are telling some of the stories in it, you will see a smile pass over the faces of your congregation at the familiarity of the story. And someone may come up to you at the close of the sermon and say, "I always liked that story."

C. Study the masters in illustration.

Study such men as Moody, Spurgeon, Guthrie. Do not adopt their illustrations too extensively, but see how they do it.

D. Cultivate the habit of talking to children.

I do not know of anything that will make a man more gifted in the power of illustration than talking to children. You are simply obliged to use illustrations when you talk to children, and thus you acquire the power to do it. By talking to children, you will not only cultivate the gift of using illustrations, but also using pure English style.

IV. HOW TO USE ILLUSTRATIONS

A. Be sure you have something to illustrate.

Do not preach a sermon for the sake of the illustrations. One hears many sermons where it is hard to avoid the conclusion that the sermon was gotten up for the sake of the stories that are told in it, rather than for the sake of the truth it professes to teach. Indeed, it is sometimes hard to tell what the truth is that the man is trying to illustrate. A literary friend once came to me in great disgust after a service he had attended. I asked him how he enjoyed the service. "It was all bosh. The man preached his whole sermon to work up to the point of getting off a quotation from Scott's *Marmion* at the end. He did that well, but the whole performance was disgusting." Yet this preacher was considered by some a great pulpit orator.

B. Be sure that your illustrations illustrate.

C. Avoid threadbare stories.

But it is well to bear in mind that a story that is threadbare in one place may be perfectly new in another. It is well, however, to be overcautious rather than undercautious in the matter of threadbare stories.

D. Do not make up stories.

If you make up a story and tell it as if it were true, it is a lie. There are religious adventurers in our country, sometimes calling themselves by the noble name of evangelists, who go here and there making up the stories that they tell. It is time this sort of thing was stamped out. True evangelists are suffering much injury from those who are making up stories.

E. When you tell a true story, tell it exactly as it is, or do not tell it at all.

There are some who exaggerate their stories because they think in this way they will be more impressive. Perhaps they call this a pious fraud, but pious frauds are the most impious and blasphemous on earth. Do not take a story that someone else told of his friend, and say, "A friend of mine" did so and so.

F. Often begin your sermon with an illustration.

In this way, you get the attention and gain the interest of your audience at the very outset.

G. Often close your sermon with an illustration.

This, if wisely done, will not only serve to fix the truth but to touch the heart.

TEACHING
THE BIBLE

I. THE IMPORTANCE OF BIBLE TEACHING

A. The Bible is the Word of God.

The one who is really teaching the Bible may be confident that it is a good work, for beyond a doubt the truth of God is being taught.

B. There is a great demand in our day for Bible teachers.

The one who takes up the teaching of the Bible, and does it in an interesting way and in the power of the Spirit, is bound to get a hearing and to do great good. In the city of Chicago, a popular evening Bible class has been in operation for four years. The first year there was one class, the second year four classes, the third year five classes, and the fourth year it was necessary to reduce the number of classes in order that the teacher might go two evenings in the week to Detroit and St. Louis. In the five classes there was a weekly average attendance of about six thousand. The great interest people have today in studying the Bible is illustrated by the Saturday evening class at the Chicago Avenue Church. People come out at five o'clock and remain until nine. From five until six there are about seven hundred in attendance, from seven until nine between two thousand and twenty-five hundred. Similar interest in Bible study has been shown in other cities. In every city and village there should be systematic Bible teaching; nothing else will draw and hold such large and interested audiences.

II. METHODS OF BIBLE TEACHING

A. Expounding the Scriptures

This consists in the simple reading of a passage of Scripture with such comments as illuminate its meaning and enforce its teaching. Mr. Spurgeon had a great gift in this direction. Mr. Moody used to say, "I would rather hear Mr. Spurgeon expound the Scripture than preach; I get more out of it." The following suggestions are offered to aid in expounding the Scripture to edification:

1. *Make thorough preparation.*

There are those who think that it takes no preparation to expound the Scripture, that all that is necessary is to go into the pulpit and read a chapter and make such desultory comments as come to mind. There may be some profit even in that slipshod way of expounding the Scripture, but it has done much to bring Bible exposition into disrepute.

2. *Avoid rambling.*

There is a great temptation to the expositor, when he has started out upon one line of thought, to branch from that on to another and from that still on to another, until it is almost impossible to get back to the chapter.

3. *Avoid tediousness.*

4. *Seek for connected lines of thought.*

Suppose, for example, you are expounding the fourth chapter of Philippians. Instead of reading through with disconnected comments, go through the chapter with this line of thought: "Seven Present Privileges of the Believer":

a. Constant joy (verse 4)
b. Absolute freedom from care (verse 6)
c. Abounding peace (verse 7)
d. An ever-present Friend (verse 9)
e. Never-failing contentment (verse 11)

f. All-prevailing strength (verse 13)

g. Inexhaustible supplies for every need (verse 19)

Or suppose you are expounding the second chapter of 1 John. Your exposition might begin with the introduction, "This chapter presents to us seven comforting views of Jesus":

a. Jesus as an Advocate with the Father (verse 1)

b. Jesus as a propitiation for our sins (verse 2)

c. Jesus as our Light (verse 8)

d. Jesus as the Anointer with the Holy Ghost (verses 20–27)

e. Jesus as the Christ and Son of God (verses 22–23)

f. Jesus as the great promiser (verse 25)

g. Jesus as the Coming One (verse 28)

Of course these are only outlines, and the points made are the headings for different divisions of the exposition.

5. *A Bible with a wide margin or an interleaved Bible is very useful in expository work.*

6. *A resource book is helpful.*

Horatius Bonar's *Bible Thoughts and Themes* is a very helpful book for one who would know how to expound the Scriptures interestingly and profitably.

7. *The book of Psalms is a good book with which to begin your expository work.*

Of course, we do not intend by this that every Psalm should be expounded.

B. The conversational Bible class

This is a very interesting method of teaching the Bible.

1. *Have the class meet in a very informal way, if possible around a long table.*

2. *Take some book in the Bible and assign a portion for careful study.*

3. *Read verse by verse, and give each one an opportunity to state what he has gotten out of the verse; or ask questions upon the verse.*

4. Hold your class to the passage and subject in hand.

5. Avoid trifles.

In almost every class, there is likely to be some member who will want to spend all the time in discussing some trifle.

6. It is often well to assign questions beforehand to be looked up by individual members of the class.

C. The topical or doctrinal Bible class

Such a class is of immense importance in a church. Very few people in our day are being carefully indoctrinated in the great fundamental truths of the Bible. In consequence of this, they are likely to be led off by any false teacher who comes along and is a bright talker, or skillful in producing the impression of an unusual amount of Bible knowledge. The following are suggestions as to how to conduct these classes:

1. *Make a careful list beforehand of the great doctrines that you wish to teach. Take these doctrines up in systematic order.*

2. *Arrange all the Scriptures that bear upon these doctrines in an orderly and logical way.*

3. *In the class, you can either read from the Bible and expound what the Scripture says on these doctrines, or you can have the different passages of Scripture read by members of the class; and let the class put the contents of the Scripture into systematic form for themselves.*

The latter is the better way, provided your class is of sufficient intelligence to do the work well. Sometimes it is better yet to give out the Scripture beforehand, and have the class bring in the results of their own study and thought in systematic shape.

D. Study of individual books

This is the best and most important of all methods for continuous work. By this method of study, a class can be continued from five to ten years, or indefinitely.

1. *Introductory work*

Assign the lessons to the class beforehand; have them find and bring in answers to the following questions:

a. Who wrote the book?

b. To whom was it written?

c. Where was it written?

d. When was it written?

e. Occasion of writing?

f. Purpose for which written?

g. Circumstances of the author when he wrote?

h. What were the circumstances of those to whom he wrote?

i. What glimpses does the book give us of the life and character of the author?

j. What are the leading ideas of the book?

k. What is the central truth of the book?

l. What are the characteristics of the book?

2. *Have the class divide the book into its principal sections.*

3. *Take it up verse by verse and study.*

At each lesson, have the class bring in an analysis of a certain number of verses. Insist:

a. That nothing shall be in the analysis that is not in the verse.

b. That, as far as possible, everything that is in the verse shall be in the analysis.

To accomplish this, when any member of the class gives an inadequate analysis, ask if that is all there is in the verse, and keep on asking questions until all has been brought out that you see in the verse.

c. Let what is found be stated as accurately and concisely as possible.

Do not be contented when a member of the class puts something into his analysis somewhat like to what is in the verse, but demand that it shall be a precise statement of what is in the verse.

4. Have the class bring together all the teachings on the various subjects scattered through the book.

a. To this end, have them first make a list of subjects treated in the book.

b. Arrange these subjects in their principal subdivisions.

c. Go through the analysis already made, and bring the points in the analysis under the proper headings in the classification of teaching.

E. Classes for the rapid survey of all the books in the Bible

This is sometimes called the "Synthetic Method of Bible Study." Assign the class a certain number of chapters, wherever possible an entire book, to read over and over again; and then when they come together, go over the book rapidly, bringing out the salient points about it and its teaching. Dr. James M. Gray's book *The Synthetic Study of the Bible* will be helpful for this work.

F. Classes for the study of the Bible by chapters

1. These classes can be conducted in a variety of ways.

Perhaps the simplest method is to give out four questions for the class to be prepared upon, writing answers to these questions for each chapter. The Bible can be covered in about two years in this way if two chapters are prepared each day. The questions are:

a. What is the subject of the chapter?

(State principal contents of the chapter in a single phrase or sentence.)
b. Who are the principal persons of the chapter?
c. What is the truth most emphasized in the chapter?
d. What is the best lesson in the chapter?
e. What is the best verse of the chapter (memorized)?

2. A somewhat more elaborate, and much more valuable, method is to give out eight questions.

a. What are the leading facts of the chapter and the lessons they teach?

These facts, with the corresponding lessons, should be given one by one and written out.

b. What are wrong things done and mistakes made?

That does not mean mistakes made by the author of the Bible, for there are none, but the mistakes that are recorded in the chapter as made by various persons.

c. What are things to be imitated?

That is, things different persons have done, as recorded in the chapter, that are worthy of our imitation.

d. What are the most important lessons in the chapter?

It is best to restrict the number of lessons to not more than five (or not more than ten) or such number as you deem best.

e. What is the most important lesson in the chapter?

f. What are the great texts in the chapter (written out in full)?

g. What is the truth most emphasized in the chapter?

h. What is the personal blessing received from the study of the chapter?

This is an especially helpful way to study the Acts of the Apostles. The author has obtained one of the greatest blessings that he has ever received from Bible study in the study of the Acts of the Apostles in this way.

3. *A still more elaborate method for the study of the Bible by chapters is to give the class the following twenty questions and suggestions:*

a. Read chapter five times.
b. Note any important changes in versions.
c. Discover and study parallel passages, and note variations.
d. Date of events in chapter?
e. Name of chapter?
f. Outline of chapter?
g. Best verse? Mark and commit to memory.
h. Verses for meditation; note and mark.
i. Verses for thorough study; note and mark.

j. Texts for sermons; note, mark and outline the sermons.

k. Characteristic, striking, and picturesque words and phrases; mark and study.

l. Leading incidents?

m. Persons; what light upon their character and lessons from their lives?

n. The most important lessons in chapter?

o. The most important lesson in chapter?

p. Central truth?

q. Places; locate and look up their character and history.

r. Subjects for further study suggested?

s. Difficulties in chapter?

t. Personal blessings received from the study of the chapter.

First. What new truth learned?

Second. What old truth brought home with new power?

Third. What new course of action decided upon?

Fourth. Any other blessing received from the study of the chapter?

Of course, these suggestions and questions can be varied to suit the class and the judgment of the teacher.

G. Classes for the study of the Bible for use in personal work

Such a class should exist in every church and mission. This volume gives hints for the conduct of such a class.

H. Teaching from a prepared curriculum

Whatever other lines of Bible teaching we may take up, we cannot afford to exclude the curriculum prepared by denominations and publishing houses. Helps for the study and teaching of these lessons are so abundant and so excellent that often there is no need that anything be added .

LEARNING ACTIVITIES

1. Identify two or three contexts in which you might have an opportunity to present a message from God's Word to a group of people. Would your pastor or a professional ministry be likely to have these opportunities?

2. What are appropriate passages of Scripture and points of emphasis for these contexts? Use this occasion as a chance to sketch out what you might present if given these opportunities. Then pray for God to give you the chance to present these messages.

3. What are two or three of your favorite passages of Scripture? Follow Torrey's instructions and prepare Bible readings on each of these passages. Identify illustrations that could accompany these Bible readings.

4. Reflect on several of the best illustrations that you have heard or that you have given regarding a truth in Scripture. Write down a few notes regarding these illustrations so that you have a few ready to use at any moment. Perhaps you will want to add them to your "Textbook."

5. Are you actively involved in a systematic study of God's Word? What place ought this to have in your personal life? How does it fit within your church life and ministry activities? What else might need to be adjusted to make room for it?

More Quality Life Essentials Books

What Every Christian Should Believe

Getting grounded in the essentials of the faith is the key to a deep, abiding relationship with Christ. *What Every Christian Should Believe* is a classic primer on the basics of the Christian faith. Whether you're a new believer needing a primer on the basics of Christianity or a seasoned Christian desiring a comprehensive refresher, this book is a timeless classic to prepare you for today's Christian walk.

ISBN #0-8024-5220-5, Paperback

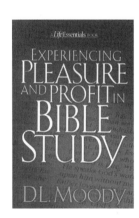

Experiencing Pleasure and Profit in Bible Study

Dwight L. Moody recognized the common struggle people have to regularly and thoroughly study the Bible. Knowing God's Word is essential for you to have a vibrant, growing Christian life. This classic work, refreshed and updated, will renew your enthusiasm to discover the life-changing truths contained in the precious Word of God.

ISBN #0-8024-5222-1, Paperback

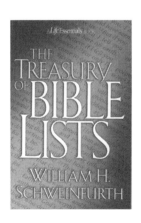

The Treasury of Bible Lists

The Treasury of Bible Lists is a rich compilation of Bible truths. They are designed to equip you to do in-depth study of a topic in Scripture, prepare presentations, or meditate upon a multitude of principles within Christianity.

ISBN #0-8024-5221-3, Paperback

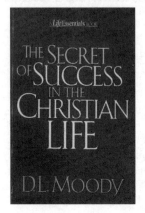
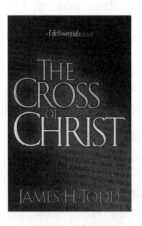